D1558646

The publisher gratefully acknowledges the generous support of the Valerie Barth and Peter Booth Wiley Endowment Fund in History of the University of California Press Foundation.

California on the Breadlines

California
on the Breadlines

*Dorothea Lange, Paul Taylor, and the
Making of a New Deal Narrative*

Jan Goggans

UNIVERSITY OF CALIFORNIA PRESS

Berkeley   Los Angeles   London

Frontispiece: Dorothea and Paul Taylor, 1939. Photo by Imogen
Cunningham. © Imogen Cunningham Trust. www.imogen
cunningham.com.

University of California Press, one of the most distinguished
university presses in the United States, enriches lives around the
world by advancing scholarship in the humanities, social sciences,
and natural sciences. Its activities are supported by the UC Press
Foundation and by philanthropic contributions from individuals
and institutions. For more information, visit www.ucpress.edu.

University of California Press
Berkeley and Los Angeles, California

University of California Press, Ltd.
London, England

Library of Congress Cataloging-in-Publication Data
Goggans, Jan.
   California on the breadlines : Dorothea Lange, Paul Taylor,
and the making of a New Deal narrative / Jan Goggans.
      p.   cm.
   Includes bibliographical references and index.
   ISBN 978-0-520-26621-6 (cloth : alk. paper)
   1. Lange, Dorothea.   2. Women photographers — United
States — Biography.   3. Taylor, Paul Schuster, 1895 – 1984.
4. Social scientists — United States — Biography.   5. Rural
poor — United States — History.   6. Depressions — 1929 —
United States.   I. Title.
TR140.L36G645   2010
770.92'2 — dc22   2009038130

Manufactured in the United States of America

19   18   17   16   15   14   13   12   11   10
10   9   8   7   6   5   4   3   2   1

This book is printed on Cascades Enviro 100, a 100% post
consumer waste, recycled, de-inked fiber. FSC recycled certified
and processed chlorine free. It is acid free, Ecologo certified, and
manufactured by BioGas energy.

In memoriam:
Charles Edward Goggans
Born August 7, 1928
Arrived in California in 1932
Died June 25, 1991

CONTENTS

ILLUSTRATIONS

xi

ACKNOWLEDGMENTS

Like many first books, this one seems to have begun long before its debut. Perhaps unlike many, it has changed radically over time. Despite the likelihood that few who were involved in the initial stages will recognize the final outcome, all who have contributed along the way deserve thanks.

At the University of California, Davis, professors Linda Morris, David Robertson, and Jack Hicks all provided the mysterious spark that began my work on Paul Taylor and Dorothea Lange, and all three have remained, since then, enthusiastic supporters. In addition, the Davis Humanities Institute provided a working space for me while I brought the first version into existence. I was also helped by a generous award from the American Association of University Women.

That first version began its initial transformation as the result of a Kevin Starr California Studies Postdoctoral Fellowship. The award funded my research and revisions, and introduced me to the University of California Press, and while the fellowship itself no longer exists, I remain grateful to it, and to Kevin Starr's vision of California Studies.

The final version owes much to many people, particularly the dedicated and tireless staff of the Bancroft Library. I spent hours poring through box after box of Paul Taylor's archives, and everyone in the library was not simply helpful and informed, but genuinely enthusiastic. None, however, was more so than David Kessler, whom I simply cannot thank enough. His dedication and his boundless energy and helpfulness are, in a word, unsurpassed. Additionally, Susan Snyder has been a pleasure to work with, swiftly and efficiently obtaining permissions to use crucial sources. I hope I have been able to do all their work justice.

Just as important have been the Oakland Museum and those who have worked with me in the archives. I extend special gratitude to curator of photography Drew Johnson and to Robin Doolin, whose hard work in Rights and Reproductions provided me with essential interviews, photographs, and sources.

The text that finds its way to print came into existence at the University of California–Merced, and I owe a deep dept of gratitude to many who are there. My current dean, Hans Bjornsson, has been unfailingly supportive of this project. While here, I have benefited from a stimulating intellectual climate created by my colleagues, many of whom have offered helpful advice and encouragement, particularly Gregg Camfield, Robin DeLugan, Kevin Fellezs, Gregg Herken, Kathleen Hull, Shawn Kantor, Sean Malloy, and Cristian Ricci. Beyond Merced, I have benefited from participation with a diverse group of colleagues involved in California Studies, particularly those with me on the steering committee of the California Studies Consortium: Roberto Alvaraz, Catherine Candee, Kerwin Kline, Mariam Lam, Catherine Mitchell, Dante Noto, Kim Robinson, Lynne Withey, Clyde Woods, and especially David Theo Goldberg and David Wellman. To all of these people, thank you.

The book benefited in more ways than I can describe from the generous contributions of various individuals whose work has shaped it, bettered it, and enriched it. Sally Stein contributed Katharine Whiteside Taylor's unpublished memoir, and Paul Taylor's son-in-law Donald Fanger provided permission. Paul Taylor's grandson William Loesch and Dorothea Lange's son Daniel Dixon generously granted interviews. Paul Taylor's daughter Katharine Taylor Loesch was kind enough to respond to my questions in writing, and his granddaughter Dyanna Taylor provided crucial feedback and context. I am grateful to each of these important people. For access to photographs from the Bancroft Library, courtesy of Susan Snyder; the Oakland Museum, with the help of Robin Doolin; the Library of Congress, with Paul Hogroian's assistance; and the Imogen Cunningham Trust, courtesy of the always wonderful Betsy and Meg Partridge, I am profoundly grateful.

No matter how solitary an act writing may sometimes seem, it depends on the help of others. I was fortunate to have the help of three intelligent, insightful, and energetic student researchers. To Walter Knops, who helped me more than I can describe in researching the radical movements of the 1930s; to Michael Barba, who worked with me on theories of subaltern identities; and to Kacy Marume, who worked tirelessly to produce brilliant work on women's reading habits of the 1920s and 1930s, I offer humble, profound thanks, and admiration. You are the students who pave the future for UC–Merced.

Beyond this, I depended on a generous group of colleagues

who were willing to read versions of my manuscript and provide valuable feedback, without which the book surely would have suffered. Kacy Marume edited the entire manuscript, and Linda Morris, Gregg Camfield, Michael Barba, and Sean Malloy all contributed immensely to chapters they read on my behalf. To Sean I extend special acknowledgment; whether he was offering a quick lesson on Populism and suggestions for sources, pragmatic help in issues of formatting and footnoting, or encouragement, empathy, and a willing ear, he remained consistently available to me, always when I needed help the most. I learned much from him, always, and can only hope the book reflects his intelligence, sensitivity, and understanding of how history works.

All books need a press, and to the University of California Press I extend my gratitude and admiration. For their vision and abilities, Director Lynne Withey and Associate Director Sheila Levine deserve unbounded admiration. For assistance in moving the book ahead, in the laborious process of reviews, and in the endless details of production, I extend deep and profound thanks to Niels Hooper and Nick Arrivo, who literally brought the book into a form that was ready to enter the world on its own.

No book exists without taking a toll on the author's family and friends, and to mine, I extend deep thanks and acknowledgment for your patience. No one, however, deserves more credit than my daughter Ellen, who has weathered countless storms in the course of the years, always by my side. Her bright, enduring enthusiasm for this book, and for life itself, has been a sweet and welcome beacon through the darkest of times.

Uncommon Ground

On Christmas Day in 1958, photographer Dorothea Lange and her husband, University of California professor Paul Taylor, were in Afghanistan.[1] Lange's journal holds the record of the trip, and it describes a brisk pace, one that seems to have worn at the photographer, who was by then sixty-three years old and who had struggled for years with a variety of health problems. She made no photographs in Moscow because the stay there was "a struggle. The cold was terrible. Snow. The fever. And the 2 days in bed, and the white lace curtains in the still warm room." Always visual, even in sickness, Lange wrote of seeing "Hitler's funeral pyre" in Berlin, "and bombed buildings whose sections [were] still wiped out." The sight obviously moved Lange, who had made a career of photographing people whose lives had been in some way or another "wiped out."[2]

The old European ways seemed to intensify her feelings, bringing her to points of almost helpless morbidity even as she rallied to retain a sense of her independent and upbeat self. She felt increasingly that "the past" was overtaking them and described herself in writing as a gradual and unwilling victim of history, a feeling that seems to have been intensified by the presence of Rose Schuster Taylor, her husband's indomitable mother, who traveled with them, and by what Lange felt was Paul's "reliance" on his mother. "I don't want to live with her and her ways, and Paul, brave as he is, is also timid . . . and dense. God Damn. The cold got me. Berlin I am glad to leave."

Nearly a week later, on January 8, they were still in Germany, in Stuttgart. As if to brace herself, she put down the following: "I have the battlefields ahead. I have those battlefields ahead and it will be a thorough job." Those battlefields, where her husband earned a Purple Heart in World War I, were perhaps Taylor's primary reason for the trip. The war changed his life, and the battle at Belleau Wood is still commemorated as one of the worst, and bravest, and noblest—in military terms—that American soldiers waged. Taylor revisited the Chateau Thierry sector battlefield three times. The first was one week after Armistice Day, 1918, when German prisoners were clearing up the battle debris. The second was this trip. Years after Lange's death in 1965, Taylor went a third time, in 1972. She went just once.

The day after shoring herself up for the trip, in a wonderful turn of psychology, Lange moved within her own emotional and psychological framework, writing a long passage about the book she planned to write about the people in her life—all details, "just a mass of tiny details. The brooches they wore, for instance. The winter hat of Aunt Caroline and her black shoes with bunions, then her summer hat."[3] At the end, she mused, "I wonder if I could ever write of my father. So hard that would be?" It is a lovely passage, one that shows this remarkably resilient mind gathering itself together, reaching inward to confirm the separate identity of the woman, Dorothea Lange.

On their way to the battlefields, they stopped "for a warm room and a good bed and a cheering meal." Sometime after that, while musing about the causes of war, she wrote, "What can be substituted to relieve these insane compulsions?"

> Then, traveler, what can be done closer to home? Very close to home? You, yourself, are one prone to wage war on those around you. You attack and when you do not have your own way, when you must give way to another route, you imagine yourself persecuted. You attack in a variety of petty criticism, spoken and unspoken. You are not a man of blessed peace, world traveler. You punish Paul, because we cannot easily go to Paris. You get yourself up as a Paris-sort-of a person. You make him feel like a one too dull to be a Paris-sort-of person. This is not true, but it is *revenge*.

And then, in a tribute to the compromise that marked their extraordinary marriage, she ended the page both conceding the "surrender to history" and honoring her own frustrations: "We are not going to go to Paris. We will visit the Goddamn [that word then crossed out] battle fields of World War I. Plaques and monuments. Paul will revisit his youth—40 years ago. I go and will try to go."

Slightly more than one week later, on January 16, Taylor and Lange recorded their day at Belleau Wood on opposite sides of the same notebook pages, a tactic they had been using since their first days together, in the mid 1930s, while documenting the lives of Dust Bowl migrants in California's agricultural fields. In their linked but individual responses, it is easy to see the crucial distinction that would characterize their work, bringing to it a narrative tension even as it produced a coherent text. She had an innate, even intuitive, sense of the future inscribed within the object of her gaze, and it brought a modernist quality to many of her photographs, whether in the spare, stubbled jawline of a stoic field laborer or the relief of shadow against light in a field at harvest time. He had a deep, intellectual, passionate sense of history, of what had been, that was as vivid and clear as the present, and it drove him relentlessly to work at making the present retract to what had been good and carry hope into the future. In those first years they spent together documenting the widespread poverty of Dust Bowl migrants, there were many times at which that divergent vision marked out separate paths toward the same goal: better treatment of the Americans who had come west in hopes of finding work and homes; however, not until the Great Depression neared its end would they find a way to reach their goal. In their metaphoric conflation of physical soil erosion with societal human erosion in *An American Exodus: A Record of Human Erosion* (1939),[4] Lange and Taylor combined their voices to narrate the story of what they saw. It was a text that thrived on tension and difference, the extraordinary result of the extraordinary five years they had spent working together.

At Belleau Wood, their dual-entry notebook shows the same tension at this one moment, twenty-three years into their marriage, capturing how each could look at the same thing, their perceptions veering from each other, yet somehow together, producing a common vision wholly uncommon in its depth and meaning. Lange's side of the notebook lists the visual beauty of snow-covered villages, "beautiful patterns of bare snow-clad trees in wood and orchard. The French woods. The war memorials. The Sword, black, plunged into the white Earth." She writes about the congeniality of men in a little town's restaurant, "the rounds of draughts and cigarettes." Lange recorded the details, particularly the visual details, as signs of the present, but also as the symbolic aspect of a landscape not quite maimed, but forever changed, as it struggled to move forward from events forty years ago. Most of all, she noted the patterns—light and dark, hard against soft, face among faces—as they appeared to her. She was always looking at *things*.

Taylor's entry reads quite differently:

> No sign of life at triangle, because everyone here was indoors. At Bouresches, two youths waiting under a shelter eyed us but made no move. Outside the village, an elderly couple—not peasant type—had been in Paris during the war. "They say there were many dead around triangle." I had chosen a "mauvais moment" ([indecipherable word] & cold) to come to Bouresches."—Yes, I had also chosen a "mauvais moment" in 1918.
>
> Memory played no trick—the farms, towns, trains. The house in Bouresches where Captain Randolph Lange was eating chicken the night I established contact for the 78th C. The creekbed down [which] we moved, east of Lucy, to prepare for counterattack that proved unnecessary. The road to the right over the culvert where we got the men out—back from the forward position in the woods . . . Belleau Wood & the cemetery—the vestiges are vivid reminders—and the cemetery, and the woods & farms & the villages almost without life in the cold & under the snow seem so final, and quiet—& to have closed what in memory was so vivid and living.[5]

His experience is, indeed, closed in memory, as much as hers moves forward, creating the photograph it could become. Yet from husband and wife emerges the same story—war in its horror, the starkness of death on the landscape, the irony of memory. All are there, whether in image or text. While only one had been at the battle, both knew its impact on their lives. Their story starts there.

"White Angel Breadline, San Francisco," 1933. Dorothea Lange, American, 1895–1965. © The Dorothea Lange Collection, Oakland Museum of California, City of Oakland. Gift of Paul S. Taylor.

CHAPTER I

From Belleau Wood
to Berkeley

On June 24, 1919, at 4:30 P.M., the University of Wisconsin–
Madison conducted a ceremony that set out to do double duty,
both a formal tribute to "her Men of the Service and the Dedication of Lincoln Terrace." Sunny skies gave way to a trace of pre-
cipitation, and it remained cloudy afterward, with a gentle wind
blowing from the northwest. The university's program began
with the playing of "Semper Fidelis," followed by assembly of the
men of service, the bugle's clear notes likely sustained solemnly
by the breeze. A procession to "Stars and Stripes Forever" wound
through the campus's Column of Honor and halted at the Lincoln Monument, where the band played "On, Wisconsin." The
national anthem preceded an invocation by Bishop Samuel Fallows, class of 1859. Then the university president took the stage,
leading the varsity toast and offering a welcome to alumni, soldiers, sailors, and marines. Wisconsin Governor Philipp extended
an official welcome, and University Regent Colonel Gilbert Sea-
man's address, "Our Men in Action Overseas," followed, after

which George Haight, class of 1899, delivered a speech entitled "The Alumni Tribute to our Men of the Service."[1]

Finally, the youngest man on the program, Captain Paul S. Taylor, class of 1917, stepped up to the podium. He had arrived home from Europe only two months before. Facing those gathered before him, he gave a short address,[2] beginning with thanks on behalf of all servicemen for the "generous tributes" they had received and informing his listeners that he wished to speak not of what he and other men had done in the war, but of what they could do as citizens of the present and future. He declared that in the war, soldiers had come to know one another "as never before." In such an idea, he transcended decades of regional strife that had in combat been significantly reduced, his words reinforcing the soldiers' experience of solidarity in the eyes of other nations. "We have seen ourselves in foreign countries, among foreign peoples," he stated, asserting that when servicemen became aware of how "others see us," they found "their strengths and weaknesses, and learn[ed] our own." Ultimately, he claimed, the soldiers came back with "a wider, clearer conception of world problems" and a greater awareness of their "responsibilities for their solution."[3]

That solution, which would become a permanent ideology to which he dedicated his life, was collectivity, cooperation, and interdependence: "We have learned how dependent we are upon each other—the man at the front upon the army behind the lines, upon the camps in the States which trained and sent overseas the replacements and reinforcements which staved off defeat and brought final victory, upon the Navy which carried them over, and the dependence of the country upon all of us, and of all of us upon the country." To emphasize his belief in the important message behind that interdependence, he expanded it from the soldiers to those at home, claiming that morale remained high only because "our fellow countrymen and women were determined to make our efforts victorious." He widened this vision to the global scale, pointing out that "only when we completely acknowledged the interdependence of the Allies, one upon the other, and placed Marshall Foch in Supreme Command, did the tide of battle turn in our favor." Such a lesson, he maintained, would take the country and the world forward, leading to a "new world order which is only beginning to be established." In that new world, he urged that all must remember the crucial lesson of the war: "that man is dependent upon man, group upon group, and nation upon nation." To conclude, Taylor urged his listeners to think of the returning soldier not as a hero but as something more important—"as a man, broadened in knowledge and viewpoint, deepened by experience, humanized by intimate association with his brother-man, with stronger convictions of right and justice—a man come back with a strong resolution to be a factor in the guidance of this nation, not for what he can get from it, but for what he can contribute to increasing its peace, honor, and well-being."

Taylor's remarkable speech received a standing ovation from the crowd, and his fiancée, Katharine Whiteside, remembered "how deeply moved everyone was" at the closing line.[4] Then, before the ceremony ended, the university awarded honor medals to those who had survived, and read the Gold Star roll, a long and tragic list of those who had not. One hundred and twenty-five men were on the Gold Star roll that day, and the newly returned captain Taylor knew, intimately, of the kinds of deaths it tallied. His Purple Heart testified to the massacre he had survived at Bouresches-Belleau Wood. When the Germans broke through the French-British front, the French soldiers retreated, leaving the American Marines holding the line. Taylor's battalion, the 78th Company of Marines, arrived around June 5 and received orders the next day to attack and take Bouresches. In letters to his mother, Taylor described shelling and gassing, men being shot by snipers and taken to the dressing station, marines attacking by "running top speed through a hail of machine gun bullets." While he watched some fall, others were trying to crawl away from the bullets, and then, "an interval and another wave rushes across that same bullet-swept area, [and] this time there are even more sheaves of bullets spraying them."[5]

The marines lost the town to the Germans, and the fighting continued. By June 10, confined to a foxhole he shared with his captain, weakened by lack of food and movement, Taylor was unable to talk or eat. He was sent to the first aid station, and when he returned, he found his company being moved back from the front. The Germans attacked two days later, and Taylor's description is vivid and detailed, describing a bombardment of "big stuff, little stuff, gas shells, shrapnel, high explosives, etc. . . . The woods are torn to pieces." In order to lead his men in the growing darkness, he took off his mask, an action that would end up affecting him permanently. They plunged through the woods, stumbling "over everything, fallen men included," the smell of gas "pungent" and "[c]ries for aid all around." Only after he had secured his men in a safe place did Taylor begin to feel the effects of the gas, and by the time he was at the hospital, he was blind. Ultimately, the battle at Belleau Wood claimed 5,711 official casualties out of a 7,200-man brigade. In Taylor's unit, there was a 90 percent mortality rate, "overwhelmingly from gas, mostly 'mustard' with some phosgene."[6]

Taylor's sight returned, and after the war he moved west and enrolled at the University of California, partially for the health of his lungs, which had also suffered from the gas. He took his M.A. and then brought out his fiancée; marriage followed, then a doctoral degree and a faculty position at the university. In the years afterward, he would learn to put into practice the ideas the war had taught him were most crucial not simply to the quality of life in general, but to every human life: community, interdependence, honor, and integrity. It is this simple but crucial coalescence of the individual experience with the social principle that most distinguishes the work he did in California. He began studying communities of migrant Mexican fieldworkers, first in California and then, for a year, in Mexico. From there, he turned to the self-help cooperatives that had begun to spring up in the state in response to the Great Depression. When conditions in California worsened, the Division of Rural Rehabilitation of the State Emergency Relief Administration asked him to study the growing migrant population. It was an invitation that fit naturally with both his academic experience and his personal philosophy; indeed, his studies of how disenfranchised people learn to structure effective communities inspired work by graduate students. Anthropologist Walter Goldschmidt, who worked with Taylor, would go on to publish groundbreaking work on Arvin and Dinuba, two rural communities in the Central Valley; Clark Kerr, who would go on to become president of the University of California, left Stanford to study self-help cooperatives under Taylor's guidance. Taylor thus had much in common with Rexford Tugwell, the "unconventional economist"[7] who, as head of the Farm Security Administration (FSA), would have such an impact on Taylor's work with Dorothea Lange; indeed, he had much in common with the entire "think tank" of young, liberal Democrats whom Roosevelt enlisted to put the New Deal into effect. Under their guidance, the notion of social justice would grow to encompass a number of specific interests, including agriculture and labor, all creating, in FDR's words, "a genuine period of good feeling sustained by a sense of purposeful progress."[8]

Yet it was in the shambled battlefield that Paul Taylor saw his first glimpse of the new world order he sought to express in his speech that day. And significantly, it was the Great War that Taylor would cite in his oral history as being the thing he could not forget, something "burned into one's memory."[9] Like many soldiers, he sought to put that early experience into some kind of ideology. War, its great losses and heroic tragedies, is often represented as a watershed event that changes a life permanently. For Taylor, it *did* change his life, moving him in a new direction academically and professionally, relocating him, and, in that relocation, awakening him to new ways of thinking. He told oral historian Suzanne Reiss that the war taught him "to bear a responsibility for the lives of others." The Great Depression and its effect on California farm workers provided for him the conditions to put that ideology into practice.

Academically a labor economist and social scientist, morally a Progressive reformer in the Populist tradition, Taylor believed that his work, a combination of social science reporting and what he termed "nonstatistical notes from the field,"[10] could effectively awaken the sleeping moral conscience of a state and a nation, changing their hostility toward California's migrant agricultural workers. It was both the starting point and the goal of his research; he argued tirelessly, never losing hold of his belief in the innate goodness of the American people, a goodness that had been plunged, through whatever circumstances, into social despair and disparagement, yet could be literally re-formed into the "lost" Jeffersonian ideal—a communal and cooperative agriculture that Taylor evoked in his vision of "man . . . dependent upon man, group upon group, and nation upon nation." In writing, Taylor followed a recognizable literary pattern, structuring the devastation of the Great Depression as a "fall" from which every individual could be raised, "humanized by intimate association with his brother-man, with stronger convictions of right and justice—a man come back with a strong resolution to be a factor in the guidance of this nation, not for what he can get from it, but for what he can contribute to increasing its peace, honor, and well-being."

In that belief he was joined by a group of thinkers who emerged from World War I believing that catastrophic devastation could create the hope of a new world order and for whom the Crash, and the economic, political, and social conditions that followed, became the mechanism by which to achieve it. A diverse group—artists, filmmakers, authors, photographers—became, in David Peeler's term, "social artists."[11] All struggled to resurrect from the fallen society not simply hope, but a vision of something better, based on what had been there before. Diverse in their influences and methods, they relied on the same ideology and terminology, a "new world order," to articulate the future they insisted should and could rise from the devastation of the Great Depression.

WOMEN ON THE BREADLINES

The woman with whom Taylor crafted that vision was, in May 1918 (the same year and month that the battle at Belleau Wood broke out), arriving somewhat circuitously to life in California. After apprenticing in various New York City photography studios, twenty-two-year-old Dorothea Lange had reason to feel confident in her skills, for she had been a diligent student. She had taken classes at Columbia from Clarence White, the famed "soft-focus" photographer and friend of modernist innovator and photographer Alfred Stieglitz. She learned from working in the formal portrait studios of a number of New York photographers: Arnold Genthe, a man named only Kazanjian, and, right before her departure, Charles H. Davis, a photographer whose once-successful portrait studio business ("he did all the Metropolitan Opera singers," Lange remembered) had taken a downturn. Working over a saloon, she recalled, "he had this whole floor where he had—with a good deal of style—his laboratory, and all his drapes, and all his leftover grandeur."[12] It is not clear exactly what Lange's job was, for she says of that winter only that she was "sort of a pet" of Davis's. But from him, she learned a handful of technical tricks, including Davis's stylized notion of how to "pose the model"—with the head, the fingers, even the knees placed in certain ways, "all posed," she remembered later, "and then he would induce the atmosphere, and then he'd photograph."[13] Just as she had been with Clarence White, with Davis she was a "sponge," studying the trade, certainly, but also soaking up the entire idea of photography, learning everything that went into the business of photography and into the making of photographs. After her internship she had more ideas than any one photographer could put to good use, and she and her best friend left the East Coast, thinking they would go around the world. Perhaps she felt that with so much, she could not possibly fail; perhaps her

decision to leave was a means of refining and distilling the knowledge, finding out what worked for her. As Lange herself said, "I
guess it was just the time that comes in most young people's lives
where they just, for some reason or other, know they have to go.
I wanted to go away as far as I could go. Not that I was bitterly
unhappy at home, or where I was, or doing what I was doing.
But it was a matter of really testing yourself out. Could you or
couldn't you."[14]

After traveling no further than California, she set up a studio
in San Francisco, its main clientele socialites and western money.
Marriage to Maynard Dixon, the painter, followed in 1922; then
two sons, Dan and John, and then, suddenly, the Crash. The
advent of the Great Depression and the absolute shattering of
the lives in front of her drove her, literally, out of the studio and
into the streets to photograph the human wreckage. The pull was
highly urban; her initial photographs were all of displaced workers, strikers, people whose unemployment forced them into idle
roaming of the city's streets. The most famous of these, "White
Angel Breadline," she took in 1933, when, in her own words,
"the discrepancy between what I was working on in the printing
frames [in the studio] and what was going on in the street was
more than I could assimilate."[15]

Knowing that she had, in the photograph, captured a moment
"when time stands still," one that "encompassed the thing generally," Lange titled the photograph after the rich woman, called
"White Angel," who had set up a breadline, and the line itself.[16]
Lange's choice of topic and title focused on one of the more
remarkable symbols of the Great Depression, the breadline. Seen
in some ways as a vast agent of democratization, the breadline

suggested a shared experience. The fear of hunger, the need for assistance, the difficulty and determination it took to stand in the long lines—all seemed to speak to the common ground on which former millionaires might stand with shoe-shine boys, the two ends of the economic spectrum reduced, but somehow ennobled, by the Crash.

In addition, breadlines spoke to the reality of what the New Deal itself had to address most immediately: food. Even John Steinbeck noted in a letter about a flood in Visalia that "there are about five thousand families starving to death over there, not just hungry but actually starving."[17] Thus, the great political shift that moved the government directly into the lives of citizens in ways unknown in the previous decade may have entered through the kitchen door. The interiors of people's lives, formerly unregulated and certainly not documented, opened for an involved president who was, as one woman said, "the head of the household since he gives me the money."[18] The movement from the kitchen to the breadline, as Lange's photograph structures it, puts the soup kitchen in the role of a maternal and providing figure. Yet, as Meridel Le Sueur was reporting that same year, the breadline was not democratic, and its providing kitchen was not maternal. Indeed, Le Sueur's article "Women on the Breadlines" sets out to demonstrate that despite its title, there *were* no women on the breadlines. For that very reason Le Sueur was criticized roundly for her "defeatism" by the communist editors of the journal that published it. Implicitly, Le Sueur's stance suggested that narratives about the breadlines needed modification when it was women who stood on them. Without social presence, or power, women were absent from the breadlines and the headlines.[19]

A NEW DEAL NARRATIVE

The term *breadline,* both a symbol and a product of the Great Depression, thus serves as a starting point for this exploration of the work Paul Taylor and Dorothea Lange created together in California during the Great Depression.[20] Meeting in 1934, after both had individually turned their attention to the human toll of the Great Depression, Lange and Taylor set out together to construct a written and visual narrative that fused the fragmented lives before them into recognizable ideas and images that not only pled the economic case of the impoverished, but elevated them from the lowest level of society. Because that narrative developed over their years of listening to the migrant workers whose lives they set out to document, like the breadline, it was both a real and an imagined response to the 1930s and the many social, economic, and cultural shifts they brought; it was also a narrative that necessarily began in California. Lange and Taylor created work that did not simply document Californians on breadlines. Instead, they took the concept of California as a way to understand everything breadlines signified: hope in the face of unmet want, deprivation, need, dignity, individuality, and, perhaps most of all, the many motives that led to a desire for a new deal for Americans. California's exploitive, rigidly classed agricultural system housed a subculture created by long-standing Western immigration patterns that rejected workers on the heels of inviting them. At the same time, and in the same breath, that pattern of immigration highlighted the crucial place of California in the national narrative of manifest destiny, the state's long-standing symbolic function as a new Eden. Because of that unique combination, thousands of rural Americans migrated to the West Coast during the ecological and economic crises of the 1930s, in the process colliding with long-standing agricultural practices but also, in their cultural makeup and their expectations, bringing changes.

The visual and textual narratives that Lange and Taylor created between 1934 and 1939, the date they published *An American Exodus: A Record of Human Erosion,* suggest how much and how thoroughly they collaborated; but Lange's work and Taylor's also differed in significant ways. Looking at their work narratively highlights these differences, illuminating not simply structural contrasts but the reasons for them. At the same time, the great similarities the two shared in their work and thinking become apparent, starting with the clear understanding that their work belongs within the continuum of narratives that influenced the 1930s, and which the 1930s ultimately influenced: a genre taught in high schools and universities as American Protest literature. This is a literature long associated at its most insistent—and often least aesthetically successful—with the Great Depression: *Years of Protest,* to use the title of Jack Salzman's anthology of writing from the 1930s.[21] This wide-ranging, discursive field—including in its textual definition photographs as well as song and film, to name a few—came sharply into focus in the 1930s in tandem with two distinct developments of that decade: the rapid advancement of what would come to be defined as documentary photography and the unprecedented social tolerance for ideologies of radicalism, communism, and socialism.[22]

Lange and Taylor worked within this intellectual and political milieu, creating articles, photographs, reports, and, ultimately, a book—all of which contributed to a new way of understanding "protest in print." At the same time, essential components of what we can call protest discourse, identified in John Stauffer's anthology, *American Protest Literature,* formed the foundation on which their work was built. Stauffer identifies three distinct "rhetorical strategies": "The first two are empathy and shock value. Empathy is central to all humanitarian reform, and protest literature encourages its readers to participate in the experiences of the victims, to 'feel their pain.' Shock value inspires outrage, agitation, and a desire to correct social ills. The third characteristic of protest literature is 'symbolic action.'" Stauffer explains that symbolic action implies an "open-endedness in the text, which goes beyond the author's intent."[23] Such ambiguity separates the discourse of protest from, for example, advertisements, which rely on both empathy and shock value but do not provide an ambiguous enough message to allow for anything beyond the intent of the advertisement. Such a distinction opens up, literally, the far-ranging intent of all forms of protest discourse, which is not simply to convert (although conversion is essential), but to convert to action, the symbolic introduction of the possibility of action being the first step.

Stauffer's generalized rubric carries even more force when it encompasses photography. As Cara Finnegan has argued, the meaning of photographs—documentary included—"is not fixed or univocal, but rather multiple and ambiguous. There is no one identifiable meaning for a photograph, even when it is isolated as part of a specific rhetorical situation."[24] The photograph's insistence on freezing a moment in time while still remaining an incomplete glimpse into that moment invites the audience to, in John Berger's explanation, pursue "the connection between the image and the 'story,'"[25] forcing meaning into a discovery on the audience's part. In such an experience, the audience is, literally, compelled to perceive the multivalent possibilities of the photograph. And, while all photographs carry this open-ended, symbolic potentiality, the photographs that emerged from Lange and Taylor's work together in the Great Depression carry it to a greater and more complicated extent than is readily apparent.[26] While many of Lange's photographs would ultimately travel back to Washington for archiving, with Taylor, she learned to create and present documents insisting on a photo-textual interaction between image and voice that urged large-scale action on the part of the audience. Indeed, despite efforts to aestheticize Lange's photographs, Richard Steven Street devotes much of his massive volume on farm labor photography to Lange and her broad influence on "activist" photography, and Linda Gordon recently showed that the FSA photographic project was, as a whole, aggressively political and based on the ideology not simply of reform, but of protest. Noting that the FSA "was at the left edge of the Department of Agriculture, and its photography project was at the left edge of the FSA," Gordon argues that the photographers "challenged an entire agricultural political economy," exposing, among other inequities, "unjust race relations in the West"[27] and gendered conditions within agricultural labor and its perception.

FROM THE GROUND (BACK) UP

Paul Taylor worked passionately for the rights of the "forgotten man," the "one-third of a nation" against which the other two-thirds seemed willing to turn their backs. In his belief that all agricultural laborers should have the opportunity to participate in the Jeffersonian notion of the "agricultural ladder," the socioeconomic mechanism by which an individual laborer is imagined to move, rung by rung, up from worker to owner, he combined the Populist belief that a return to an earlier, better time was necessary with the Progressive-era conviction that "the present is 'better' than the past and the future will bring still more betterment."[28] Taylor believed in conserving certain past values, but, more radically, he believed in conserving them for the sake of those who had not traditionally benefited from them. His vision of the future relied heavily on a combination of nostalgic faith in small farms and land ownership and a firm belief in contemporary economic principles, including the mass redistribution of California farmland to those who labored on the land. In essence, he sought to *re*build a *new* order. His interest and faith in the self-help cooperative as a viable solution to California's migrant population did not wane throughout the entire decade. The last chapter of Lange and Taylor's book, *An American Exodus,* called for, among other things, a labor and machine cooperative that would allow poor farmers to use the technology that was changing the landscape of agriculture in the West. The fact that in the West an equitable distribution of land had never existed was not lost on Taylor. His abrupt introduction to the California farming system, with its large farms and seasonal workforces that were often at the mercy of corporate or absent—or both—owners, goaded him to argue for reforms that were radical in both scope and intent.

Some historians would argue that reform, the goal of any form of protest, rests within the heart of all American history and much of its literature. Certainly, our founding documents sought reform in the wake of a large-scale protest—the American Revolution. Even before that, however, American religious writing was based on the idea of reform, taking the discursive shape of the jeremiad, with a distinctively American element. Whereas this European sermonic mode began as "a lament over the ways of the world," decrying sin and warning of "God's wrath to follow," the Puritan mission in America was so distinct that the form shifted, adding a third movement to the jeremiad that constituted God's wrath as a corrective, "a father's rod used to improve the errant child," who was therefore capable of redemption.[29] Given the emotional resonance of this form and its importance to early notions of American identity, even the increasing secularization of the country did not diminish its power. Michael Kazin points to a "republican jeremiad" that Ignatius Donnelley read to the gathered reformers in establishing the first Populist Party's platform.[30]

While written as social science, Taylor's work was far more about human life, sometimes the individual human life, than it was about the statistics that quantified an abstract or academic understanding of "society." Thus, it is better understood in terms of what Janet Galligani Casey identifies as the "social-realist 'conversion narratives'" distinctive to the 1930s.[31] Much of what Taylor published during the Great Depression is built, discursively, on the narrative structure and some of the principles of the jeremiadic reform narrative, with reform reliant on conversion. His pleas on behalf of the migrants' individuality and dignity, his insistence on their right to a place to live and enough food to eat—all assume that, if recognized, such pleas could and should instigate a change for the better, a true conversion of society. The work Taylor produced with Lange can be read in the larger category of the social protest novel, but because it is so distinctly grounded in the matrix of social, economic, and political issues that were distinctive not simply to the Great Depression but to California during the Great Depression, it is better understood by looking also at significant aspects of the writing that characterized 1930s fiction and reportage, a genre that often relied on the conversion of the protagonist into a redeemed state, often "red."[32] Like John Steinbeck, Taylor was influenced by, but not writing in, the burgeoning genre of radical fiction. The social conversion he sought that would lead California to treat its migrant class as human beings followed, ideologically, the classic conversion trajectory. Casting the migrants as pioneers, Taylor viewed them as having, through a variety of social and economic mechanisms, fallen: their journey west marked them as both followers of a long-standing tradition and wandering exiles victimized by drought and despair. Once arrived, they were treated as outcasts, as human refuse, in a land that was both physically and socially hostile—their failed Eden. But, just as in the early Puritan sermons, the biblical framework, apparent in the titles of both Steinbeck's and Lange and Taylor's books, structures a redemptive vision and makes it accessible to readers. Reform comes as a corrective, a means to regain something lost.

While "triumphing over adversity" and a general "redemptive genre" had become a part of American culture by the mid 1930s,[33] Taylor both drew on the strength of that cultural genre and veered from it in significant ways. For Taylor, the means by which to pull society up was just as clear as the paths by which it had fallen. Taylor believed that with politically enforced small-acreage farms, the cultural as well as the geographic landscape could be changed, converted into a network of small family farms, each grouped into working communities based on shared labor systems but characterized by individual profits based on crop yields that went only to the landowner, not the land renter. Taylor's belief was economically sound, in general, even if there was at the time no precedent for the permanent success of such a system in California.[34] For Taylor, the key lay in homemaking—his overall metaphor and phrase for describing the complex means by which families settle (into) the land: they learn the soil, the climate, and the seasons, and, in so doing, take possession in ways that those whose relationship with the land is strictly financial never will. For Lange, however, the term *homemaking,* which she clearly understood in the ways Taylor articulated it, also meant much more for women in the West.

NO ROOMS OF THEIR OWN

Lange's own evolving approach to her work with Taylor is under-scored by a shift in the formulations of protest that occurred before she was born. Wide-ranging changes occurring in the nineteenth century had a profound impact on America's understanding of literary forms and literature in general, with increasing delineations among genres of literature—essays, poems, novels, and drama—combining with new categories of "high" and "low" literature, to create a much more diverse, if codified, system of literary production. When Harriet Beecher Stowe published *Uncle Tom's Cabin* in 1852, it was already understood that she was fashioning protest in a new model, something very different from that which the framing fathers had utilized decades before. In Stowe's novel, the urge to convert readers into a force capable of concentrated, mobilized action against the status quo is articulated through a highly sentimental rhetoric that draws on Stowe's willingness to put mothers at the heart of her country. Her intent was to change the political face of the nation, simply and literally, and to do it by relying on maternal sympathy and the ability of women to transform their feelings into actions. As Lange worked with Taylor to document the agricultural crisis as it unfolded in America's Great Depression, her work in California addressed the problem of changing female subjectivity in the mythic West. While Taylor seemed determined to resurrect or even reconstruct the western mythos of the hardy pioneer, referring again and again to Dust Bowl migrants as pioneers, many of Lange's photographs of women suggest a collision of ideology, reality, and expectation that women faced in California—and specifically because they were in California—in the 1930s. Much of this collision occurs in a domestic space, appropriately, for after the initial steps toward emancipation had culminated in the 1920s, the Great Depression saw, for a variety of reasons, women's return to domestic spaces. Susan Ware has written at length about the Depression-era pressure on women to demonstrate ingenuity in the household, to "make it do or do without." For both economic and cultural reasons, domestic service declined during the Great Depression, and women often sought to maintain a standard of living comparable to that which they had experienced before the Crash by returning to a variety of hand-labor tasks within the household. Indeed, the household turned "inward," so that "women's roles at the center of the family took on an even greater significance."[35]

By focusing on the story of how the Great Depression both continued the social destabilization of woman's role in society and simultaneously introduced new and unique complications of that role—including questions of domestic worth, professional value,

"Daughter of migrant Tennessee coal miner. Living in American River Camp near Sacramento, California." November 1936. Library of Congress, Prints and Photographs Division, FSA-OWI Collection, LC-USF34-009907-C (LC-DIG fsa 8b29876).

and sociopolitical place—Lange's photographs reveal a text less concerned with the reconstruction of a great social order and more concerned with an exploration of increasingly diverse, even antagonistic, social practices and messages. Because this narrative is neither overt nor independently presented as a separate text, it exists rather as a subtext, an unconscious narrative that the audience must unearth. This type of text, what Frederic Jameson would identify as an "ideology of form,"[36] relies, for Lange, on both time and place. Responding to long-standing cultural practices created and perpetuated in California, it both acknowledges her husband's use of the sharply delineated jeremiad of 1930s social realism and the humanitarian narrative, and breaks from it, responding to concerns that dominated portrayals of women in fiction, film, and photography of the thirties and to the social issues behind those portrayals, including the hostility that many women encountered in seeking employment outside the home (thereby "stealing" jobs from unemployed men). Such hostilities resulted in a reaffirmation of the separate spheres that had in the nineteenth century divided men's lives from women's, and which were once again, in new ways, doing the same. The women on the breadline were indeed, her photographic subtext argues, different. But the breadline meant widely different things for women.

In photographing migrant women whose domestic lives were lived out in the public space, or spectacle, of roadside, ditch bank, and even government camps, Lange documented the physical and demonstrable reality that, for the western migrant mother, the "separate sphere" debate was, truly, impossible. Taylor's energetic yet conservative appeal to a unity and order to which California could return is contested in photographs that juxtapose all the markers of domestic unity and order—pans hanging on walls, pots on stoves, brooms—with the fact that such markers cannot bring about either unity or order when walls are made of bamboo reeds, stoves are constructed of gathered refuse, and brooms sweep nothing but dirt. As greater America was turning inward, reaffirming the ideology of the family as a domestic interior space held together by the wife/mother—and the oppositional stance of the male sphere as public—the migrant farm women Lange photographed were denied such interiority, forced by governmental ignorance or denial of their problem to engage in the futile task of attempting to set up interior spaces in relentlessly public spaces: tents or roofless shacks constructed overnight next to ditch banks. As Depression-era women turned to housekeeping to create stability and permanence in a struggling society, Lange's photographic subjects "kept" house in cars, by highways, within the time frame of a harvest. Lange's photographic narrative does much more than simply expose the fact that the dream of the West had failed for Dust Bowl migrants; it interrogates the validity of that dream, suggesting that for 50 percent of its citizens, it *never* existed. Moreover, many of these women's futile attempts at the oxymoron of public homemaking were accompanied by their insistence, via visual constructions of the attractive and fashionable female, that they be accepted as part of the society to which they were denied access. Not only did Lange's visual representations of women in the California migrant system reveal the entire traditional western myth as a fraud *for* women, they went beyond that to suggest that, in their ability to construct themselves as part of a changing California social system, these disenfranchised women were an integral part of what California would become to the changing nation.

AN AMERICAN EXODUS TO THE GOLDEN STATE

As goes California, so goes the nation. The catch phrase has resonated in profoundly different ways in the more than one hundred and fifty years since California was given statehood, but perhaps never as uniquely as it did during the Great Depression. Still grappling for a fixed national identity and already entrenched in an agricultural labor system that received little attention and less understanding from the federal government, California stood in an uncomfortable and problematic position, clearly finding it difficult to fit into the New Deal's programs. Plagued by ongoing labor problems that had nothing to do with urban life, grappling with ingresses and egresses of workers whose working habits remained uncovered by relief policies, California threatened to tarnish its own image and take down the rest of country's with devilish glee. And it was not an empty threat. Democrats and Republicans responded not simply with concern but action to Upton Sinclair's attempt to grab the governorship; the Ham and Eggs movement stole the hearts of millions, and the migrant exodus, the "Okie" story that John Steinbeck's *The Grapes of Wrath* insisted on making public, provided a deeply disturbing look at the failures of the state and the nation.

Political responses indicate just how serious California's anomalous status was. FDR's patronizing meeting with Sinclair afforded the gubernatorial candidate enough respect to prevent him from protesting, but little enough to let those outside of Sinclair's camp view the meeting as "proof" that Sinclair was a certifiable nutcase, an unrealistic candidate for anything beyond dog catcher. Ham and Eggs became part of the social lexicon for crazy schemes, yet another successful PR scheme to belittle and infantilize a serious threat.[37] And the three hundred and fifty thousand migrants? Despite earnest attempts by several talented people to establish their place in the American historical continuum, both

"Migrant Mother." February or March 1936. This is a print from the
original nitrate negative (LC-USF34-009058-C). It was retouched
in the 1930s to erase the thumb holding the tent pole in the lower
right-hand corner. The file print made before the thumb was
retouched is available in copy negative LC-USZ62-95653. Library
of Congress, Prints and Photographs Division, FSA-OWI Collection
(LC-DIG fsa 8b29516).

Californians and the politics of the day encouraged the public to see the Dust Bowl migrants not as American citizens but as part of a foreign stream of field-workers that had moved in and out of the state, their identities exoticized and fetishized.

It is difficult to imagine the Great Depression without calling to mind the face of Florence Thompson, the subject of "Migrant Mother," a photograph whose circulation has been so widespread over the years that it deserves the title of iconic. The thirty-two-year-old migrant worker in Nipomo, California, and her three children, two with faces buried in her gaunt shoulders and a third lolling listlessly at her breast, all seem to articulate the pain, deprivation, and perseverance of what Richard Steven Street identifies as a subclass of the California labor class, and James Gregory names as a subculture: the migrant field-worker.[38] The stream of disenfranchised white American citizens pouring into California during the decade of the 1930s was both part of and distinctly separate from the continual waves of nonresident workers who sought employment in a state that is still called, for its astonishing agricultural output, the nation's "breadbasket."

Lange's and Taylor's individual journeys to California are also, like those of the Dust Bowl exodus, both similar to others before theirs and quite distinctive. Unlike many men who had preceded him, Taylor came not for fortune, fame, or even a new life, but because of his health and a desire to attend college. Lange was literally waylaid, her temporary stop in California turning into permanent residence. Yet both came with similarly Progressive-era mottoes, Lange's "Could you or couldn't you?" matched by Taylor's yearbook inscription, "I can and I will." In the West, both found their lives transformed in and by the state, and in that transformation, they changed the way the country, then and now, perceives the Great Depression. Their insistent relocation of the public's attention and sympathy from either urban tenements and street stories or "dusted out" Great Plains farms to the migratory farm laborers, the families in their threadbare clothes seeking work in the "factories in the field," carried within it the understanding that none of those pictures was separate from the others, and therefore none of the circumstances depicted could be remedied without California. Once World War II mobilization provided employment opportunities that helped the white "Okie" assimilate culturally and economically into California's landscape, the nation's understanding of field labor and its attendant requirements for immigration and migration, remained, and remains, unchanged. While Lange and Taylor were not the only ones working to expose conditions during that decade, their understanding of what they witnessed, and the forms in which they recorded it, would shape the country's understanding of immigration as a national, not a local, issue. As Rebecca Solnit wrote of Eadweard Muybridge and Leland Stanford, had either of them "stayed where he was he might have lived and died having made hardly a ripple in history." It was, she insists, "California that set them free to become more influential than they could have imagined."[39] California's legendary power to transform and shift shapes, an idea admitted into the union along with its physical land mass, has long been part of the state's mystique and has lured migrants and immigrants within its borders. It wreathed early settlers like Muybridge and Stanford, drove Lange and Taylor and, ultimately, fueled the migration of more than three hundred and fifty thousand Americans during the 1930s.

James Quay's claim that the stories collected in *California*

Uncovered: California Stories for the Twenty-first Century "show us many different Californias," providing readers with the means "to imagine the lives of others,"[40] is both naively innocent and starkly true. All narrative allows us to understand others, although the "others" can be grossly misrepresented and often expose the narrator far more than the narrated; that is as true in the West as it is anywhere. The West is, however, the subject of a cult of exploration, much of it into California's unique role and reputation. "The stories that shape[d] us," to play on the title of Teresa Jordan's and James Hepworth's anthology, are found multifariously in the story of the West; *The Way West,*[41] another book, created a master narrative that remains well known, although it is frequently contested in terms of gender, race, and class. Particularly in terms of California's fictional heritage, western narratives from Richard Henry Dana's nineteenth-century sea adventure to Sui Sin Far's eastern trajectory across the Pacific Ocean and Les Savage's post–World War II dime novels about how the West was won all rely on the dream that drew migrants to California and the often antagonistic reality that challenged that lure. Even the earliest creation narratives of California's hundreds of original tribes focus on how the first peoples arrived, following initial combat between Coyote and Earthmaker. The road to California fractures into hundreds and thousands of narratives, and beyond those, into millions of individual stories. Yet all share the pull of the dream and its counterpoint: the shaped stories document the reality of the dream along with, as Jack Hicks writes, "the ironies, looking around the edges of the promise where so many Donner Passes have lurked right beside the seams of gold."[42] As much as anything, tales of the West have made the West.

Thus, while Lange and Taylor continued to live in California long after the Great Depression, one element of the story of their California years ends with their own tale of the West, the book *An American Exodus: A Record of Human Erosion.* Five years in the making, it sought to put into photographs and words their intimate understanding of the story playing out in California's fields: its causes, its consequences, and its solutions. Tracing a cultural, historical, and geographic trajectory in which all roads have indeed led west, the book recognized in profound and radical ways the role of California in the Great Depression, its locus as both the failed dream and the "new order" that intellectuals and visionaries dared to dream into existence in the face of abject poverty. It would be the only book they would publish together, despite a private and public partnership that lasted unabated until Lange's death in 1965. Both groundbreaking harbinger of the future and unintentional swan song, the book serves to close this unique chapter in their lives. At the same time, as did so much of their work, it opened up something new.

Viewed as narrative, the visual and textual images that Lange and Taylor recorded in the course of their fieldwork in California provide a complex vision of this country, one that both invokes our history and interrogates it, that recognizes the emergence of new realities as well as the powerful pull of old beliefs. Above all, they have shaped the nation's memory. During her time, Lange's photographs were more frequently requested than those of any of her FSA contemporaries, and Jacqueline Ellis argues, along with many others, that "it was through Lange's eye that contemporaneous impressions, and subsequently visual memories of the Depression—and of migrant labor in particular—were formulated."[43] Lange's production of those images relied on her working relationship with her husband, Paul Taylor, a relationship that was equal parts intellect and emotion, ideology and compassion. California, the site of their intellectual and emotional engagement with the world, became the textual representation of their beliefs and their understanding of the flawed dream of the New Deal.

"Southeast Missouri. Horse and wagon is still a common means of transportation." August 1938. Library of Congress, Prints and Photographs Division, FSA-OWI Collection, LC-USF34-018981-E (LC-DIG fsa 8b33039).

CHAPTER 2

The Magnet of the West

The geological formation of Sioux City, Iowa, noted Paul Taylor, is "wind-blown loess—a very fine yellow dust [that] was blown up from Kansas during geological time after recession of the ice-age."[1] The loess, which remained for much of Taylor's early life covered by buffalo grass, seemed to him "a very beautiful formation . . . like the waves of the sea," with a "gently rolling" surface so smooth that he "never saw a pebble" during his boyhood. But when the buffalo grass gave way to development, the fine-grained yellow loam that moves like dust began to fly. Taylor remembered that when a street was graded for paving, it was "just like living in a dust storm. The mules and the graders would come, and they'd expose all this flour-like dust, so breathing the air almost choked you."[2] This clear recollection, vivid and precise, is not so much a predictor but an element of the attitude that would mark his reaction, years later, when he would face thousands of migrants dislocated by dust storms much thicker and blacker than those he'd known as a child, the results of which transformed the face of the state he had adopted as his own. Taylor migrated to California, as would Dorothea Lange, learning its unique physical and cultural formation through events both national and local in scope and effect. Ultimately, each brought to the state a sensibility shaped elsewhere, and both would find themselves grappling as much with their earlier experiences as with those before them in their responses to the problem they set out to document in 1934.

The boy born in 1895 in Sioux City was "third generation American, half English, and that English is Cornish, with apparently a touch of Welsh, and on the maternal side, half German and half Swiss."[3] Taylor knew his lineage and could tell with ease the story of his immigrant maternal grandparents, a Swiss grandmother and German grandfather, one of whose ten children, Rose Eugenia Schuster, married Henry James Taylor. He was the "Cornish" in Taylor's lineage, son of a miner who followed the gold rush to Australia, then to the Cape of Good Hope, and finally ended up in Black Earth, Wisconsin, a scant fifteen miles from Middleton, where Paul Taylor's mother was growing up. From her parents' farm, Rose Schuster could walk the short distance to a neighboring farm, from which she could see the main buildings of the University of Wisconsin in Madison. Inspired by that vision, Taylor's mother made her way to and through that university, in her son's own words, "by main force," teaching school to save up enough money to pay her own way and completing in three years the usual four-year course.[4] Taylor was proud of his mother, pointing out that women didn't "[attend college] much in those days. But, she made up her mind that she was going, and she did."[5] Rose Schuster began teaching immediately after receiving her degree, and it was at her post that she met Henry Taylor, by then a Civil War veteran and Dane County superintendent of schools. They married in 1887, and set up their first home in Sioux City, Iowa, where Taylor had moved in either 1885 or 1886 as a result of a political disaster with the senior Robert La Follette.[6]

Still in many ways a frontier town at the end of the nineteenth century, Sioux City was a hybrid of progress and history, and thus served as an apt representative of much the country's political and cultural state. Even as America was becoming more urban and industrial, many Americans clung to the old Jeffersonian ideals of the independent small farmer. The persistence of a sizable rural population (soon to be a minority) in the United States helped fuel simmering tensions between the values and interests of the predominantly agrarian South and Midwest and the concentrated power of urban interests in the industrialized Northeast. For farmers, increases in productivity had brought lower prices at the same time that the costs for producing and selling those crops remained the same or in many cases went up. Farmers depended on railroads to get the crops to markets in the big city, and following the financial panic of 1893, many of the smaller railroad companies collapsed. Those remaining came under the control of a few large railroads with monopolies on particular routes and the ability to increase the prices charged to farmers to ship their products. Increased costs and decreased land availability forced more farmers into tenant farming and sharecropping, and, ultimately, increased debt for overpriced supplies "furnished" by suppliers. The economic vise grip contributed to growing calls for agrarian reforms and eventually led to the Populist revolt, a short-lived political movement focusing on economic reform but espousing ideologies that would profoundly affect American thought, particularly through the casting of its anti–"big money"/pro-labor stance into the mold of the ennobled American worker.[7]

The markers of rail travel, westward movement, and tumultuous economics all remained with Taylor well into his adulthood. In a 1942 essay published in the *Land Policy Review,* Taylor recalled in his youth "hearing people consider whether to keep their job in the city or to take up a homestead on the plains." In the early part of the century, land openings on the Rosebud Indian Reservation in South Dakota became available via a government lottery, and Taylor recalled "trainloads of land seekers going through Sioux City bound for the Rosebud when word came to the winners of the drawings, when trips were made to see the lands that were won, to decide finally whether or not to homestead the claim."[8]

Taylor's awareness of the changing world around him may have been heightened by his own position as an adolescent in a fatherless home. In March of 1902, Taylor's father had become ill enough that doctors advised a break from the legal practice that had kept the family afloat during the Panic. "They never did get [the illness] diagnosed," Taylor recalled, "and as happened frequently, then, they said, 'Well, take a sea voyage.'"[9] On May 5, 1902, Henry Taylor wrote to his brother what would be his last letter, assuring him that he was "getting along well" and that he and his wife would leave the next day for San Francisco to begin a trip that was to take them from Honolulu to Australia, returning home on August 25.[10] Two months later, Henry Taylor died in Auckland, New Zealand, at forty-seven years of age.

He left behind four children, the eldest thirteen, the youngest four, and his widow just thirty-nine. The day after her husband's death, Rose wrote to his brother, telling him that Taylor had experienced problems "in the motor nerves of the spine, until the muscles of respiration became more and more inactive." "The last few hours, Henry's head rested in a wife's loving arm and with his hand clasped in mine. I went down into the valley of the shadow of death and when at four minutes before four in the morning of July 21, I could go no farther with my loved one, the idol of my heart, I closed his eyes, and returned with my aching heart, trying to battle on bravely for the sake of our dear little ones."[11]

The "dear little ones" that brought Rose Schuster Taylor back from the "valley of the shadow" would prove to be a challenge. Few single parents move comfortably into the role once inhabited by the departed spouse, and she was no exception. "I know my mother felt very heavily upon herself the responsibility of being left alone to bring up that family," Taylor recalled, "which in many ways she did well, but with a heavier hand than would be recognized as desirable today. In fact, I'm sure that she, in her later years, had some comprehension of this, too."[12] Taylor, too, felt the pressure, recalling "many, many happy aspects" of his childhood, but also "the responsibility of going on and fulfilling in some kind of way what [Henry Taylor] couldn't complete. I am sure that at times this feeling was oppressive. No one intended it to be that way, but it was there all the time."[13] Paul sang in the church choir and spent summers at the family's small vacation cabin, "Ambleside," a one-room building his father had worked in when he didn't want to walk downtown. His mother hired movers to haul it to the river, and there, on an acre of rented farmland, the family was directly across river from the Sioux City Boat Club. Taylor occasionally caddied at the golf course, danced until ten o'clock on the weekends, ate macaroni and cheese at family gatherings on the river, and pestered his sister's friends. But he was no Tom Sawyer. Under his photograph in the high school yearbook appeared the motto "I Can and I Will," a phrase Taylor insisted applied to his whole generation. "That was the motivation. What was before you was the question, 'Could you make good?' That was the common phrase, 'make good,' and you felt a responsibility to do it."[14]

THE PROGRESSIVE MANDATE

The country as whole was trying to "make good." The 1896 defeat of William Jennings Bryan, perhaps more than anything a rejection of political protest of any kind, led into two decades called by one historian the "springtime of social movements."[15] Increased prosperity and a proliferation of causes and their corresponding organizations encouraged Americans to identify themselves with, among other movements, segregation, immigration, rural and urban labor, socialism, temperance, and suffrage. Nearly all focused on reform, a concept that was evolving under the direction of a new group of middle- and upper-class progressive thinkers, most of them professional and generally well educated. Legislative changes were designed to improve, or "progress," the nation's well-being as it moved helter-skelter into industrialization, and encourage the belief that Americans were duty-bound to help those who were increasingly seen by progressives as unable, perhaps even unwilling, to help themselves.[16] Unregulated labor, among a host of other social concerns, brought about a new interest in the working class and a patriarchal desire to protect the downtrodden. As a result, social work, which had its genesis in economics departments, came into a professional-ized existence.[17]

With a family "deeply rooted in Wisconsin," Taylor "re-sponded" to family expectations and chose the University of Wis-consin at Madison for his college career.[18] At the time of Taylor's undergraduate work at the University of Wisconsin, President Charles Van Hise was putting Progressive-era doctrine into ac-tion, positioning Wisconsin as one of the top state universities in the country. "If you wanted to know where to send your son to get a vigorous contact with the problems of the day, Wisconsin was certainly one of the places to think of first," Taylor said, noting that FDR had purportedly considered sending his son Jimmy to Wisconsin.[19] Indeed, in the new field of labor economics, Wis-consin professors such as John R. Commons, who wrote the first bill for Workman's Compensation, produced a cadre of students who went on to provide FDR with the bulk of his New Deal ad-ministration. Wisconsin, Taylor says of the university during his tenure, "was a university where professors were concerned with political and labor problems of the day." There was a feeling, Tay-lor remembered, of not only "I Can and I Will," "but anybody could; if you had the stuff, you could do it."[20] One of his courses from Commons used as a text *The Pittsburgh Survey* (New York: Charity Organization Society of the City of New York, 1909), a landmark study of steelworkers enduring twelve-hour days, seven days a week. His understanding of the iniquities of life came "pretty fast," he said, in the field of labor economics, especially as he studied the pre–World War I tide of immigration and the influx of labor "at the bottom level" that pointed out a disparity between skilled and unskilled working conditions. "That was impressive," he recalled.[21]

On farms, though, "labor was somewhat different," and in college, farm labor seemed to Taylor to be the standard against which other labor conditions should be measured. Taylor himself had experienced two farms. One, a "decidedly unusual 2,000 acre farm" where he worked for a few summers during high school, showed him the agricultural ladder that would later play such a large role in his vision of California's future. While some of the laborers were seasonal, migrating north to earn some cash and leaving just as quickly, there was also a Danish immigrant employed yearly and paid monthly. Taylor's wages matched the Dane's, but Taylor knew that by the next year, "the Dane was going to rent and operate a farm. He was on the way to ownership, on the agricultural ladder." In industry, he knew, there was not "much of a ladder. So at that time it was very different to be on the bottom rung in agriculture, from being on the bottom rung in industry."[22] That awareness drew him to the "liberal" side, as he called it. But he was also quite conservative in his thinking about farm labor, and remained throughout his life convinced that the small-acreage model of operating and owning land was the best way to make agriculture work in America. He experienced that model firsthand at his uncle's farm, where he stayed from June to December 1908 and a few other times. At one hundred and twenty acres, it was a typical midwestern farm, just northwest of Madison, on wooded, rolling terrain. Taylor's memory of it suggests a Norman Rockwell painting:

The time when neighbors came was notably when harvesting grain—oats and wheat. My uncle was one of about eight neighboring farmers served by one among them, a Czech. The Czech farmer owned a steam threshing rig. The steam engine would travel down the roads at three or four miles an hour, pulling the thresher behind it. The whole rig would pull up to each of these neighboring farms, one after another. When it was set up you'd pitch the bundles of grain into his thresher, you see, and he would take as his pay a percentage of the kernels of threshed grain.[23]

Taylor's extended memory includes a work allocation that divides necessary, even crucial, chores equally between men and women. He notes that there was "really an exchange of labor in both house and field," with farm women preparing meals for the harvest crew at each harvest site. Taylor's delighted memory of sitting at the dinner table "like anybody else" when the team came to his uncle's farm includes pumpkin pies and a wholesale belief in the value of exchange labor: "In a little book, my uncle would keep track of how many days' labor he owed to whom, and who owed him. His neighbors probably kept track the same way."[24]

The Populist cast of Taylor's nostalgic memory includes all the elements that would ultimately shape his response to labor in California's fields: the communal nature of agricultural labor at harvest, the stark contrast between seasonal, migratory laborers and permanent stewards of the land, and the near idyllic system of true exchange labor. Farming offered the possibility of a sensible, tangible social utopia, a community in which men and women were afforded position and pay equal to the work they were willing to do. Such a vision was no doubt best articulated in the "producerism" tenet of the Populist ideology. While crop prices, shipping rates, and bank loans were at the heart of the party's platform, Populism also expressed a fundamental cultural resistance to the values associated with the new urban, industrial America of the Northeast. It held that those who actually produced the nation's wealth with their own hands, workers—especially farmers—should receive a fair share of that wealth rather than see that wealth being monopolized by a handful of factory owners and bankers who produced nothing. Moreover, producers had the responsibility to act for the common good of the community.[25]

And while the Populist Party cast itself in unflinchingly pro-American, Jeffersonian democratic terms, much of its platform reflected ideological concerns and concepts that, quite simply, sounded socialist. And in some ways, the era was a socialist time, even in the most Progressive years; Eugene Debs garnered nearly a million popular votes in 1912.[26] Taylor, a Wilsonian Democrat in Republican Iowa, was never a registered Socialist, but like many serious and social-minded men and women, much of his thinking reflected a concern for the position of laborers and their chances at self respect, and a belief in the power of reform. The thriving communal exchanges Taylor recalled at his uncle's must have, in light of some of the political talk going around during that time, seemed like the best possible direction for a country whose working poor were habitually abused in so many ways. And, whether the farming life he recalled was actually as smoothly idyllic as Taylor's description claimed became a moot point by the time he arrived in California; it remained the standard against which he contrasted the golden state's highly industrialized and inequitable agricultural system, the corporate-owned structure that Frank Norris aptly represented in the shape of a tentacled octopus.

HOW THE OTHER HALF LIVED

Perhaps one of the best examples of the progressive mindset came in a book. Jacob Riis's *How the Other Half Lives: Studies among the Tenements of New York* (New York: Charles Scribner's Sons, 1890), a photo-textual exposé of working-class lives in urban New York, sold eleven editions in five years and prompted Police Commissioner Theodore Roosevelt to call Riis "the most useful citizen of New York."[27] After arriving at Ellis Island in 1870, Riis, a young Danish immigrant, began taking pictures of the New York slums. *How the Other Half Lives* presents photographs that are still startlingly bold and bleak, capable of evoking pity, horror, and a grim fascination. Using flash powder, Riis was able to take interior photographs of New York City's most tragic ghettoes, and his pictures of "the other half" really show how they lived. Yet the photographs fall into an odd netherworld; they are not presented as art, and he did not consider himself to be an artist. Neither are they what we would define today as documentary, for their sensationalist tone and lurid qualities make us think of the *World Weekly News* rather than the *New York Times*.[28]

Riis was the original social service worker with a camera, but he was followed, and in many ways his work was improved upon, by Lewis Hine, whose work in East Coast factories exposed inhumane child-labor practices and brought public attention to the plight of the working poor. Working fully within the Progressive mandate, Hine used photography to investigate child labor in mines and factories in Indiana, Ohio, and West Virginia; glassworks and textile mills in North Carolina, Georgia, Connecticut, and New England; canneries in New York, Delaware, and Illinois; cotton mills in Alabama; cranberry bogs in Massachusetts; and the oyster-packing industry along the Gulf Coast. The annual conference of the National Child Labor Committee arranged for a showing of his work, and many of his photographs appear in *The Pittsburgh Survey,* the book Taylor read in his Wisconsin class with John Commons. Like Riis, Hine did not show his work in art galleries. He did not call himself an artist, yet he knew his photographs had an effect on people, and he sought to remain true to the scene in front of him while working to achieve that effect. It is this complicit relationship between the photographer, who does indeed have a purpose in taking the picture, and the subject, who participates, either willingly or not, in achieving that purpose, that makes the kind of photography going on at the turn of the century, and the entire notion of Progressive-era social work, so complicated, for it was built upon the clear division between the "other half" and the class of those better able to help that Riis's title identifies. Thus, while social work was taking place in charitable houses, a host of "social artists" sought reform through other channels: photography sought to expose conditions, and fiction, in its great realist and naturalist social critiques, sought to dramatize those same conditions through narratives of protest and redemption. Specifically, they protested the conditions in which the lower class lived by pointing out the absence of a solution, the lack of any redemptive pathways: Stephen Crane's *Maggie: A Girl of the Streets* (published by the author, 1893) protests the urban condition by focusing on its protagonist's inescapable downward spiral, just as did the photographs of Riis and Hine.

In the Progressive era, the earliest and rockiest forms of what would one day become documentary photography were being produced. Building on the legacy of Mathew Brady's Civil War photographs, which had been a startling counterpoint to the studio settings that marked the advent of photography, Riis's exposés of New York slums, taken at the time of Carleton Watkins's photographic accounts of Yosemite and California's Central Valley, were ideologically similar.[29] Bending the trajectory of photography to that point, they sought to capture events, not portraits, and the world that produced those events. In response, the American public demanded a constant supply of "realistic" photographs, everything from the rugged living conditions of Clarence King and the U.S. Geological Survey expeditions to any "real life" Maggies who might be roaming the streets. Photographers had to shift quickly, facing not simply rapid changes in technology but a growing awareness that photographs could serve a purpose, providing the kind of "shock value" necessary to move people to reform. Only a few decades after photography's introduction to the United States, the Progressive era was making it a tool.

Despite her eventual move to this brand of photography, Dorothea Lange, who was at this time training as a photographer, did not seem initially interested in much beyond the studio. Histories of Lange are almost universal in locating her choice of studio photography in her biography. When she was twelve, Lange's father disappeared, and she never saw him again. Lange, her brother, and her mother had to leave their home in Highwood, New Jersey, and move back to Hoboken with Lange's grandmother. Sophie Lange was a German immigrant; she arrived in Hoboken when her brothers were in their twenties, and, in Lange's amused recollection, they simply "plomped themselves down, right there," without moving any farther.[30] Lange remembered her grandmother as "temperamental, difficult, talented," a woman with legends and stories "crushed" around her. The family made money in lithography, and Lange referred to "rich German relatives" paying her way through school.[31]

Yet any family wealth seemed not to reach Lange's daily existence. Joan Lange Nutzhorn, Dorothea's mother, was lucky to find work at a library, but her pay, although double the average immigrant family's salary (including wife and children) in 1907, was still below the eight hundred dollars a year declared the minimum needed for a decent lifestyle in New York City.[32] Financial insecurity intensified Lange's isolation at her school, PS 62, where more than 95 percent of the pupils came from non-English-speaking families, and where Lange felt she was "the only Gentile among 3,000 Jews." Twice a week, Lange joined her mother at the library after school and from there walked home alone through the Bowery. "I became acquainted with the Bowery," she recalled in a 1963 interview, "the New York Bowery, down which I walked, every evening, at about five o'clock, alone. Now if you know anything about the Bowery in the winter, on a winter night, a little girl, a lame little girl, walking down that street unprotected was an ordeal. I had to do this for reasons that, well, there were certain arrangements—my mother worked in that neighborhood at the library, and I learned to be unseen at that age. I could step over drunks easily after a while. I learned that unless, that if one is not afraid, and doesn't look personally at anyone, they will let you go by."[33] Polio had left Lange with a rolling gait, a hitch to her left shoulder that accompanied a step of her right foot. Children called her "Limpy," and her sense of not belonging seems grounded in reality. She learned early that she had "more iron" in her than her mother, she says, but perhaps only because she had so little security, so few opportunities to sink into the adolescent's blissful knowledge that she looks, talks, and acts like her friends. Lange hardly had any friends. High school was hard, so hard that later she would simply refer to "years when I don't remember much. Nothing." Certain images, however, "the hands of Stokowski," for example, she retained, as well as the awareness that wherever she went, "there were all kinds of pictures. . . . My love of pictures is not limited to photographs. I love visual representations of all kinds, in all media, for all purposes."[34]

With that in mind, it is not so surprising as it initially seems that after high school, when faced with the question of what she would do, she said, "I want to be a photographer." She had never made a formal portrait, however, and set out to learn how to became a photographer by working in studios in New York, "nights and Saturdays and Sunday." She studied with a handful of mentors, including one of the leading California pictorialist photographers and an early innovator of candid photography, Arnold Genthe.[35] Like Riis, Genthe immigrated to the United States, coming to San Francisco as a tutor. When he was not tutoring, he wandered through San Francisco's Chinatown, using the smallest camera then available to take a wealth of startlingly vivid and candid photographs. He braved bad lighting and conditions, standing, in his words "for hours at a corner or . . . in some wretched courtyard, immobile and apparently disinterested" as he waited "eager and alert, for the sun to filter through the shadows or for some picturesque group or character to appear—a smoker to squat with his pipe, or a group of children in holiday attire."[36] In these early photographs, Genthe did not, as did Jacob Riis, photograph those whose lives were unlike his in order to help them somehow, thereby positioning himself socially above and apart from them; but he was nonetheless apart from them, his choice of subject highly aesthetic. He was drawn to the color, the movement, the spectacle, and the mix of old ways formulating themselves in a new place and through new types of gesture. In his naive belief that the Chinatown residents he photographed were picturesque, he exoticized them and distanced them from mainstream society; at the same time, his work candidly presents a remarkably accurate record of a group of people living wholly beneath the radar of what was already the West's master narrative, the story of assimilation and success in mainstream society. That narrative would strongly influence the work of Lange.

Oddly, while others have pointed to the similarities between his early street photography and Lange's, Genthe is not often recognized as a significant influence on the woman who worked in his studio after he relocated to New York. Perhaps Lange's own recollections of working for him, which distinctly downplay his importance as a photographer, have been responsible. By the time Genthe hired Lange, he had turned his attention to photographing portraits of women, many of them famous. It was in his studio that Lange saw Isadora Duncan close up (she suspected the dancer had been drinking, but did not seem too concerned about it); it was also there that under the tutelage of this "old roué," as she called him, Lange found "that this man was very properly a photographer of women because he really loved them. I found out something there," she continued, "that you can photograph what you are really involved with."[37] In Genthe's studio, Lange learned the trade, answering telephones, making proofs, and spotting the pictures—using India ink to cover any dust flecks on the photograph. She learned retouching on glass plate, learning to "slightly modify a feature—you could do it with an etching knife—and you filled it in."[38]

In New York, Lange dedicated herself to her craft, but she was not cut off from human life and emotions. The difficult childhood produced a woman open to human possibility and human frailty, a woman who valued the unexpected even if it disappointed her. Isadora Duncan, whom she had seen perform a handful of times at the Metropolitan Opera, had enriched her, transported her, changed her permanently, and Lange remained in awe of the great dancer many years later, remembering acutely the woman who was "rather sloppy-looking, rather fat, with very heavy upper legs, yet with a peculiar grace, not grace as I had preconceived it, but different."[39] Lange always seemed unable to avoid the particulars of people, describing herself as horribly disappointed when she found out that Teddy Roosevelt had a high, squeaky voice. In her "training" days in the studio, she did not simply soak up information but, literally, extracted it. Like Taylor, but in a hugely different world from Taylor's, she was a product of the fervent and vibrant times in which she came of age.

THE ROAD WEST

When World War I broke out, Taylor, who was between his freshman and sophomore years, went with his best friend to the president's office to request a special appointment as a second lieutenant, contingent on passing a physical exam. Both passed, and Taylor entered the marines. After being gassed, he was hospitalized for three months' convalescence, and returned to duty in September, just months before the Armistice. He returned to Wisconsin in May, ready to continue his studies, and, on recommendation of his Wisconsin professors, he decided to attend Columbia for his doctorate in labor economics. He had a modest scholarship, enough to start on, but after military doctors advised him to go to California, he wired the University of California and asked if they would admit him. Berkeley, which started classes in August, replied that he could come at his own risk. Although his original plan was to recuperate in California for a year and then leave, he stayed. He liked his professors, liked his fellow students, and he still felt the effects of the gassing. "I used to run a low fever in the afternoon sometimes for weeks. That suggested the verge of TB, and my diagnosis had been recorded as 'Arrested TB.' They never found the bugs on me. So, on the health side, I was doing all right in Berkeley but I still needed to take care."[40] He was awarded his M.A. in the spring of 1920, and before beginning the Ph.D. work he would complete in 1922, he brought west and married his fiancée, Katharine Whiteside, the Wisconsin student who had waited for him while he served in World War I.

Born and raised in Louisville, Kentucky, Whiteside doted on her father, a free thinker who lost the family business while recuperating from tuberculosis. She admired but was less intimate with her mother, who was well educated, artistic, and such a powerful speaker that she became a lecturer for Theodore Roosevelt and the Progressive Party, as well as for conservation. Katharine led a sheltered, protected life, her early memories marked by ponies, puppies, and fantasies of being a fairy princess. Given to intense responses to music and literature, and prone to spiritual raptures, she confesses that as a child, "the outer world . . .

was pleasant enough but seemed less meaningful than my own imagination."[41] She was an undergraduate at Wisconsin when she met Taylor, and was a serious, ardent, student—French, German, philosophy, biology, and sociology—who belonged to a variety of clubs, including a pacifist group, unrecognized by the university, whose antiwar stance put her into difficult situations.[42] Taylor was set to enter the military when Katharine accepted his fraternity pin, and when Katharine and her mother went to Alexandria to watch Paul drill his platoon, Katharine found, despite her pacifist activities and antiwar stance, that "though I deeply hated the war, I thought he looked extra handsome in his dark green uniform and was thrilled with the masculine strength in his voice when he called out 'March' to his men."[43] Ultimately, as it had been for so many women in those years, it was the thought of his going to war "almost immediately" that made her want "to give him all the happiness and reassurance" she could give. Then, suddenly, the war was over, and the men were coming home, and Whiteside found herself "all eagerness" to see Taylor. She had received word of his being burned and blinded for six weeks by mustard gas and being brought back to health with full sight, with only a little weakness in his eyes. Recalling her anticipation of his arrival, Whiteside writes that by that point, "He had become my hero, all I wanted in a man."[44] She determined to quell some earlier doubts she had experienced about marrying Taylor, reflecting that "marrying Paul seemed logical. . . . I did love him as a winning, handsome and really splendid person who was fully devoted to me, [although] I realized that marriage with him would not enlist my particular powers or fulfill my intellectual and spiritual longings."[45]

Yet when Katharine received a letter from Paul saying he

had been advised by a famous physician to go to California, she recalls feeling neither ready nor willing to disrupt her life so completely. She agreed, however, and writes nothing about the trip west beyond "the advice of a sophisticated older woman who asked me how old I was when she heard I was going out to be married. When I said, 'Twenty-two,' she said, 'That's too young. Don't hurry. A beautiful girl like you can always get married!'"[46] Despite her internal conflict, after her marriage, the new Mrs. Taylor took her responsibilities as homemaker "very seriously," learning to keep house, to polish silver and wood and brass, to sweep and dust, and to cook, all things that had been done by servants in her own home. Yet her initial disillusionment with marriage was profound, reaching from her disappointment at Taylor's feeling that her trousseau was too extravagant to a lack of much sexual compatibility.[47]

Both forced west, Taylor and his new wife struggled to adapt to this new scenario. Taylor's work at the university provided him with an immediate sense of purpose that his wife longed for but did not have. Lange's route west, on the other hand, hinged on a master plan with the title "Let's See What Happens." Just as she had, at eighteen, announced seemingly out of nowhere that she would become a photographer, she decided that after six years apprenticing in New York, she was ready to head west with her best friend, Fronsie Ahlstrom. In January of 1918, the two sailed down to New Orleans and caught a train west, armed with two large suitcases, a camera case, and the vague and impractical idea that they would be taken care of along the way. From friends, they took letters of introduction, one of which took them to live on a ranch in New Mexico "with people who were extraordinarily kind," Lange said later. It was, she recalled, one of those periods in a person's life "where everything seems to happen all right," and "you make friends with great rapidity."[48] They had little money when they set out, and after paying rail fare, they had even less, "only a few dollars," Lange recalled. They did not reach the West Coast until May and had already decided to stay and find work in San Francisco when Fronsie's pocketbook was picked. They looked at the little change they had left from breakfast, and Lange said, simply, "Well, here we are. What will we do today?"

Fronsie suggested going over to the University of California; Lange, pointing out the obvious, said that they had no money, and opted for a job search. She prevailed, and in light of the women's need for money and lodging, it was perhaps the only decision that could have been made. Much later, realizing Taylor had arrived at that campus only months after her decision to reject it, Lange could look back and wonder at what a good story it would have been, "in view of later happenings, if we had given the University a whirl."[49] The two women moved into an Episcopal home for working girls at 1040 Bush Street in San Francisco. Lange did not take the situation seriously at all; she knew she could get money from home if she needed it and still felt herself very much caught up in the entire mood and temper of the trip. It was the test she had longed to take, and she was still passing it, even to the point of talking her way past the Episcopalian deaconesses who twice caught her smoking before she was finally asked to leave. By then it did not matter. The home was for poor working girls, and both she and Fronsie had secured jobs the day after their arrival, Fronsie at a Western Union and Lange at Marsh and Company, a luggage and stationery store that did photo-finishing in the back.

From her perch behind the high counter, Lange watched the store:

> The boss was a very anxious and uncertain man, and the employ-
> ees had to be busy every minute or else he was afraid he wasn't
> getting his money's worth. He had a store manager who was
> cross-eyed, one of those good store managers, rather lazy but he
> knew how to sell. The boss used to get nervous; . . . if he'd see
> somebody coming into the store and hesitating for a moment (this
> always used to make me laugh) he would go up so fast he'd just
> slide, and then he'd stop short and say, "Was you waited on?"[50]

Her job was to take in the developing and printing, and to try
to sell as many enlargements as she could; if the store was not too
busy, she did framing. It was not long before she met some of the
city's most prominent photographers. "Usually the girl behind the
counter [at Marsh's] would be one of those gum-chewers who'd
write up the order and then you'd go," Roi Partridge recalled.
"But one day I found a new girl there, one who showed an interest in what you were doing. When I came back for the prints she
said they were good pictures."[51] Partridge, an etcher married to
Imogen Cunningham, who was at that point already a famous
photographer, probably knew the pictures were good without
Lange pointing it out to him. But he found out that *she* knew
what good photography was.

In a matter of months, Sidney Franklin, a rich young business-
man whom Lange met in a camera club, offered to underwrite
the lease of a building she had chosen for a studio. Right next to
Elizabeth Arden, 540 Sutter Street was a richly detailed, beautiful
building. Lange was to have the basement and back half of the
building; in the front was Hill-Tollerton, which sold etchings and

fine prints. But before they closed the deal, another young man came onto the scene. Joe O'Connor had access to three thousand dollars, the money of an Irish friend who was, Lange recalled, "awfully rich . . . and he liked me and he liked Fronsie very much and he gave the money to Joe and he said, 'Here, you give it to her. She can make this by herself. She needn't share the results of her work with Sidney Franklin.'"[52]

Lange's studio became a meeting place where members of San Francisco society commingled after having their portraits taken. Lange, developing in the basement, heard them above her, coming in each evening, and sometimes she knew them by the sound of their footsteps. "One night," she recounted, "there came some very peculiar sharp, clicking footsteps, and I wondered who that was. A couple of nights later I heard the same steps." Asking somebody who it was she'd heard with the sharp heels, she was told, "Oh, that's Maynard Dixon. Haven't you met him?" Lange had not, but, she recalled, "I did meet him up there a few evenings later. And about six or eight months after that we were married."[53]

Claiming a distinguished lineage that went back to Williamsburg, Dixon was born in Fresno, where the family had migrated from Virginia, and his father was Fresno's first county clerk. Maynard Dixon was old-school California and had moved to San Francisco as a young man, assured of the Californian's golden success in his own land. For Lange, he remained, even up to the marriage, intimidating:

> I was very hesitant in a way, about this marriage. I remember being in that darkroom and hearing those footsteps. He wore cowboy boots, that was it, with very high heels, Texas boots. He

had slim and beautiful feet, and he was inordinately vain of those feet. They were very wonderful-looking feet and hands that man had, and those slim cowboy boots showed it, with those high arches. Well, at any rate, I used to hear those footsteps and then for awhile I was very much afraid of those footsteps and when I heard them I wouldn't go upstairs. I avoided him.[54]

Bright, elegant, witty, and highly original, Dixon was a figure in bohemian San Francisco, the kind of man people noticed and talked about wherever he went. Lange recalled in her oral history that he was "the kind legends cluster about, without his making any particular effort." They married in Lange's studio on March 21, 1920. The newspaper report noted that "the only decorations were a few branches of the flowering peach and hazel, which gave charming color note while the soft glow of candles added to the artistic effect."[55] Roi Partridge's daughter, Elizabeth Partridge, describes the wedding couple as "striking: Maynard tall and arrow-thin, casually carrying a silver-tipped cane; Dorothea, short and compact, with her beautiful silver necklace and long, fluid skirt."[56]

Within a few years, Lange was managing a successful career in San Francisco, raising two sons and a third child, Maynard Dixon's daughter Consie, from his first marriage. The homescape was sometimes turbulent. The new wife clashed with the step-daughter, sometimes physically, and then repented bitterly her temper. No one who has spent time under a roof with an adolescent can deny the difficulties, and they alone can know how painful it is to raise a child wrongly. Neither Lange's remorse at her difficulties with Consie nor the difficulties themselves abated. It could not have helped that Dixon was gone as often as not: "It was his life's practice," Lange recalled, "to go on painting expeditions as often as he could," expeditions that took weeks to materialize and then ended up taking him away from home for extended periods. Lange said, "He was one of those people who could never get off! We were always meeting people who'd say, 'I thought you were in New Mexico.' And Maynard would say, 'I'm going next week.' Next month he'd still be around! It was interminable. Then he was always going 'for a month or six weeks,' but he never came back inside of four months."[57]

Lange stayed home, raising the children and meeting commitments. The separation between the couple was not simply physical: "It was sort of myself and the little boys, and he. It wasn't so much he and I, and the little boys. I thought I was protecting him, helping him in his work."[58] When Dixon left the advertising world to devote himself to painting, Lange saw her desire to support him as crucial, taking on the financial responsibility of regular paychecks to free him from that particular worry. Later, Lange would look back and declare, "See, I helped him the wrong way; I helped him by protecting him from economic difficulties, where I shouldn't have done that; I should have helped him in other ways. It wasn't necessary but I guess it was for his security, and my thought was that if there wasn't any money my work would keep us afloat, would keep us going."[59]

It is hard to know whose "security" Lange's work addressed. Her role as Maynard Dixon wife's offered her an odd variation on the cloak of invisibility she had developed in the Bowery: while she was in some respects highly visible, the lovely, energetic wife of this popular "San Francisco figure," Dixon's public mythos overtook him and his family so much that outside of her studio, Lange was not often called on to be anyone but Mrs. Maynard Dixon. That guise became simply a different way for her to remain invisible; at least her real self was hidden, and it became especially effective when she incorporated her own photography into the role of Dixon's wife. In recasting her work as a means of support for her husband's, subsuming her original desire to be a photographer into something she did out of financial necessity, she created at the same time a role for herself and yet another aspect of the Maynard Dixon myth: his need for a reliable source of income to support his talent. Her studio, started for her own needs before she met Dixon, she now envisioned as some sort of patronage, providing funds for his many sketching trips. Later, Lange would concede that the Dixons never went without money, and that they may have been able to live on what Maynard took in during the 1920s for commissioned mural work. Instead, she allowed her work to exist for his sake. Whoever Dorothea Lange considered herself to be when she arrived in San Francisco, she was hiding beneath a self-constructed cloak of invisibility by the decade's end.

BERKELEY AND BEYOND

During this time, Taylor was busy at the university, where he had become a sort of understudy for his major professor, Solomon Blum. "Blummie" had tuberculosis, and one of Taylor's assignments was to "stand ready" to take his morning class if he was not physically able. Taylor would get a call, often at 8:00 A.M., from Blum's wife, who would say, "'This isn't a day for Blummie to go out, would you take his class at 11?' The answer," Taylor adds, "of course, was 'Yes.'"[60] Taylor saw himself as Blum's protégée, a relationship affected intensely by the tubercular condition they shared. After Blum died in 1925, Taylor inherited his courseload, including a seminar on labor economics, which he took up without hesitation. By then, Taylor felt "up to [his] neck in teaching" and longed to get out into the field, as he had been encouraged to do back at Wisconsin. He joined with four colleagues to propose a study of labor on the Pacific Coast. The proposal showed clearly that Taylor was pushing his colleagues in the direction of what Commons called "applied economics," and that he had focused his interest in labor on California's fields.[61] Taylor wanted to use that approach to study the West Coast "because this agricultural labor situation was so peculiar, so unique."[62]

He received funding for a modified proposal from the newly formed Social Science Research Council. The council was just one indication of the rapid changes taking place in the social sciences, which were still new fields, at least academically. Few universities had sociology courses, and those that did offered them as part of the economics department. The same held true for social work departments, which grew out of economics departments and only slowly professionalized themselves. In California, Taylor explained, "almost nobody had taken doctorates in the social sciences."[63] But Edith Abbott, dean of the Graduate School of Social Welfare Administration at the University of Chicago and chair of the Committee on Scientific Aspects of Human Migration, wanted a study in California; sociologists at the time assumed that the wave of Mexicans immigrating into California would be one of the last of the great migrations. With the country's western and eastern borders effectively closed as the result of the Immigration Act of 1924,[64] only the southern border remained open, and Mexican immigration was left free to increase. "In 1926 the

Mexican migration was at high tide," Taylor wrote, resulting in "a focus of sharp political controversy between restrictionists, on the one hand, and those demanding unlimited supplies of 'cheap' farm labor, on the other."[65]

Working with surveys, interviews, and an intuitive process fed by his increasing knowledge of the problem, Taylor set out to answer his initial question: "Where are the Mexicans?" He went to Napa, where an agricultural extension representative told him he would find them working in the vineyards. But, he recalled, "It was in February, the wrong season." In the vineyards, they told Taylor to try the cities, so he went to the Southern Pacific railyard in San Francisco and asked for records of Mexican employees. He spent a month there "trying to see what data might be available in governmental offices or in employers' offices" before starting down the Great Central Valley. At Merced, he began to encounter Mexican settlements. By Los Angeles, he recalls, "I got a glimpse of the magnitude and spread of the Mexican population. When I got into Imperial Valley, I found that a third of the population there was Mexican."[66]

Taylor's field research attuned him to the seasonal migratory patterns of California's agricultural labor. Over a decade before writers such as Carey McWilliams and John Steinbeck dramatized the problem, Taylor saw firsthand the way large-scale farms worked: when thousands of acres of lettuce came ready for harvest, huge numbers of workers were needed in the fields, but when the harvest was in, the farm owners were done with the workers. In a pool hall in Brawley, he recorded one worker's complaint that "Americans want Mex [sic] only while able to work. When no longer able to work will go back to Mex." A fellow worker challenged that response, saying, "No. . . . Don't go back and be a burden to your own country."[67] While California's labor market had always relied on non-native workers, immigrants from various countries who built the railroads, worked the mines, and harvested the crops, the Mexican labor force was in many ways unique. The Guest Worker program—the government's perky euphemism—began in May 1917 when the U.S. Department of Labor issued an order to bring Mexican workers into the country exempt from the usual head tax, literary test, or any other restriction as long as they came for the sole purpose of agricultural labor. Mexican labor proved to be so economically efficient for the state that after the wartime emergency order expired in 1920, the policies that worked so relentlessly to prevent many immigrants from entering the country steadfastly ignored Mexicans.[68] The response was terrific. In 1920, "an estimated 88,771 Mexicans were residing in California, mainly in the South. By 1930 that figure had jumped fourfold to 368,013," 6.5 percent of California's total population.[69] "Informal arrangements," Howard Rosenberg calls them in a paper reviewing the farm labor tradition in California,[70] explaining that legislative attempts to control Mexican immigration in the way Chinese or Japanese immigration had been controlled often failed to get out of the state capitol. California's landowners simply loved the "arrangement," and it would not be challenged until the Great Depression sent hundreds of thousands of midwestern and southern farmers into the state, offering a comparable supply of labor.

Ironically, the Mexican migration prepared California for the Dust Bowl exodus. Mexican migrants were in many ways unlike the often solitary Chinese and Filipino migrants who preceded them, with qualities more like those of the European immigrants who for two decades sailed unceasingly into Ellis Island. Like the German, Greek, Irish, and Italian immigrants, Mexicans came in families, and they set up familial structures and communities. However, they differed from their East Coast counterparts in their lack of family chains, extended family members who would arrive first to pave the way for the rest into the new land. Because Mexican immigrants generally did not follow each other, they knew little about the established communities into which they moved, and, with a nuclear family structure already in place, they made little effort to integrate themselves into their new communities. Mexican workers had a shorter route home than any other immigrants and a culture more transportable than those of the immigrants who came before and with them. The *barrios* and *colonias* in which they were forced to live were as culturally rich as they were economically poor. Isolation, in some ways, simply affirmed the Mexicans' strength and heritage. Their work forced them to move from field to field, so they had little time to organize—although Mexican laborers did strike, with some Communist Party help, in the late 1920s, and by the 1930s they had begun to organize quite effectively. Overall, however, like the agricultural workers who came before them, and unlike the Irish or Italians, they had little political voice, despite the fact that Mexicans had once ruled the state.[71]

For many Californians, that sort of entitlement was a memory best buried or ignored. Response to Mexicans on the part of the white, landowning population, was typical—in an effort to "control" the rising population and at the same time enjoy the economic benefits it offered, the equivalent of Jim Crow laws appeared under the rubric of "local ordinance." The Imperial Valley had laws on the books that excluded Mexicans from restaurants, soda fountains, beauty parlors, and barbershops. They had special seating sections in movie theaters and public schools. Taylor himself noted the racial division and the attitude that Mexicans were inferior,[72] pointing to hazing in schools and, in employment, a racial "line" similar to the South's color line: "The shade of brown on the cheek may determine whether a man is employed in an industrial establishment, or whether a girl is accepted as a clerk or stenographer."[73]

What he saw in the Imperial Valley, he wrote, "hit me in the face," for it was "a labor pattern the opposite of all that as a youth I had known in the Middlewest."[74] Later in his life, he would repeat and elaborate on the impact of that experience, referring back to this time that turned the tide for him, so to speak, and brought him into a new and galvanized understanding of California labor. "I saw the great difference between the agriculture of the middle west and the agriculture of California. I saw the class distinctions, race distinctions. Domiciliary isolation, isolation in education. In land ownership. I think I found about half a dozen Mexicans in the whole valley that owned farm land. The contrasts were beyond my experience, almost beyond my belief."[75]

In *On the Ground in the Thirties,* Taylor cited the highly organized labor patterns structured around seasonal needs that led to the complete separation of Mexicans from the American population. "For them there was no 'agricultural ladder,'" he wrote, nor was there any bridge, geographic or cultural, to help them out of their economic plight. In California, he concluded, "Mexicans and Americans live socially in two worlds."[76] Along with creating restrictive ordinances against Mexicans, white Californians also created a popular mythos by which they could comfortably normalize the disparity, a way to "tell the tale" in terms that made it palatable. Taylor's book, which he liberally infuses with anecdotal research, provides an example of the typical view from one farmer: "If they were miserable or unhappy, I would say, 'All right; Mr. Educator, do your damndest.' But the Mexicans are a happy people. Happier than we are; they don't want responsibility, they want just to float along, sing songs, smoke cigarettes. Education doesn't make they *[sic]* any happier; most of them continue the same sort of work at the same wages as if they had never attended school. It only makes them dissatisfied, and teaches them to read the wrong kind of literature (IWW) and listen to the wrong kind of talk."[77]

The study Taylor did for Edith Abbott's fledging Social Science Research Council was perhaps the first of its kind. Studies existed on European immigration, but they were all conducted after the fact, when immigrant colonies had already established themselves. Taylor's study, done at the moment of what he called a "flood tide"[78] of Mexican migration, occurred while the Mexican labor force was still on the move in response to changes as they took place. Of the many difficulties Taylor faced in his work, one was the fact that non-academics, civic-minded people in charge of adult Americanization programs in the public schools, had done and continued to do what little research existed on the subject. Many of them, Taylor remembered, were apt to have educational or religious orientations, and some were ministers. Their studies assumed the Mexicans were culturally and spiritually inferior to Americans and sought ways to "improve" their lives, a term in this case fraught with all the predictably colonial connotations.

Their work affected Taylor primarily with regard to ideas for ways to set up camps and to improve daily life in material terms.

Further complicating the process was the fact that Taylor was an academic, and academic studies always take place in response to other academic studies. The lengthy literature review that prefaces any scientific article is but one example of the homage to the past that academics must pay when they set out to talk about any given subject. Scholars and professors are trained to put their work in the context of all related work that precedes it. Academically, Taylor's subject had no precedents;[79] it was not simply new ground, but startling ground, and in the confines of his own university, academically suspect. When Taylor spent two years in the field, the professional fallout was not small. The university president granted Taylor repeated leaves of absence, from January 1, 1927, through December 31, 1929, all in six-month increments.[80] But there were problems in his status. A 1927 letter sought to explain to department chair Carl Plehn that leaves of absence would not in general prevent a professor from receiving a promotion. Were there not, the letter asks, "some special complications prevailing in the case of Taylor," among these "perhaps the particular nature of the research, which involves delicate points of policy which might have embarrassed the University if it had retained Taylor on the active list and thereby more definitely sponsored his particular investigation?"[81]

There was additional controversy brewing in Taylor's academic status. The "pressures" Taylor mentions in his oral history refer mainly to agricultural employers, who demanded conclusions that confirmed the state's need for "more and more laborers from Mexico in order to have an ample if not a surplus, labor supply."[82] When university president William Wallace Campbell read Taylor's fourth study, on Mexican migrant patterns and practices, he "went up to the ceiling of his office on the second floor of California Hall and stayed there all morning!" Taylor recalled.[83] Campbell appointed a faculty committee to determine whether Taylor's study was scientific. When the committee found the study to be scientific, Taylor was allowed to go on with his research. In *There Was Light,* Taylor explained that his cooperative study, done with Standard Oil, had been focused on a daily count of automobiles with farm laborers passing over the Tehachapi Mountains, a geographical point of departure that James Gregory noted as determining the migrants' future economic success.[84] The university's relationship with growers was so strong that while the data was intended to let growers know of the availability of laborers, via informational releases from the university itself, those releases had to carry a disclaimer that the study was not affiliated with the university in any way.[85] Later, in his oral history, Taylor stated that the pressures on Campbell "undoubtedly" came from big employers down in the San Joaquin Valley, some of whom were at one time or another regents of the university.

"Straws in the wind," Taylor later called these difficulties, and in *There Was Light,* he stressed that the university supported his work entirely and liberally. Certainly, he was one of the first social scientists, if not the first, to be granted so many years of research and publication without carrying an equal teaching load. In return, Taylor seemed able to absolve the university itself of any animosity toward him, though he held the record for being an associate professor for eleven years,[86] which trapped him beneath a salary ceiling surpassed by colleagues who arrived when or even after he did. He had enough money to do what he wanted to do—field research. And the most important thing to him came neither with raises nor advancement up the academic ladder. In these early days, when he was forging the mold for social science research done "on the ground," what he wanted to know was if the university would give him freedom to do his work.

Taylor's path may have been just as challenging at home. In 1927, Katharine Whiteside Taylor organized California's first cooperative preschool, the Children's Community, and became its director; her pioneering work in that area would continue for the rest of her life, earning her widespread respect and a place in the Cooperative Hall of Fame. But she was far from achieving a professional reputation in her initial years at Berkeley, and with a husband engrossed in research, she could not have felt much personal satisfaction in the life of a university professor's wife. In July 1926, she had the first of what would ultimately become a series of affairs. While brief, and never fully sexual, the affair was apparently intense enough that her lover wrote to her after his departure, saying "he had heard of some murmurings about us in the University." Katharine, who had been reading books about open marriage and believed her husband would agree with the concept, accepted her lover's decision to leave, perhaps understanding that her ideas would not be accepted in the rigid university community. As to Taylor's feelings, they are hard to fathom. Katharine suffered periodically from bouts of depression that eventually gave way to more manic emotions and periods of intense social activity, and these mood swings were hard for Taylor to accept. In an interview with Therese Heyman, Rondal Partridge pointed to Katharine's ambition as a factor in a marriage he characterized as difficult.[87] Taylor's grandson put the situation in a gentler perspective: "Katharine suffered from manic depression. Paul was stoic and even-keeled, and I don't know [that] he was able to deal with the kinds of things that have to be done to deal with that condition."[88]

In the summer of 1927, Katharine fell in love with the director of the university's Institute of Child Welfare, whose classes led her to open up the Children's Community. Herbert Stolz immediately infused her life at all levels. When Stolz did not immediately reciprocate, Katharine wrote to Taylor, then in Chicago, asking him to return. His decision to finish his work before he came back was, in Katharine's words, "fatal to our marriage."[89] When he did return, she decided to tell him about her new love. Explaining that she wanted to follow Bertrand Russell's plan for open marriage, she found her husband "dismayed but [he] tried to accept it and adjust to it as best he could." The extent of his inability to do so was probably clearest one night when, after the Taylors and the Stolzes had been at the same dinner party, Taylor looked at his wife and said, "It hurt when I saw you looking at Herbert the way you used to look at me."[90] In December 1929, the third Taylor child was born, but there is some speculation that she was not biologically Taylor's daughter. Taylor, his wife, and the children continued living together, and by every account, his youngest daughter was as much a joy to him as his first two children. Taylor's grandson says his relationship with her "would be like this—I'm not going to take it out on her." Katharine writes that because her husband was feeling more established at the university, having published a number of volumes on Mexican labor, he "spent more time enjoying and playing with this Babe than either of the others. . . . They just loved each other from the start."[91] Still, given the struggles husband and wife faced within the marriage, it's not surprising that in 1931 and 1932, Taylor's résumé lists research "in Mexico on a rural community in Jalisco." Thinking, perhaps, that things would somehow resolve themselves, he could have had no idea that when he returned, California would be, literally, a different place.

"San Francisco, California. After forty-four years of Republican administration, California gets a Democratic administration. The California 'New Deal' faces same opposition as the national 'New Deal.'" January 1939. Library of Congress, Prints and Photographs Division, FSA-OWI Collection, LC-USF34-018791-E.

CHAPTER 3

Labor on the Land

Neither Taylor's oral history nor his wife's memoir makes much mention of the Crash as affecting their lives. Indeed, while Margot Taylor was born only a month after Black Thursday, Katharine's memoir focuses on the Taylors' move to a larger home and her efforts to make the open marriage work, both philosophically and practically. Yet when Taylor returned to teaching, the nation was undergoing large-scale, permanent changes. In the initial years following the Crash, President Hoover continued the optimistic front that he had adopted in his first few months as president, a time characterized by market instability. He encouraged Americans to address local problems locally, and they did so with a provincial fervor. As residents in all forty-eight states spun from the sudden and unexpected economic disasters that followed Black Thursday, Californians did not know what Mississippi farmers or West Virginia miners were doing; Omaha lived in ignorance of Lincoln City; Cleveland was a mystery to Cincinnati. It was not until the country moved into its fourth year of unemployment and poverty that politicians and public alike demanded a broad national program to improve not simply the economy but the daily lives of America's people. That program began on March 4, 1933, the first of Franklin Delano Roosevelt's famous "One Hundred Days." FDR's request for "broad Executive power to wage a war against the emergency, as great as the power that would be given to me if we were in fact invaded by a foreign foe"[1] underscored the fact that for many, the country *had* been invaded. Or, as historian James Burns put it, "It was worse than an invading army; it was everywhere and nowhere, for it was in the minds of men. It was fear."[2] Banks closed daily, thirteen million Americans faced unemployment, and evictions and foreclosures characterized the American rural landscape. Labor strikes were as frequent as factory closures, and men and women facing their eighth or ninth month without income found themselves forced to starve or steal.[3]

Labor strikes took on a decidedly different aspect in the West, where agriculture remained the largest source of capital. Despite the administration's attention to agricultural programs, its failure to understand the distinctive structure of western farming led to a severe crisis, especially in California. During Roosevelt's campaign, acknowledging how long agricultural America had been struggling and how important its products were, he reportedly pledged to the Farm Bureau's head, "One of the first things I am going to do is take steps to restore farm prices."[4] His promise to "call farmers' leaders together, lock them in a room, and tell them not to come out until they have agreed on a plan," was nearly fulfilled when the nation's agricultural leaders met on March 10 with the president and his secretary of agriculture to begin hammering out what would become the Agricultural Adjustment Act

(AAA). By March 16, Roosevelt was ready. He sent to Congress a request for an agriculture bill that would raise farmers' purchasing power, relieve the pressure of farm mortgages, and increase the value of farm loans made by banks. The bill passed the House on March 22 after five and a half hours of debate; five weeks later, it passed the Senate as well. On May 12, FDR was able to sign into law the Agricultural Adjustment Act.[5]

Diverse in both its goals and its plans for achieving them, the act had at its heart one unwavering purpose: to return farmers to the kind of economic livelihood they had known before World War I. The idea of "parity prices" was as much ideological as it was economic, as evidenced by the bill's term, "economic justice." What we now know as the farm subsidy bill did indeed create a system of income supplements in exchange for supervised cutbacks in production. It paid Oklahoma wheat farmers not to grow wheat; it bought steers from Texas ranchers and cows from Wisconsin and Minnesotan dairymen.[6] But the act soon revealed a fatal bias. The American Farm Bureau and the National Grange were both heavily involved in the writing of the act; the Farmers Union, which represented smaller farmers on more marginal lands, was largely absent. Subsequently, small farmers lost out in a number of ways, particularly when AAA checks were cut for farm machinery purchase, always with low and often no interest rates. As farmers—or corporations that owned farmland—bought machines, tenant farmers and sharecroppers who had farmed the land for generations, often buying plows and animals at their own expense, were put off the land. It was a scene John Steinbeck described dramatically in the opening chapters of *The Grapes of Wrath,* when the nameless tenant farmers put up a frustrated and futile cry against the absent landowners.[7] The tenant farmers' expulsion unveiled an economic mechanism that led Taylor to fully understand the Dust Bowl exodus from the South and Midwest to the West. In that unfortunate amalgamation of states, a forty-acre tenant farmer whose parents and grandparents had been on the same plot for decades suddenly found himself "tractored out."

Just as pernicious was the plan to put land out of production. Landlords soon figured out that they could collect the subsidy for putting forty acres out of production, with a fair economic windfall to themselves, simply by putting forty acres' worth of tenant farmers and sharecroppers off the land. Sharecroppers and tenant farmers who did stay and put land out of production never received subsidy checks. Landlords, who paid their croppers with a share of the crop, would take the government check, promise to pass on a share to their renters, and simply not do it. Their renters then had neither a share of the crop nor a subsidy check for leaving it out of production.

Both problems played a major role in the western exodus that ultimately sent more than three hundred and fifty thousand migrants to California. But California was already struggling with loopholes in the act that created some distinct problems for western farmers. "Basic crops," as defined by the act—wheat, cotton, corn, and tobacco—got quick benefits via government checks for crop limitation, but not all of those crops were grown in the West and those that were—mainly cotton and wheat—demanded large acreage and thus were grown on single-owner farms so large they boggled the mind. The amount of money that J. G. Boswell, who owned thousands of acres of cotton, made in subsidies is still not clear, but Mark Arax and Rick Wartzman make a good estimate simply in the title of their book, *The King of California: J. G. Boswell and the Making of a Secret American Empire.*[8] Small farmers were left, in more ways than one, high and dry, "the only effect of the program [being] to raise their hopes and expectations," historian James Burns writes, adding, "By fall Roosevelt admitted that the West was seething with unrest."[9]

WORK OR WALK OUT

Back from his work in Jalisco, Mexico, Taylor found in 1932 an accomplice of sorts. A young student from Swarthmore, a Quaker college, was working on his master's degree at Stanford. Receiving only a tepid response to his planned research there, Clark Kerr came over from Stanford to work with Taylor, studying the self-help cooperatives, a radical movement that by 1933 would include about three hundred and forty thousand members in more than two hundred groups.[10] Kerr's interest in the self-help cooperatives sprang from his academic interests: he hoped to make the movement the topic of his thesis, studying "the effort of the unemployed to support themselves and do so with self-respect." Such a stance was soundly within the Progressive tradition, for, at heart, it bespoke the "other half" as its target of observation and the goal of its program. Yet Kerr, like Taylor, added to that stance something quite personal, not fully academic. They shared what Kerr called a "rural background," something "that made one want to be in contact with the hard facts, made one want to be 'on the ground' where things were happening."[11]

Kerr became Taylor's research assistant in 1933, and his first assignment solidified in his mind how the cooperatives and labor exchanges could remediate current conditions in California, where workers were coalescing into a strike mentality. This was particularly true in the Imperial Valley, which was a time bomb, albeit one that had been ticking for years. In late 1932, prune pickers went on strike in Vacaville, and in the spring of 1933, a number of strikes occurred, many under Communist leadership.[12] Taylor lists them in *On the Ground;* beginning in the Santa Clara Valley and El Monte, east of Los Angeles, a succession of strikes moved across the state—"sugar beet, apricot, peach, lettuce, and grape harvests—reaching a climax in the cotton harvest."[13] The cotton strike, California's biggest and most complex, began clearly enough. On September 21, 1933, growers set the price of cotton at sixty cents for each one hundred pounds of cotton picked. Up twenty cents a pound from the previous year, it was, however, still forty cents a pound shy of the dollar a pound the pickers' union demanded. On September 25,[14] an announcement in the Communist paper *The San Francisco Western Worker* made it clear that battle was imminent. The subsequent cotton strike "directly involved over 10,000 pickers, held up harvesting for more than three weeks, and threatened, with longer duration, to spread to areas where the harvest was late and thus tie up practically the entire crop of the state."[15]

The role of cotton in California is, to say the least, contentious. Cotton, an imported crop, is difficult to grow in the state because of the scarcity of water that characterizes all farming practices in the West and because cotton needs a large area in which to grow if the grower is to be successful.[16] That combination encouraged large-scale growers to sequester federally reclaimed waters, legally available only to smaller farms, by whatever means possible. With water secured, farms expanded, instituting an ingrained hierarchy of owner, managers, and workers, the latter of which were routinely exploited in a system that brought not simply the crops of the south to California, but the plantation system as a whole. Exploitive land practices shifted cotton-growing from the Imperial Valley to the state's Central Valley. By the time of Taylor's studies, the Central Valley grew 96 percent of the state's cotton, and its harvest demanded a vast number of workers: ten to fifteen thousand.[17]

Kerr went into the cotton fields with two instructions from Taylor: "(1) to record what people said in their own words; and (2) to send him my notes as soon as possible."[18] What he brought back was the revelation of "the alignment of groups, their opinions, and behavior under stress," all of which "were exposed by the cotton pickers' strike of 1933, when thousands of agricultural workers, largely of alien race and under Communist influence, clashed with conservative American growers."[19] For both Taylor and Kerr, the strikes were a symptom of the great problem of labor exploitation and its institutionalized program of stripping agricultural laborers of dignity, self-esteem, and a meaningful sense of their own contributions. The answer they sought was not in strikes, but self-help co-ops.

The burgeoning "co-op movement" seemed to both men to be a potentially successful solution to labor exploitation and loss of self-respect. In an article published in *Survey Graphic,* the two men explained that in California, where cooperatives "far outnumber[ed] those in the remainder of the United States altogether,"[20] the glaring difference "between the literally overflowing Horn of Plenty and the desperate need of industry's human outcasts" had created a fertile ground in which the seeds of the "self-help-beats-charity" program grew swiftly. They found only one group, the Unemployed Exchange Association (UXA), an Oakland organization with a unit in Marysville, north of Sacramento, that demonstrated in its exchange of labor and services for food and dental and medical care a system that was "cooperative in any sense akin to what students of social movement understand by the term." The UXA unit offered a real and right future—a way to assimilate migrants into California's cultural landscape that benefited both the migrants and the state in which they lived. Here, in a unit that declined donations, maintained a rigorous accounting system, and had "genuine hopes to make repayments" on its grants, Taylor saw a productive community providing work and education to its members, one that had no need of Communists, "for [only] in a politically rather than economically functioning organization, [does] the typical communist leadership come more readily to the top."[21]

Communism did indeed threaten those whom winter had left with "depleted commissaries, [which produced] fertile soil for radicals," Taylor and Kerr wrote in the same article. Discontent within the communities combined with a myriad of factors—including the "genuine sympathy of citizens who wished to alleviate their neighbors' distress" via gifts of food and gasoline—to turn the "cooperators" to "chiseling" for handouts from local agencies rather than setting up true exchange programs.[22] One unit in Compton was a scavenger unit held together by the will of its leader, not the equal exchange of labor by its men and women for the things they needed. Another was run by an "energetic leader [who] had developed a chiseling organization par excellence," did little or no work, and leveraged its community aid from businesses based on the threat of Communist takeovers. "One man's boy died here," Taylor quotes the manager as telling him. "I called up the funeral director, the cemetery, and a preacher, and told them I wanted a burial. The boy was buried. If he had been cremated by the county, as planned, the father would have turned Bolshevik."[23]

The threat to landowners and local businesses of Communist-led strikes was real enough. With 142 agricultural workers for every hundred jobs in 1934, low wages and the harsh laws of supply and demand created a welcome zone for the Cannery and Agricultural Workers Industrial Union, founded in 1930. When the canneries announced a wage cut in July 1931, "nearly two thousand workers, almost spontaneously, walked off the job," but within days, Communists had seized leadership of the strike, "which spread to sixteen thousand workers."[24] Steinbeck's *In Dubious Battle,* a novel about the California agricultural strikes, has Mac, the Communist organizer, early on hoping to "start the fun in the apples," so that "maybe it will just naturally spread over into the cotton."[25] But it is Doc Burton, the novel's disinterested moral register, who describes the process that nonworkers feared: "When you cut your finger, and streptococci get in the wound, there's a swelling and a soreness. That swelling is the fight your body puts up, the pain is the battle. You can't tell which one is going to win, but the wound is the first battleground. If the cells lose the first fight, the streptococci invade, and the fight goes on up the arm. Mac, these little strikes are like the infection. Something has got into the men; a little fever had started and the lymphatic glands are shooting in reinforcements."[26]

At the very moment that Communist organizers were experiencing increasing success among laborers, the countermovement arose: the Associated Farmers of California, Inc., a highly conservative group with support from large-acreage farmers and landowners. Ignoring the heart of California's problems—why farm labor had become such an inviting field for Communist organizers' skills—the Associated Farmers were, in Kevin Starr's words, "using the language and psychosis of a Red Scare to protect their hegemony and investments."[27] Starr describes a "shadowboxing" match, with Communist organizers dreaming of utopian communes rising from the ashes of a united workers uprising, and Associated Farmers moving from counter-revolutionary rhetoric into overt persecution.

"RECORDS OF ACTUALITY"

California's tumult and upheaval were not confined to its large-scale agricultural landscapes. Within cities, and particularly in San Francisco, a city characterized both by unionized labor and ethnic enclaves of retail enterprise, unemployment created significant social and political tensions. Lange's financial success as a portrait photographer was threatened by the Great Depression, and like so many intellectuals and artists, she retrenched both physically and mentally in response to what she faced. When she and Dixon returned from eight months in Taos, New Mexico, living in a house owned by Southwestern icon Mabel Dodge Luhan, the couple split up their family and their living situation, an economic move with long-lasting repercussions. Under a special arrangement, they boarded their two sons, John and Dan, at a day school in San Anselmo, the cost of which was lower than the cost of renting a home and studios. Years later, Lange could describe the pain of separating from her children, the things she still carried inside because of it. "Even now when I speak of it I can feel the pain," she said in her oral history, "and it hurts me in the same spot that it did then."[28] The separation emphasized the world Lange suddenly lived in. Unlike many, she had enough to eat, but all around her, even people in the same economic situation were "shocked and panicky." Everything changed; everyone began, at some level, struggling to survive. Lange and Dixon each found studios and lived in them. Dixon's was at 728 Montgomery Street, a building with walnut balustrades that visitors—adults and children alike—freely slid down. "That studio was fine for him," Lange remembered. She returned to her former studio, where she had been before they left for Taos, at 802 Montgomery, three blocks down from her husband's. Lange's studio had taken on a notorious cast during her absence. Her brother had rented it out to "some kind of maniac, [who] tried to commit suicide there, unsuccessfully." But the unsuccessful suicide was the least of it, Lange explained:

> He cut his throat and his wrists, and the indications of what he'd tried to do were there. The police got him and he was very drunk and so on. But it was all in the paper, including my name, and also before this fellow did this, he had gone on a rampage with Prussian blue paint, and to this day I don't like Prussian blue as a color. He had taken it and he had just daubed wherever he felt like it. I had a portfolio of drawings, original drawings, some of them Diego Rivera had given me, and this maniac ha[d] improved on the drawings in Prussian blue . . . there was nothing that I could salvage.[29]

In Taos, Lange had been busy with the boys and Consie: "I baked and cooked and you know when there's deep snow on the ground you're kept busy. The gloves, the galoshes, the wet clothes—you put them on and you take them off."[30] Once back in San Francisco, without the girl whose upbringing had continually baffled and frustrated Lange, and haunted by a constant longing for the boys, Lange survived on work. As she spent the day engaged in countless "cold calls," telephone calls to ask potential clients about their desire to be photographed, her eye traveled restlessly to the scene below her studio, a point at which San Francisco's financial district, Chinatown, and Italian town all converged: "The unemployed would drift up there, would stop, and I could just see they did not know where next."[31]

She looked as long as she could until the day she said to herself, "I'd better make this happen." She made a print of what she saw below her, put it on the studio wall, and waited for her customers' reactions. The reaction was most commonly "Yes, but what are you going to do with it?" Not soft focused, not sensational, neither landscapes nor portraits—the prints she displayed had few photographic precedents. For two years she continued balancing her paid studio work with forays onto the street, and although she often photographed an event, the event was often distilled into a single person. "People that my life touched" is how she phrased it, meaning, probably, not the false studio environment of posed portraiture. Instead, she sought photographs of people whose poverty, indecision, and poignant hopes were indeed daily touching her life, people whose struggles with labor Lange empathized with at party meetings, even as her husband's "leery" feelings about Communism kept her uninvolved with the burgeoning movement.[32] When she saw these people, she photographed them, feeling "almost pursued," as she later put it, explaining that for artists "there's something constantly acting upon them from the outside world that shapes their existence . . . it's what belongs to the artist as a solitary."[33]

Of a collection of this work that she showed in December of 1934, Ansel Adams had this to say: "To my mind, she presents the almost perfect balance between artist and human being. I am frankly critical of her technique in reference to the standards of purist photography, but have nothing but admiration for the more important things—perception and intention. Her pictures are both records of actuality and exquisitely sensitive emotional documents. Her pictures tell you of many things; they tell you these things with conviction, directness, completeness. There is never propaganda. . . . If any documents of this turbulent age are justified to endure, the photographs of Dorothea Lange shall, most certainly."[34] On the streets, she had indeed begun to find the images that told stories, and she was flush in the age of storytelling—not romances or fantasies, but the burgeoning genre of protest literature. It would remain for her to begin shaping a narrative with which to do that.

In 1933, she photographed the May Day demonstrations at the Civic Center in San Francisco. Admitting she should not take time away from her studio but simultaneously acknowledging that she wanted to, she told herself she could "set limits" on herself: "I've got to photograph it, develop it, print it, get it out of my system, in twenty-four hours. I can't let it spill over."[35] Lange herself observed that the urge to portion out her work, to keep such tight boundaries that none of her own work would "spill over" into her studio work and home life, shows that it already *was* spilling over. As 1933 turned to 1934, the Dixon family all moved into a house together, a two-story on Gough Street. Lange gave up her studio on Montgomery, converting some upper-story space into a workroom. By April, Maynard was gone, sent by the government to Boulder Dam. The Public Works of Art Project (PWAP), which opened the door to the Works Progress Administration and Federal Art Project murals, made some funds available for murals, paintings, and sculpture to adorn public buildings. Based as much on boosterism as on relief, the PWAP murals often waxed patriotic about characteristically American scenes and themes—farm fields and, in the first days of FDR's colossal public works administration programs, dams. Dixon returned by summer, with a check for $450, just as the San Francisco General Strike was mobilizing and Lange was down on the waterfront taking pictures.[36] That moment was, for many historians, a turning point.

THE SAN FRANCISCO GENERAL STRIKE

"WOMEN, CHILDREN PERILED BY BULLETS," the *Daily News* headline gasped. The newspaper reported three killed and thirty-one shot, as officers poured gunfire into the crowds on the first day of the San Francisco Waterfront and General Strike. Commuters were the victims of tear gas when rioters "grabbed up gas bombs and hurled them back at police." Bullets and rocks flew in the melee, along with tear gas bombs and, the paper reported, "the new 'vomiting gas,'" used "for the first time in this battle." Rioting broke out around noon at the International Longshoremen's Association headquarters, where H. F. Sperry, a striker, was killed, and "within an hour two other men had died, one of gunshot wounds, the other from the effects of a tear gas bomb which struck him in the head." Strikers were shot at varying locales, including the Embarcadero, the Seaboard Hotel, and the Ferry building. At its height, the riot raged at the intersection of Mission and the Embarcadero, where fifteen hundred had gathered, while across the Embarcadero "were fully 5000 spectators."[37]

The strike was, even for a state already besieged by violent agricultural strikes, bloody and profound. Its violent upsurge, during which "so much tear gas was used that officers had to send for a fresh supply," was matched only by its aftermath. The National Guard was called in, and they continued to arrive, so that by July 17, nearly five thousand soldiers had flooded the Bay Area. After leading a delegation to the mayor's office to protest the police tactics used on "Bloody Thursday," Harry Bridges, chairman of the joint strike committee, decided against any further attempts to stand up against police machine guns; rather, he called for a general strike. The strike hushed the city, descending after the madness of riots like a muffling snowfall: streetcars, taxis, and automobiles were silent. The strike ran from Sunday July 15 until, against Bridges's wishes, the Strike Strategy committee voted to end it on July 18.

The strike emphasized a shift in California's economy that would lead to political and social repercussions at all class levels. By 1934, employment levels were actually up, but wages were down. It was, Kevin Starr asserts, a state of "partial recovery and partial impoverishment" that "created its own special form of restlessness."[38]

It was this "partial recovery and partial impoverishment" that formed the crux of Taylor's analysis of the strike, published soon after it took place. "San Francisco and the General Strike" (September 1934), which Taylor coauthored with Norman Leon Gold, makes a claim similar to Starr's, pointing to "the numerous unemployed and under-employed unionists" who were "ready for aggressive action."[39] While acknowledging that for "most Americans," strikes suggest "the 'dole' storm-trooper, socialists, communists, and fascists," Taylor and Gold put the General Strike into a historical context, drawing on Taylor's knowledge of the sailor's union and its work, and extending the "beginnings" of the strike back to the 1880s. The article moves through the initial confrontation, the declaration of a state of riot by the governor, and the subsequent violence culminating in "Bloody Thursday." The futility of standing up to heavy militia combined with the lack of negotiations and growing public sympathy for the picketers ultimately led to the call for a general strike. "In all my thirty years of leading these men," a teamster officer says, "I have never seen them so worked up, so determined to walk out."[40] The article then chronicles the strike, its effect, its cessation, and, most important, its aftermath. A "leading" capitalist argues that the strike was the best thing "that ever happened to San Francisco," for men "learned their lesson. . . . Labor is licked."[41] The article exposes a process of deliberate propaganda to create "an hysteria the likes of which California had not witnessed since the war," convincing the general public of communist infiltration. Taylor and Gold discuss the public's willingness to accept the "storm troop tactics to 'save America,'" and their docile relinquishing of civil rights,[42] and maintain that the real crime is the "smear" campaign that allows the majority of the public to miss the actual subject of protest: the mistreatment of workers.

What the article omits are the quotations and observations, filed on notecards, that Taylor recorded while down on the streets during the strike.[43] On July 18, three days into the strike, he was down on the waterfront and noted the following: "Walking down waterfront—west of ferry building—tall trooper—about 6' 4"— very young. Bayonetted gun—5 tanks—frequent guard. Double line of empty trucks." Heading to the Ferry Building that evening, he received a meal ticket to a soup kitchen on Embarcadero Street. There he observed a "large room holding about 150– 200—wooden tables and benches—tin plate, tin cup and spoon,

Beans with wilted lettuce on top and coffee—coffee good. Beans cooked," he added, "but I don't like beans carrots and cucumbers mixed in." Using a reportorial technique, Taylor apparently fit in easily with those he came to observe, writing down details that never made their way into his article, but that undoubtedly influenced his perception of what would form the core of its argument. It was the same technique that would, quite simply, revolutionize documentary photography in California.

Unknown to him were the parallel movements of the woman who, like himself, felt compelled to be down on the waterfront, recording as much of what was happening as possible. Lange felt herself pushed to take pictures, no matter what the physical dangers, of this event that was further changing the world she knew. Rondal Partridge, son of Lange's good friend Imogen Cunningham, wanted to go out with her, but she refused, telling him it was "too dangerous."[44] Years later, Ansel Adams would look back at that point in Lange's life as profound, not simply for what it did for Lange's photography but also for what it pointed out in terms of the escalating gap between the direction she wanted to take and that of her husband: "The general strike I remember was the turning point. Dorothea was very active. . . . Then she tried to get Maynard to paint the scenes of the strike, of the dock strike and the bread lines, and that wasn't Maynard's dish of tea at all. He just couldn't take it. . . . I don't know if that had something to do with their break-up."[45] Adams believed that Lange's understanding of both the general politics and the individual's response ran deep, and he looked back on the time as one that highlighted for her the disparity between the California dream and its reality. "She . . . lived in this area because it was very rewarding for her," Adams reflected. "It had [that] pioneer spirit." But at this point, the pioneer spirit that had drawn her was in sharp contrast to the dockworkers' experiences. For Adams at least, the proletarians of the East were "trapped by urban conditions, [and when] you get to the ship yards, the docks,—they were trapped . . . just like an Eastern person would be and that's where Harry Bridges came in. He created a world for the people that were literally trapped in their circumstances. . . . [Dorothea] was a great friend of Harry's. Oh, they were very close."[46]

THE STATE AS PEOPLE

For two years, Lange had been photographing people whose circumstances continually narrowed; at the same time, her own emotional life was narrowing, her home feeling more and more like a trap. Still, she walked the dual line, resisting everything that threatened the marriage and family while at the same time needing to pursue the work that, in its deeply emotional significance, brought out the woman who could tolerate none of her marital conditions. She continued to seek ways to make the marriage work. For the summer, the family went to Fallen Leaf Lake, a retreat in the Sierra. There, even while she relaxed in unusual family harmony, her boys, joined by Rondal and Pad Partridge, romping in and out of a sweat lodge Maynard built for them, she was thinking back on the strike, wondering, "What am I doing here? I should be down there." Instead, she looked to her surroundings, trying to photograph "young pine trees," the late afternoon sunlight and "some big-leaved plants with a horrible name, skunk cabbage, with big pale leaves and the afternoon sun showing all the veins."[47] Her recollection of attempting to photograph the cabbage made beautiful by her good friend Imogen

Cunningham locates almost precisely the moment at which she made the decision to photograph only people. Trying to photograph plants and trees because she "liked them," she came to an understanding that her "area" was people: "Difficult as it was, I could freely move in that area, whereas I was not free when I was trying to photograph those things which were not mine."[48]

Lange felt the extra burden: her studio portraiture was already supporting her husband's work, and now it must also support her "other" work. To do so, she worked alone for long hours, and while she did continue to place her sons in others' care, she did not ever say it was easy for her, or that she pretended it was easy for them. She remained entrenched in the role she had fashioned a decade before—the stable, solid source of domestic arrangements and income, a wife whose child-rearing abilities were as important as the paycheck she earned, allowing her husband his artistic freedom. It was of course a socially conventional role, for if not all husbands needed their wives to support them while they pursued careers as painters, most women were charged with full responsibility for children and housekeeping. Such social expectations sink deeply into the individual, and women who did not at least profess to want to raise their children and keep their homes were rare. In her oral history, Lange said of her child-rearing years that she kept herself too busy, that she was not "temperamentally sufficiently mature" to have dedicated herself to photography, that she had not yet stated her "terms with life." Convinced that she could best help Maynard by cooking and keeping the children happy, Lange formulated the belief that women were not able to focus entirely on their profession, "unless they're not living a woman's life."[49]

Significantly, Lange's work began to define itself to her only in the tumult of this time. She had begun her career as a photographer in the studio; when she came west, her intent had been to keep up the kind of work she had learned as an apprentice on the East Coast: portrait work that fell soundly into the tradition of European photographic salons. She began to take pictures of events and the world that produced those events only when her environment interceded into her life. Her move out of the studio came to her as a narrative vision: speaking of a street photograph she took in 1933, she said, "Five years earlier, I would have thought it enough to take a picture of man, no more. But now, I wanted to take a picture of a man as he stood in his world—in this case, a man with his head down, with his back against the wall, with his livelihood, like the wheelbarrow, overturned."[50] Attuned to detail, she could create highly symbolic photographs that sought to tell the whole story.

As the Great Depression continued, Lange increasingly thought in terms of contextual information, a filling in of the details necessary to tell not just the story of the moment she captured, but the story behind it, a photograph that could carry "the full meaning and significance of the episode or the circumstance or the situation that can only be revealed—because you can't really recapture it—by this other quality."[51] That other quality she was never able to put fully into words, although it is clear she knew precisely what she meant. Calling it sometimes the "vision of the possibility," she claimed that those who don't have that vision "are innocent and they live effortless lives meeting their little troubles as they come in a very noble way"; those who possess it, however, share a burden, the social as well as emotional responsibility of showing in a photograph how the person and scene before the lens are "really."[52] She spoke easily of "emotional correctness," working comfortably with the possibility of representing the interiors of life. Lange sought a angle of vision that was almost 360 degrees; "sometimes I'm aware of what's going on behind me," she told one interviewer, and early on she tried to capture what she saw in front of and behind her, not simply in terms of the photograph's visual information but also its ability to document "the state as people, in an area of San Francisco which revealed how deep the [Great D]epression was."[53] She wanted her photographs to tell not *a* story, but *the* story of the world down on the street, and she wanted somehow to insure that what she saw below her was not limited to her perspective. What she lacked at that point was the clear understanding, or at least a workable version, of all that she was seeing. She would attain that vision only after she began working with Taylor.

FORGING A SOCIAL PHOTOGRAPHY

Like Lange, Taylor had come to a point in his own research that had shown him the *state* of California—from the cotton strike in 1933 to its subsequent economic and demographic fallout. He had spent time applying his economic training to the social and political realities of California's factory farms, and understood that much of what the San Francisco General Strike represented was identical to issues in rural areas up and down the state. There was an inherent injustice, he saw, in the manipulation of the workers themselves for the economic gains of the larger group, and he saw in the wave of strikes a broad, ideological sea change. Workers were at the bottom and were striving for ways to rise up.

The radical left had moved already to translate the story of FDR's forgotten man into the narrative of the American jeremiad. The "red," or proletarian, writing sought regularly, and often formulaically, to fashion the inverted triangle of the religious narrative into a secular conversion that cast the workers down via the capitalist forces of industrialization and raised them up through their awareness of their condition and a resultant solidarity. Not everyone who adopted the conversion narrative of the 1930s believed in the proletarian ideal, but the pattern rang true for those who sought to balance the social inequities. Taylor, like many New Deal reformers, wanted his article on the waterfront strike to move beyond simple labor economics and to make a clear indictment of the conditions that provided such an efficient incubator for strike leaders' ideologies.

To heighten the effect of that protest, Taylor decided to accompany his article with photographs.[54] *Survey Graphic* believed in using photographs, and Taylor included a few photographs with his manuscript and sent it all to editor Paul Kellogg in New York, where it sat awaiting publication. Then a friend sent Taylor to an exhibit in Oakland, and he saw "this striking array of relevant photographs by Dorothea Lange," one of which Taylor decided he wanted to use as a frontispiece for his article. With his article on the San Francisco strike already on Kellogg's desk, Taylor secured Lange's number from the museum's owner, Willard Van Dyke, and telephoned the photographer to ask if he could use the photograph with his article. "She was agreeable and asked the terms," Taylor remembers, and he gave her Kellogg's number in New York. For the photograph, Lange received fifteen dollars and a credit—it was not at all bad money, and the acknowledgment beside the photograph, the equivalent of a journalistic by-line, was unusual at that time. Taylor says, "She didn't give any particular evidence of excitement. She was interested and co-operative; I am sure she welcomed the prospect. But there were no clues that she was suddenly overjoyed at this recognition by a professor whom she had never heard and by a journal she may or may not have heard of." Yet, Taylor insists, he was sure that she welcomed the use of her work for a good cause.[55]

Lange recalled her own response as somewhat mixed. "*Survey Graphic* wrote and asked me for some of those photographs of the May Day communist demonstrations to accompany an article, and I sent them two or three. They printed one, full-page, with their own caption underneath." Twenty-five years later, the act still seemed to gall her. "It wasn't my caption and it, of course, gave the picture a turn which a good documentary photographer is very punctilious about."[56]

It is not likely that Lange was either as aware of or bothered by that "turn" in 1934 as she was years later, after she had come not simply to recognize the structures of power within photography, but to differentiate, as she could not have then, between documentary and other forms of photography. The genre as she would come to practice it simply did not yet exist. It was due to an alignment of the stars rarely replicated in time that she arrived in California, that she turned her camera to events outside her studio, that after two years the fruits of that work were so quietly displayed in the tiny gallery at the same moment that Taylor, amid the accumulating responsibilities in *his* personal and professional lives, found an unencumbered moment to walk down to 683 Brockhurst and see the image that connected, somehow,

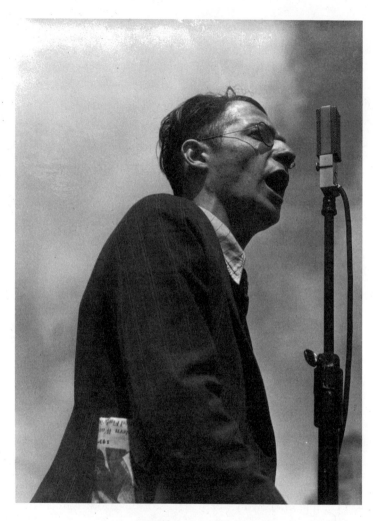

"Labor Rally Speaker," c. 1934. Dorothea Lange, American, 1895–1965. This photo was in the 1934 display where Taylor first saw Lange's photography. © The Dorothea Lange Collection, Oakland Museum of California, City of Oakland. Gift of Paul S. Taylor.

to his belief in the rhetorical power of photography and words. Lange became "punctilious" about documentary photography only after she all but invented it, and the genre that came into such focused form in her hands was largely the result of the work she did with Taylor.

That work began with a call from Willard Van Dyke, the studio owner, who contacted Taylor again to say he had some photographer friends, including Lange, who were eager to photograph the conditions of people in the Depression. Taylor, whose year-long grant for studying self-help cooperatives was drawing to a close, had made a number of contacts at the Oakland-based Unemployed Exchange Association. He scheduled a trip—his field notes indicate the date as September 29, 1934—to Marysville, where a group of men had taken over a sawmill, exchanging labor for a share of the profits. Taylor describes the trip: "So Willard got this little group together, Mary Jeanette Edwards, Imogen Cunningham, Dorothea Lange, himself and Preston Holder, an anthropologist. They turned up at my Cragmont Avenue home, on the morning of the day agreed upon. That's when I met Imogen and Dorothea for the first time."[57] The two women, friends for more than fifteen years by then, set upon the assignment quite differently. Lange had for more than two years been taking pictures "on the wing," to use Taylor's phrase, grabbing shots when and where she could before dashing back to Gough Street to continue her commercial trade; Cunningham was an established gallery photographer, her reputation, talent, and skill establishing her among the best in this era of artistic innovation. Karen Becker Ohrn's *Dorothea Lange and the Documentary Tradition* includes a study of Lange's and Cunningham's portrait work, noting how different were their attitudes toward their subjects. Cunningham, Ohrn says, emphasized the photograph: "She did not dwell on the value that photographs had for her subjects, but instead placed more emphasis on her interpretation of their character."[58] Lange tried to photograph her subjects in a way that would be useful to the subject—not the photograph. "My personal interpretation was second to the need of the other fellow,"[59] Lange said. At Oroville, Lange worked unobtrusively. She was "quiet, intent on her work," Taylor recalled. "Dorothea moved around inconspicuously. Imogen set up and made a few studied, well-arranged, well-executed photographs."[60] "You could see even then the difference in the way those photographers saw. You could see the difference between Imogen's and Dorothea's work very clearly. Both of them very fine, but very different."[61]

On that trip, Lange had an opportunity to immerse herself in the situation, to seek out that "other quality" that would get to the "full meaning and significance of the episode or the circumstance or the situation." Contextual information was clear, visual, accessible; the small details she had been seeking sprang up abundantly, creating the narrative of each photographic subject's life. On a wooden porch, two young boys, their faces dirty, their shoes old, their coveralls baggy, watch over their toddler sister. In the middle of the unit, four women in cotton stockings, flowered dresses, and baggy sweaters huddle in communal discussion. A ruddy-faced woman stands in front of her line-dried wash, proudly holding her baby. The cavernous entrance to the machine shop dwarfs a machinist, and in a profile view of a worker, hands grasp oversized machinery.

While the photographers worked, Taylor sat in one of the wood cabins in which the group was housed and talked with

"UXA Workers, Oroville, 1934." BANC PIC 1905.17139:1-80—A.
Personalities and Activities in the Self-Help Cooperatives of
California: Photographs from the Exhibition, 1933–1934. Courtesy
of The Bancroft Library, University of California, Berkeley.

the workers. "I always had my notebook out," Taylor recalled. "It helped me and I did it in a way which did not impede the conversation, but I think on the whole was pleasing and acceptable to the people I was interviewing." His phrasing and philosophy were, at the time, quite similar to Lange's. The idea that the work he was doing was somehow "pleasing and acceptable to the people" was almost a direct echo of Lange's wish to be "useful" to her clients, which meant, to her, "filling a need, really pleasing the people for whom I was working."[62]

Many years later, Lange recalled the trip for Suzanne Reiss, meditating on the difficulty of being "useful" to such clients. With the vantage of hindsight, Lange remembered "the whole business of being up there as something very sad and dreary and doomed." It was a dream, she felt, that the sawmill the men had taken over would support "a lot of them down in Oakland who would in exchange send up things they needed, and so on. This has been tried many times when people are really up against it." It was, she concluded, "a most heart-breaking effort." What made it saddest, in her memory, was the fact that the people themselves had no idea of how doomed they were. "You know," she continued, "there are always a few enthusiastic souls in such things who carry the others along with them in spite of everything that goes wrong. Yet they were so very much on the bottom that they lacked everything to do with. There was nothing to hand. It was all in the hope, and in the glimmer of a possibility of success. In the meanwhile there wasn't too much to eat and what there was was old carrots and turnips. Not enough oil to run the engines, not enough shingles for the roof, not enough of anything excepting courage on the part of a few. It was a sad thing, that was."[63]

Lange's comments, made in retrospect, are colored by experience and a philosophical understanding of her work. Noting that she had gone up to Oroville "optimistically," thinking that she could "photograph something that would help them and get more people interested," she ends her memory of the trip with the realization that, were she given the opportunity at that point in her life to make the same trip, she would "have a real document, a real record. But I have none because I didn't really see it."[64] The "it" to which she referred at the time was the whole story, the reality that agricultural labor is not only about people, but about "the story of our natural resources," the manipulation of land and water that has marked California commercial farming from its inception, dispossessing those who came before and after the Dust Bowl.

For Taylor, already by then highly aware of those practices, the UXA represented a very different "hope," a very real "glimmer of a possibility of success." Beyond the likelihood of the initial Exchange working, he saw independence in the attempt and community, a group of self-reliant workers capable of working toward a shared goal. Their intent was to make the individual life good via the communal interworkings of the members and vice versa, a social system in which, as Taylor's postwar speech had declared, man is dependent upon man, group upon group. To broaden that practice outside the Exchange, however, Taylor knew he needed a way to persuade those who could not or would not see the potential that he saw in this community. Even without knowing how, Taylor believed that the work done in those two days would help the community, and he saw Lange as central to that achievement. Indeed, Taylor's commitment to his own work and his ability to see that commitment visually articulated in Lange's photography quickly became one and the same. A document in

Taylor's archives on an untitled Xeroxed paper, with revisions in Taylor's own hand, shows exactly how he felt about Lange's work and the degree to which it encompassed his: "Careful study of Lange's photographs from the period of her earliest association with Paul Taylor clearly indicates that from the beginning she had a total grasp of what she should do with her camera to factually document the condition she found in a meaningful fashion. Paul Taylor aided Lange in her development as a social observer, and this, coupled with her own innate feelings about what she saw around her made her the best observer of the human condition within the FSA program."[65]

Like many of the onion-paper documents crammed into the hundreds of folders of Taylor's work that the Bancroft Library houses, this one indicates no author or context. Like many, it emphasizes the quiet, yet full, sense of wonder he felt that this woman upon whose work he had practically stumbled was able to "say" things with her camera that he himself had not yet been able to say, things that needed to be said. Taylor's chance discovery of Lange's abilities occurred just as Lange was ready to find a voice for her own talents. She had been photographing indigents, the needy and wounded, for a few years, but without what we would call a coherent text—a story that really made their condition both clear and palatable to an audience. Taylor's vision allowed her to move beyond simply witnessing the tragic conditions of those before her; in the implied promise of better days, days those people could help to bring upon themselves, she became able to see nobility and strength. Without hope of some kind of solution, few Americans are able to tolerate photographs or stories of poverty, starvation, and sickness. Just as significant, however, is the *shape* of that solution, the upward movement that casts remediation as redemption. Lange recognized this on a very personal level and may have been responding at that level to the fact that finally, when looking through Taylor's "lens," she was able to take pictures of people whose tragic conditions were quantifiable, explicable, and at least potentially temporary. Her photographs could bring them "up" from where they had fallen.

Taylor arranged for an exhibit of the photographs to appear at Haviland Hall, on the Berkeley campus, in early November. Before that, while nearly all accounts list the following February as her official beginning with government work, Lange seems to have done some work for Taylor.[66] Right before the show was scheduled to open, Lange sent Taylor a note: "Dear Dr. Taylor," she wrote, saying that she had finished photographing "Andy"[67] and would show him the results whenever possible; but, she continued, she had nothing of the UXA units down the peninsula because "the present boss of my SERA project couldn't see any sense in my wanting to do that." Expressing disappointment at "not being permitted to make use of what seems to me a big opportunity to make a record," she pledges patience and asks if she can "help get the UXA show on the wall Saturday night."

Among the eighty prints Taylor exhibited and then deposited in the Bancroft Library, five are by Van Dyke, thirteen by Lange, four by Cunningham, and seven by Taylor himself. The majority are unattributed, and not all come from the 1934 trip. What they demonstrate, even more than the conditions or the specific details of the camp life, is Taylor's acute awareness of the power of the visual. During his 1931–32 Guggenheim Fellowship study in Mexico, Taylor had purchased a Rolleiflex, but he had begun using a camera as far back as World War I, taking photographs of his foxhole.[68] Building on his initial photographic attempts while in France during the war, he had been slowly working toward a method of using photography not to illustrate but actually to make his point. In Mexico, he realized that "no amount or quality of words could alone convey what the situation was that I was studying. It was another language, if you will."[69] He knew, in essence, what documentary photography was, but had not been able to produce it.

Lange, on the other hand, was producing it without knowing what it was or what her photographs could do. Without knowing either, her hunger to continue grew, and it was not simply because she was receiving attention and praise (although those things, like a paycheck, helped to validate the work), and not simply because it was different from the work of those around her (although, again, the lack of precedents seems to have helped her focus on what she was doing). After more than a decade within the circle of her husband's world, her work was becoming her own, and at the very moment that she was savoring the taste of that, she was already craving more. Because she needed to find some way to continue taking photographs of these people, their plight, now entwined with her own future, became personal. Despite the street identities that they could not share with her, she knew them; she believed that they needed her, and it was quite easy for her to see that they needed her more than her studio clients did, and more than Dixon did. It is not clear if she knew at the time, if she ever knew, how much she needed them, that their mended hosiery and bent hat rims had somehow set her free. Truly, only one person's needs may have been at that moment as clear to her as this large and nebulous need she felt from the street—and those would be Taylor's, whose ability to recognize Lange's street photographs as work, not a hobby, helped convince her of her own future. From the start, Taylor made it clear that he needed Lange to help make happen what he felt, to his core, must happen in California.

"Pea pickers from Vermont—6 weeks earnings $7.00—at squatter's camp, Nipomo." 1935. Library of Congress, Prints and Photographs Division, FSA-OWI Collection, LC-USZ62-69104.

CHAPTER 4

Far West Factories

Following the exhibit at Haviland Hall, Taylor and Lange's work
shifted in scope and content. In January, working together again,
they left for the lowest reaches of San Luis Obispo County. On
the second day, their notes and photographs produced the earliest
narrative structure of the work they would create and ultimately
perfect in a photograph of a cotton-rag tent next to a car: the tent
a testament to the impermanence of life as a seasonal laborer, the
car evidence of the relentless motion set in force by the one-in-
twenty chance of getting to the few jobs available before others
were hired. And there were the children: a "case of malnutrition,"
the scar left by chronic hunger and poverty.

The shape and intent of that narrative coalesced on this first
trip, as did the three symbols to which they would frequently
return: children, homes, and automobiles. Each represented the
social issues they faced and the domino effect in which one ineq-
uity led to the next: forced migrancy and a transient lifestyle leading to an erosion of the family structure and the social stability

"To harvest the crops of California, thousands of families live literally on wheels. San Joaquin Valley." February 1935. Library of Congress, Prints and Photographs Division, FSA-OWI Collection, LC-USZ62-69109.

"Migrant Mexican children in contractor's camp at time of early pea harvest, Nipomo, California." January 26, 1935. Library of Congress, Prints and Photographs Division, FSA-OWI Collection, LC-USF34-003803-ZE (LC-DIG fsa 8b27537).

that came with it. Yet none was simply a symbol, representative of a set of ideologies or practices. They were, in addition to the emotional charge they were capable of creating and the social significance they represented, real, tangible, materially extant; hundreds of thousands of cars on the road; as many if not more shanty shacks and rag tents; actual children, lined up according to age, that parents put before Lange's camera. All of these forced their way into both Taylor's and Lange's perceptions of the Great Depression in California as they set out into the field.

Theirs was by no means an entirely original narrative, for in its reliance on the literal showing of abhorrent conditions to protest them, in the hope that audiences would be moved to action, they joined a long tradition of social protest, perhaps the most famous of which began when Harriet Beecher Stowe wrote to her editor that she had embarked on a "series of sketches which give the lights and shadows" of slavery. *Uncle Tom's Cabin, or Life Among the Lowly,* set an early precedent for the combination of written and visual protest; "There is no arguing with pictures," Stowe wrote, "and everybody is impressed by them, whether they mean to be or not."[1] Long-standing belief in the persuasive power of the visual explains why pictorial evidence is so compelling and why so many forms of protest depend on some form of realism, a need to show as well as tell the conditions at hand. Within the genre of protest literature, some of the most powerful novels—*Life in the Iron Mills, The Grapes of Wrath, Native Son*—have relied on detailed and sometimes exhausting veracity, often visual. More-over, many of the novels we currently recognize as protest novels came in the wake of photography, whose introduction to the United States coincides with the advent of literary realism and naturalism, Progressive-era genres that relied on a writer's ability to act as both scribe and photographer and led to realist works of protest such as Upton Sinclair's *The Jungle.*

That approach fed directly into the 1930s, an era whose socio-political development of documentary photography made it a turning point in the history of photography. With the conception of the Historical Division of the Resettlement Administration, a concerted effort to produce "honest" and "realistic" photographs "that better fitted the harsh realities of the times" was underway, even in magazines.[2] Along with the political marriage of politics and protest within the frame of the camera, the f/64 movement, begun in California in 1932, inaugurated a new era of precision, their manifesto rejecting artifice but not art. Even the preceding decade's high modernist fiction, the emphasis on a plausible recreation of interiority evident in Woolf, Faulkner, and Joyce—these, too, paved the way for the turn to "honest" photography of "harsh realities," for those realities were often visually articulated within the everyday lives of the economically and socially dispossessed. This leap into visual interiority was by the 1930s so personal that Andrea Fisher called it "a crisis of the intimate," pointing to a social collapse in the decade that equaled the economic collapse. The resulting "imperative to poetically catalog every mundane detail of the Depression's effects signaled the penetration of crisis into the unspeakably intimate."[3] Such a visual narrative privileges the social and cultural over the political as ways to understand human life. Within that context Lange and Taylor were able to use the fieldwork methods they developed, which came out of the discipline of social science, to produce a protest narrative that drew on proletarian and social-realist techniques but ultimately developed new forms and ideologies to move their readers to action.

FINDING THE "LEADING EDGE"

The move into work that created this narrative was not easy, and Lange's memories of how she came to be employed by the State Emergency Relief Administration (SERA) are variously cryptic and vague. In her oral history, when talking about her growing desire to do "that kind of work" full time, she mentions that by 1935, she was doing it "wholly" when the state of California employed her as a typist, since they had no provision for a photographer. Later, when Suzanne Reiss prompts her, asking, "You began to go on field trips with Dr. Paul Taylor in 1935?" Lange blandly responds that she was indeed "on Dr. Taylor's crew." Four years later, when Richard Doud interviewed her for the Smithsonian Archives of American Art, Lange, nearer the end of her life, was trying harder to pull together the pieces and connections that would explain her life: "[Taylor] suggested that if there was any possibility that I could do field work, he had a grant from the state of California to investigate agricultural labor, and he'd want photographs as visual evidence to accompany it. . . . I went on several field trips to photograph what this social scientist and his crew were investigating. And that was the first time I saw how trained people in a field like this operated."[4]

Taylor's memory is more detailed, encompassing both his own purpose and the difficulties the government posed to him. It was toward the end of 1934 that Taylor was asked to do research for SERA's Division of Rural Rehabilitation. His assignment was to find out if the federal programs coming out of the Federal Emergency Relief Administration were actually fitted to the needs of rural California, a place with conditions both peculiar and largely unknown in Washington, D.C. "Questions were: who was in distress, what was the nature of the distress, and what would be a sensible thing to do to alleviate it?"[5]

Taylor insisted that in order to make the reports that would answer those questions, he needed a photographer. By all accounts, there was nothing personal in his request for Lange's services, only that he respected her ability and attitude, recognized something unusual, perhaps even extraordinary, in her photographs, and knew, or sensed, or guessed that she wanted to do the work enough to put her current work to the side, unlike any of the other photographers who went to Oroville.[6] Apparently, he paid her out of his own grant to do some work, made the decision, and then set out to hire her, although Lange's son Dan believes that even the first few trips were trials by fire during which Taylor was to some extent testing Lange.

If so, it was only as much as he had been tested prior to receiving approval for her to join him. Harry Drobish, director of the Rural Rehabilitation division, asked Taylor right off why he wanted a photographer. Taylor replied that after years of research in the California fields, he was familiar enough with the conditions, but "knowing the conditions and reporting them in a way to produce action were two different things."[7] Drobish then asked Taylor if social scientists generally asked for photographers on their research staff. "No," Taylor answered, they did not, "but I wanted a photographer." Taylor was not simply reporting by this point in time; he wanted to inspire change, radical change, and words would not be enough to show the conditions in such a way as to provoke a response. Perhaps the two would have remained at an impasse without the creative thinking and enthusiasm of an office manager.

Lawrence Hewes, who would go on to play a major role in the Farm Security Administration, was at the time simply a young office manager who had been a bond salesman in the 1920s. "What was his life?" Taylor asked rhetorically. "You go to Dartmouth, then you go into business, in to the stock and bond market, with the market going up—wonderful! Wonderful! Then comes the 1929 crash. Stock and bond houses don't need their sales men any more."[8] The suddenly unemployed Hewes had enough political influence to get a government job, and he met Taylor in the "grim Depression winter of 1935" at 49 Fourth Street in San Francisco, in the "dingy offices" of California's SERA. Taylor's reputation as a scholar of California agricultural labor conditions and laborers was well established. As Hewes wrote in the introduction to Taylor's oral history, he "quickly demonstrated that the problem of rural poverty, till then conceived as disparate episodes of no general significance, was in fact a major catastrophe, transcending state and local boundaries." Taylor, Hewes recalled, believed that the California problem was "the leading edge of a large regional migration" of people whose dust-blown lives would turn west and "would swamp the resources of California agricultural counties and even of the State itself."[9]

But Taylor's ideas remained theory until events turned tragic in the Imperial Valley. Several hundred migrant families were camped in Nipomo, stranded by rains that had ruined the pea crop. Hewes recounts that the little valley afforded nothing to them, "no shelter, no sanitation, and no food," not even "gas for their old jalopies."[10] Requests for aid poured into SERA from county authorities, and the agency was unprepared to help on such a scale. From their offices, Taylor and Hewes saw the disaster as an opportunity to expose the conditions in which the Dust

Bowl migrants were living; they decided to prepare a document of the disaster.[11] Hewes recalled, "Paul realized at once the drama of the situation. He felt that the Nipomo story could provide documentation necessary to attract national attention,"[12] and he knew that to attract that attention, he needed photographs. He was "insistent that somehow he and Dorothea would have to go to Nipomo."[13] Their plan was for Taylor to write a narrative of the situation that Lange would photograph. Thus, coming from two angles, they would capture the whole story. In "a sort of defiant euphoria," Hewes hired Lange as a state relief typist at about one hundred dollars a month, assigned her to Taylor, and procured photographic supplies by calling them office supplies.[14]

"I went on two expeditions," Lange would later recall, "two short field trips . . . to do specific things."[15] Lange was then a thirty-nine-year-old woman, small and somewhat slight, with a limp that was sometimes marked and sometimes unobservable, and large, pale-green eyes. She wore her brown hair cropped short and close to her face. She had been described as "a not-at-all imposing woman" who "likes books, tea with lemon, Breton trousers to work in, late parties."[16] She must have stood out from the group of graduate students Taylor brought with him on the trip. To Ed Rowell, one of those students, Taylor said, "This is the first time we've had a photographer out in the field, and I don't know how she will be received. Will you go with her? Your instructions are, see to it that nothing untoward happens. I don't want anything to disturb the relations between ourselves as a team, and those pea-pickers. Carry her cameras, she'll need somebody to do that. Just quietly stay with her, and see that nothing goes awry." To Lange, he said, "This is your first day in the field, we don't know how we will be received here, or how you will be received. If you don't make a single photograph the first day, that's all right with me."[17]

Of the trip to San Luis Obispo County, Lange also remembers that they had "somebody who had to do with the state health board" along. "We were sitting in the lobby of the hotel there and Paul was standing over by the hotel desk, writing and writing and writing, and he stood there for a couple of hours, and this man kept saying to me, 'You see how methodical he is? See? He leaves nothing to chance.' Actually what Paul's report revealed wasn't very good for this fellow. He was methodical all right."[18] The "fellow" was Ed Brown, from the State Division of Immigration and Housing, and two weeks later he said to Taylor, "I can't see any part in coddling these people. I've started on the ground lots of times when I was a young man."[19] Taylor's response goes unnoted in the tiny notebook he kept always at hand, but the juxtaposition must have hit him: a government official, his salary secure, his meals steady, calling forth the narrative trope by which Taylor would go on to shape his argument to men like Brown, along with many others. The "ground" was much lower for those Taylor hoped to lift.

On that first trip, from January 25 to 27, Lange's introduction to migrant living conditions may have "hit" her "in the face" as much as Taylor's had eight years earlier. Taylor's notes on January 26 describe a work radius of 15 to 17 miles from which "reports are spread that 10,000 will be needed." The work contractor rented ground for "those he needs," but "more [workers] than [the] labor [boss] contracted come in and camp everywhere." With three weeks' work available and "no work elsewhere," they stayed, and "a wet season delays any further work. The migratories are 100% families,"[20] Taylor wrote, and they relied on the Red Cross for health care in conditions so unsanitary that the county health officials ultimately came in and ordered them off the grounds. It was, indeed, a disaster, and Lange's photographic response was aimed at the cotton-rag tents and the children forced to live within them.

Slightly less than a month later, they returned to Nipomo and Kern County. In many ways, Lange's photographs from the second trip recreate the narrative structure of the first; children and transiency, underscored by both the car and the lack of housing, form the core of the visual protest. Then, on the heels of those short forays, a longer trip included a series of local conferences in Riverside in order to assess whatever individual and public housing needs existed, and to find out what role local officials would be willing to play in establishing new camps or housing projects and eliminating some of the worst sites currently in use.[21] After two days of meetings, Lange went out into the field, and the frustration of endless meetings came to an abrupt halt as she faced the horrifying living conditions. No foundations—indeed, no floors. The report cites frameworks of "rough Mesquite or Tamarisk poles wired together with baling wire," and walls made of palm leaves, tin, and burlap, roofed with corrugated iron, palms, cardboard, or canvas. No plumbing, no lighting but candles or kerosene lanterns. For heat, makeshift stoves built from discarded materials. Lange would see it again and again in the coming years—the stovepipe protruding from a tent, a flap pulled back to reveal "a few cooking utensils, table and chairs, cupboards made of boxes, an iron bedstead or two."[22]

Years later, people still face Lange's photographs and wonder aloud if it bothered her, or depressed her, or upset her to face such conditions. Clearly, it did. When she recalled those first few field

"Date picker's home, Coachella Valley, California." March 1935.
Library of Congress, Prints and Photographs Division, FSA-OWI
Collection, LC-USZ6-1184.

assignments, she was still outraged that at night, her colleagues
would order "dinners that cost $1.75"[23] when, according to the
report that came out of the trip, "wages most generally paid were
reported to be $1.25 to $1.75 per nine-hour day."[24] Even that figure was an estimate since, as Lange went on to explain, "with

those people you can't figure [daily wages] because the work is irregular. Sometimes they go into the fields at noon because in the morning the fields are too wet with dew. And sometimes it's picked by three o'clock." To order a dinner that exceeded the high end of a daily wage was, Lange thought, "inhuman," but nearly everything about the migrants' conditions was inhuman. The poor housing, malnutrition, transient lives, and meager wages, "typical of thousands," she wrote, made possible the crops on which California depended.[25]

CALIFORNIA'S BITTER HARVEST

Farm labor has always been not simply a part of California's agricultural history but an explanation for it, and while the migratory labor force of the 1930s contained markedly different elements than those that preceded it, California's agricultural development contributed heavily to the rejection the migrants faced during the Great Depression. At its earliest point of political organization, California established its labor system in 1769, when "an overland expedition from the Spanish missions of Baja California brought the first field hands north through the desert to plant farms in Alta (Upper) California."[26] The Spanish acquisition and planting of lands that had been for thousands of years inhabited by natives who hunted and gathered required natives to enter, by force or curiosity, into a system of labor exploitation that would continue to Taylor's time and beyond.[27] As Catholic padres developed free land into farms, they also yoked free indigenes into a farm-labor system, one that created an entrenched class structure from which California never broke free. Richard Steven Street writes, "Class exists in California agriculture as a result of one group, farm workers, locked into a permanent wage-earning position and sharing experiences—gang labor, uncertain employment, travel, domination, blisters, bad backs, camp life, fieldwork—under an exploitative labor system, in an industry whose interests were different and often opposed to them."[28]

Spanish rule over California natives and land lasted until the nineteenth century, when Mexico, having fought and defeated Spain, took control of Spain's North American territories, including Alta California. Mexican control of the missions transformed California, initiating a period of rapid economic growth, opening the doors to American explorers, trappers, and pioneers. But the arrivals of Anglo explorers such as Jedediah Smith (1826), John Sutter (1839), and John Bidwell (1841) during this time would soon diminish the impact of Mexican *rancherias*. After the United States voted in 1845 to annex Texas, a congressional declaration of war against Mexico drew California into war against the United States. During this period of troubled U.S. foreign policy, its boundaries shifting and often unregulated, California entered the union, via the Treaty of Guadalupe Hidalgo, but the American flag over Sutter's fort in Sacramento was far more symbolic than actual in its evocation of American culture and legal practices.

The discovery of gold early in 1848 resulted in a flood of immigrants, the sudden creation of enormous wealth, and a population of wildly speculative and often lawless men and women. David Igler writes that California's "instant market economy, dynamic urban cores, and large corporate enterprises" put exploitation of both agricultural labor and the state's natural resources front and center."[29] As large-scale crop production and exportation replaced the Mexican ranching economy, agricultural laborers became even more necessary. When California, which had been admitted

as a free state, legalized contract labor from China, it effectively
finished off any ideological principles by establishing a plantation labor system.[30] Natives were systematically stripped of lands
that earlier treaties had granted them, and Mexican landowners
found their claims, ensured by the Treaty of Guadalupe Hidalgo,
mired in inextricable legal proceedings. Forced to prove their
land-grant titles before the California Land Claims Commission,
a majority received *de jure* title to their lands, Igler writes, but "in
most cases, the claimants no longer held possession of the rancho
land. Instead, it belonged to well-financed buyers [who] pushed
the land claim through the confirmation and patenting process."[31]
Indeed, Wartzman and Arax write, "Many grantees hadn't bothered with surveys or filing paperwork; some couldn't muster a
single document backing up their claims."[32]

Much of California's land had come directly to the U.S. government as part of the treaty, and as land moved out of government ownership through a series of backdoor deals and grants, it
became increasingly monopolized by gifts to the railroads and,
ultimately, a handful of well-financed entrepreneurs.[33] Their
necessary absence from the farming process made production
increasingly dependent on high numbers of imported laborers.
While California had begun by growing and shipping wheat, it
quickly diversified, and farms continued to increase in size under
the hands of fewer and fewer owners. "By 1871, after twenty years
of statehood, California found itself a more stubborn oligarchy
than at any time during Mexican rule. Nine million acres of its
best land were held by 516 men,"[34] all of whose profit margin
relied on the field-workers they exploited.

Adding to the disparity was the issue of water west of the
hundredth meridian. The state's most profitable crops relied on

imported water, and after decades of water battles in court, the 1902 National Reclamation Act, or Newlands Act, succeeded in limiting "the use of water for land in private ownership" to parcels not exceeding160 acres;[35] this limitation ostensibly sought to curb the wild land grabs and rampant monopolization of California's land. Coming out of the Progressive era, the limit was presented, in Donald Worster's words, as "a family, not an individual, standard," one that demanded the farmer work his own land, suggesting to Californians that they would be better able to establish homes and farms of their own.[36] Yet the statutes were chronically ignored and openly transgressed, even utilized by irrigation districts to insure that the large landowners received the water they needed, and the entrenched system of land monopolies remained. Taylor himself recognized the difficulty of any newcomer's purchase of the kind of small homestead he believed necessary to meet the Jeffersonian agricultural ideal, and he saw the genesis of that difficulty in the state's development of intensive, large farms, made possible by California's seemingly anomalous land and water situation. "Even administrators do not find it easy to remember that the essential question is not, who owns the land, but who gets the water."[37]

Irrigation, shifts from extensive to intensive crops, increased horticulture—these are the general economic markers by which California's agricultural development has been measured, but all depended on the farm worker's labor. While California initially relied on Chinese workers, it moved through wave after wave of immigrant work forces, drawing its labor from a host of other countries. "Farm workers," Street writes, "were channeled through the landscape as routinely as if sending irrigation water down the furrows of a field."[38] It is a pattern Taylor identified in his fieldwork, and one that Carey McWilliams would dramatize in *Factories in the Fields.* Just as eastern factories were exploiting the ethnic workforce in ways that Upton Sinclair would expose in *The Jungle,* California agricultural labor worked industrially, isolating its labor force geographically and socially. What set California's workers apart from their eastern counterparts was the transient condition of their work, for while factory workers might undergo periods of unemployment, the seasonal work of California farm workers necessarily involved a pattern of cyclical job loss and a permanently migratory existence.

For hundreds of years dreamers had been drawn to California by its best and still most successful public relations scheme—the golden vision, no matter how false, of riches. Whether gold in the rivers or mountains, entrepreneurial opportunities in the new cities, or land watered to fantastic fertility at the government's expense, California's driving force, for those who felt it, has always been the money it promises. Immigrating laborers often responded not only to the lure of gold but to a driving sense of discontent that pushed them as much away from home as toward California. For the two labor forces Taylor knew, the source of that discontent varied: the Mexicans were dislocated by a revolution that shook apart their cultural and economic systems,[39] while the Dust Bowl migrants, unable to understand either the ecological destruction of their land or the governmental disassembling of their bank accounts, had no such specific moment, no locus on which to fix their upheaval. Despite those differences, the impetus was the same; they came to California because published pamphlets told them that work was abundant, and word of mouth picked up the rumor, never really true, and spread it.[40] When they arrived, there was no work, no place to build a home, and, as a result, no cultural assimilation. California was importing people, and sometimes their basic social habits, such as food or dress, but it was not providing a context in which religious or marital practices or educational ideals, for example, could take root, expand, and flourish; it had cultural practices but no sense of coherent culture. And still the nation's people continued to head west, their daily arrivals converging into a tidal wave. "California is becoming visibly and inevitably the ground upon which problems of national import must be resolved," Taylor wrote in April 1935. "Our resourcefulness and energy are challenged at the utmost as drought, flood and depression augment our destitute population." And, he concluded, the threat of "an even greater westward tide" was looming.[41] California was a troubled and turbulent Eden.

"WORDS CANNOT DESCRIBE" IT

Taylor had been studying the patterns of labor economics in California for years, had watched the social responses to agricultural unemployment and rural poverty, and knew that things were indeed about to get worse. His use of the term "leading edge," one he used in a number of articles and reports, suggests the "rising tide" he had earlier seen in the Mexican migration. Yet the situation was different enough, the climate had altered enough, that he saw in the near certainty of harder times a potential hope for the future—a "great experiment," to use Roosevelt's term. For one thing, the shift from single males to a migratory pattern of stable families—begun by Mexicans and now being extended by Dust Bowl migrants—convinced him that a federally financed, state-wide system of decent housing and community services would, initially, solve the shelter problem.

Moreover, for Taylor, the composition of the families and the settled landscape they sought promised a California that would behave in ways far more midwestern than western farms and farmers had done so far, one in which families settled down to tend their own pastures, orchards, and farms. In this light, he saw them as recreating the original passage west, married culturally, economically, and ideologically to those who had preceded them in the nineteenth century. In only a few months, Taylor would, in an article for *Survey Graphic,* draw an extended parallel between the first pioneers, who came after the Gold Rush, and the current "westward movement of rural folk from Oklahoma, Texas, Arkansas."[42] These new settlers provided the means to recreate the West, transforming California by moving it away from the absentee landlord system that had long exploited workers, land, and water in pursuit of maximized profits. In its place, Taylor envisioned the Jeffersonian family farm, a system of farms tended by owners in residence, families who cared about their land and cared about creating a community in which quality of life was both highly prized and easily attainable.[43]

But the first step had to be pragmatic. The massive wave of new arrivals had to be housed if they were going to be able to stay. The days of homesteading on rivers running with gold were gone, and neither the government nor the general populace had, to date, acted to provide housing. Taylor's work leading up to this moment suggests that he understood how, in their historical patterns of transiency and their high numbers of single men, migrant workers had been forced into leading lives the public could easily perceive as unsettled. That perception encouraged and abetted the steadfast denial of programs that would provide decent housing. Taylor's writing at the time conflated the jeremiadic point of fall, the metaphysical ground zero from which sinners could begin

to be raised, with the physical soil on which homesteaders trans-
fer land title into single homes, which multiply into community.
Through all of this he wove the pioneer story of westward migration cast historically back a hundred years and more—thousands
of years back to the first pioneers, Adam and Eve, seeking out
a new home following that first exile. Taylor believed that the
building of any new order, to use the phrase on which Steinbeck
would later base his dream in *The Grapes of Wrath,* would begin
with government housing.

Thus, when he and Lange returned from their field trip,
they threw themselves into the task of preparing not simply a
report but a proposal entitled "Rural Rehabilitation Camps for
Migrants." Their report reached Frank McLaughlin, SERA
administrator, on March 15, 1935.[44] Looking back years later, Taylor told Suzanne Reiss, "It was something."[45] Telling Taylor of a
"new wire spiral binding technique," Lange "took the initiative,"
Taylor recalled, putting the report between "good strong cardboard covers and wax[ing] them to good effect." Dixon provided
lettering and drew a map of California. In its seamless wedding
of text and photograph, the report was in many ways the culmination of all the research Taylor had done over the last ten years
as well as a starting point. It protests the government's lack of
responsibility toward workers, arguing that California workers'
right to decent housing is both a moral as well as a civic responsibility and presenting housing as the basic requirement for the
one social model Taylor seems to feel was absolutely inviolate:
the family. After the report's first two sections explain the current economic climate and the specific western conditions that
demand seasonal, migratory agricultural labor, a third describes
the migratory workforce, ending with a single underlined sen-

tence: "Most of the migrants travel with their families." On the heels of that statement, the fourth section quotes a February 11, 1934, report from the Special Commission on Agricultural Disturbances in the Imperial Valley:

> Words cannot describe some of the conditions we saw. During the warm weather, when the temperature rises considerably above 100 degrees, the flies and insects become pests, the children are fretful, the attitude of some of the parents can be imagined. . . . In this environment there is bred a social sullenness that is to be deplored, but which can be understood by those who have viewed the scenes that violate all the recognized standards of living. . . . It is horrible that children are reared in an environment as pitiable as that which we saw in more than one locality.[46]

Lange's accompanying photographs, a relentlessly grim survey covering the three days in March and the earlier trips in January and February, focus on the structures and the people within. They provide a clear visual record of the conditions that, Taylor argues, justify a Rural Rehabilitation housing program. There are only a few pictures of field labor, and, for a photographer whose professional milieu had been "portraits of people," there are few photographs of faces. One page has four photographs that zoom in on workers' faces, but it is only to show their race, in support of a caption that reads, "All races serve the crops in California." Instead, her ire emerges on page after page at the "human habitation," as one caption claims, dirty rags draped over poles from which a stovepipe protrudes, empty cans and litter covering the surrounding area. The inventory is ceaseless: poles loosely thatched with palm, or rags worn to translucence; sagging cardboard; shreds of canvas. They are photographs of where people live, but much more than that, they are photographs of the pain that comes from not having a place to live. The gap between two pieces of cardboard that serves as a door is far more a photograph of the door that is not there, a solid slab of oak or mahogany that welcomes visitors at the same time that it protects those behind it from intruders. Each photograph of the shack that *is* there is inscribed with the home that *is not* there, the absence of security, the presence of acute vulnerability, instability, and transiency.

"This is not a quarrel over a little shack—but a human being has to have a place to stand like a tree has a right to stand. The main [concern] is to have a place to stay and put his own hands on his own shelter," her notes read.[47] In such thinking, she too has entered into looking at her subjects through the redemptive narrative of the "human being" whose fallen state is not simply redeemable but the responsibility of those whom the report calls to witness. The ingrained social injustices heaped on those workers on whom "the crops of California depend" are contested in that phrase, as is the faceless subclass into which these workers, like others before them, have been cast.

MOVING THE MASSES

The photographs from a second trip, immediately following the first report's completion, shift the focus from "inhabitants" and their "habitations," to symbolic, contextual statements of why they came and how they live. Lange had begun to seek out "pictures of people," and they were, as her studio revelation had insisted, people in context, "a man as he stood in his world." At Yuma, she photographed their cars, captioning the shot with the phrase "their worldly goods." Next to a field of carrot pullers: "The hope of work draws refugees to California." One, in Holtville, shows a pregnant woman from Oklahoma poring over a map, asking, "Where is Tranquility, California?" Migrants tell her "the cotton burned up," "we got blowed out," "no work of no kind," and "It seems like God has forsaken us back there in Arkansas." There are political views, social views—families hurry to tell her they have not received any aid or that if the aid had come in "one chunk," they could have bought land and made a living. Overall, the photographs tell a broader story by focusing specifically on personal stories, opening up the individual lives that have already been lumped into the nameless, faceless social strata of indigency.

Why this approach? Taken in light of what Lange and Taylor were attempting to do at this point, it is useful to look, once again, at Stauffer's analysis of the rhetorical strategies that protest literature employs "in the quest to convert audiences."[48] There is, of course, the plea to compassion, what Stauffer calls "empathy," the humane belief that if other humans can simply see the migrants as individuals rather than as a mass, they will want to help them.[49] Shock value is also important: if others are to "feel their pain," to use Stauffer's term, the pain must be evident enough and far enough beyond the reality of everyday life that it does indeed inspire "outrage, agitation, and a desire to correct social ills." Taken as a set of principles, these two strategies posed more difficulty for Lange and Taylor than it is perhaps easy to see in the light of contemporary response.

The difficulty of instilling in audiences a full-fledged desire to correct social ills involved what can only be broadly called the public mindset, a move toward the left that for uncertain reasons never actually gelled. A newfound support for labor, for example, after a drop of three million unionists from 1920 to 1933, was notable, but not nationally constant. Robert McElvaine locates the problem in the fact that "no organizational structure existed to translate the changed attitude [of the people] into political power,"[50] and Lizabeth Cohen argues that "fragmentation of workers along geographic, skill, ethnic, and racial lines" combined with issues within the labor system to lead to "the defeat of workers' once promising challenge."[51] Lawrence Levine, noting that "the remarkable thing about the American people before reform did come was not their action but their inaction, not their demands but their passivity," points to a general feeling of economic fear and desire for security, as well as culturally induced beliefs in individual responsibility, all of which made it "difficult to build a sense of group solidarity."[52] However, many historians locate Americans' apparent tendency to support radical figures or movements without actually working to effect the changes they promised or demanded within the powerful hope inspired by Roosevelt himself. When Lange and Taylor began working, the president was engaged in effectively reforming a number of political institutions, and a public hungry for change could look to a president who was instituting change. Those who, like Lange and Taylor, were attempting large-scale, radical, grassroots changes, even those that relied on current governmental ideologies, faced a challenge.[53]

That kind of change, political transformation that begins in the hands of those most affected by conditions of the day, came closest to realization in the Populist movement. In explaining the failure of Populists, Lawrence Goodwyn provides a Marxist reading of reform movements' pervasive failure in the country, asserting that the absence in American history of effective reform— lasting radical reform of social and political structures that have oppressed large classes of peoples—is primarily the result of a resignation to prevailing ideologies, especially a clinging to vague and unsubstantiated confidence in Progressivism. Yet he also delineates crucial signposts in the reformers' own failure and outlines four stages of how mass protests happen: formation of an organization, recruitment and growth of the organization, education, and, finally, formal politicization.[54] Certainly, that is the line taken by many of those who wrote red literature during the decade of the 1930s, their hopes for change resting on a literal conversion of the masses into a collective state of political awareness. For many, the best hope was in California.

For a brief time, communist action was alive and well in California, the "fun in the apples" Mac longed for in Steinbeck's *In Dubious Battle* occurring in a series of agricultural strikes and attempts at unionization. "People who know anything about the agricultural labor situation in California hope and fear—some hope, others fear—that this summer there will be 'hell to pay' in the rural districts and in the fields along the peripheries of large cities. Unions are being formed everywhere," Louis Adamic wrote in 1936.[55] California's potential for radical reform, grounded in what Kevin Starr identifies as the "deep, very deep, roots" of radicalism,"[56] would seem to have been at an unparalleled zenith during Lange and Taylor's first years of working together. The Waterfront and General Strike had pushed the balance of labor in new directions, and the gubernatorial campaign of Upton Sinclair, "an atheist, a free lover, a communist, a man who attacked religion, learning, the institutions of America,"[57] was shaking the foundations of California's conservative establishment. Sinclair's plan called End Poverty In California (EPIC) attracted the interest of some and the near worship of others whose tearful thanks to their "savior" carried the fervor of revivals.

Why Sinclair lost the 1934 election, receiving about eight hundred thousand votes from the 2.5 million registered voters who voted that November is complicated and still under debate.[58] Similarly, why the equally popular and equally radical political and social movements of Father Coughlin and Dr. Francis Townshend, both of whom, like Sinclair, enjoyed popularity in California, did not translate into complete and lasting reform is a question still discussed.[59] But the truth remains that in the state Starr calls "The left side of the continent," Sinclair lost the election for California governor, the Townshend plan fell into ridicule, and, by 1936, Coughlin had passed the peak of his popularity. And while the factors at play continue under historical review, one constant remains: the Associated Farmers of California. This conservative group commanded during this time a growing influence on political policy and public opinion. Organized enough to introduce legislation and often push through policy that effectively decimated rights gained over half a century of political and economic struggle, a *Survey Graphic* article claimed that the Associated Farmers "demonstrated that labor excesses and the split in labor's ranks can be made the basis for sufficient public resentment to weaken organized labor."[60]

While the Associated Farmers' self-interest lay in suppressing uprisings in the agricultural fields, its tactics were far more general, seeking not simply to suppress attempts by workers to organize but to build on a growing and dangerous body of work by vigilantes,[61] as well as on the already established rightist sentiment in California, to cast any type of revolt as communist and all Communism as anti-American.[62] Although in many ways California was indeed at its most radical moment of the decade in 1934 and 1935, the fact of that moment brought on a full-scale countermovement by the right, and Starr claims that by 1936, "the

California Right had perfected its ability to manipulate social and legal procedures."[63] At once reviled by many Californians, particularly conservative and landowning rural inhabitants, for their association with "red" and communist-led strikes, and sympathized with by intellectuals and liberals for the same associations, the Dust Bowl immigrants, whether pitied or despised, were seen as a problem *because* they arrived in the state during a veritable hotbed of political and social turmoil. With radical movements still unable to bring about the changes Taylor wanted to see "on the ground," Taylor and Lange faced their problem as one of representation; they knew they needed to bring the wider public into the problems they themselves witnessed on a daily basis and allow them to connect personally with people for whom the agencies of conservatism were encouraging them to feel an outright antipathy.

Lawrence Hewes, who characterized their initial optimism as "incurable," elaborated on the shape that optimism took: "We hoped as hard as we worked that somehow the story of this great westward movement of disinherited rural people could be told to people who had the power to help."[64] Taylor would turn to that "great westward movement" for his symbolism; his approach was to put the migrants into an historical context, to assimilate all migrants into the historical narrative of the pioneer West, the long-standing American "errand" that urged Europeans further and further away from eastern shores into the wilderness, its— and their—redemption assured in the process.

AGAIN THE COVERED WAGON

That approach generated the article "Again the Covered Wagon." Published in *Survey Graphic* (July 1935), it is rich in imagery, its often melodious syntax driving a powerful and persuasive intent. In this article, Taylor's writing establishes most effectively what would become his and Lange's grandest metaphor, the process of erosion. In a dramatic move to prevent readers from denying their own role in the current tragedy, Taylor binds the country together through an opening description of "vast clouds of dust" that rose from the Midwest to move both east and west, the result of drought and agricultural practices that exposed the soil, leaving it vulnerable to wind erosion. In the same way, the "protracted depression" following the dust and drought left the people of the Great Plains "exposed," with the country now "witnessing the process of social erosion and a consequent shifting of the human sands." In this grand, continental sweep of vision, Taylor moves almost immediately to historicize the moment, noting that the westward movement from the plains is "of course . . . not new."[65] Beginning with the rise of cotton farming in the Imperial Valley, in 1910, migration accelerated at the same rate as cotton farming, he explains, which moved into the San Joaquin Valley in 1919. Thus, the "immediate factors" are put into a larger context, defusing some of the Depression-based hysteria that scholars have pointed to in seeking to explain Californians' adamant rejection of the Dust Bowl migrants.[66]

The article relies heavily on the work Taylor and Lange did that spring. Moving from the specific migrant to the general condition he or she represents, their text is rich with quotations followed by brief and illuminating social explications. There are emigrants who "got blowed out," whose pasts are literally "burned . . . up" by the drought, and those with even more detailed stories: "Negroes from Mississippi . . . reported that they had 'just beat the water out by a quarter of a mile,'" and a sharecropper's story provided "echoes of crop-restriction . . . and of conflict between cotton share-croppers on one hand and 'first tenants' and landlords on the other." The "furnish" system—at the heart of the Populist protest in the nineteenth century—and the Federal Emergency Relief Administration's inability to circumvent its inequities receive note, as does "another refugee who had been a farm laborer and oil worker in Oklahoma" who said, "'since the oil-quota, I've had no work.'" Each quotation, vernacular and heartfelt, leads to a wider story, one the article insists readers should understand as victimizing the refugees, forcing the majority of them into circumstances not of their choosing.[67]

A description of bedraggled and ragged "refugees" goes back to the days Taylor and Lange spent at Yuma, the cars they counted endlessly crossing into the state, and, especially, the pregnant young woman Lange photographed and interviewed who was looking for "Tranquility." "A pregnant Oklahoma mother living without shelter in Imperial Valley while the menfolk bunched carrots for money to enable them to move on, made a poignant request for directions. 'Where is Tranquility, California?'" "Unfortunately," the essay counters, "tranquility" is a goal "not generally reached by those seeking refuge on the coast." With land unavailable and reception not "altogether friendly," current bills in the California legislature were designed to exclude immigrants "without money," "in the spirit" of the Chinese exclusion policies and acts that began in the 1850s.[68]

The great difference between earlier farm workers and the current migrants is found in history. The article claims the Dust Bowl refugees are "seeking individual protection in the traditional spirit of the American frontier by westward migration," unaware, upon setting out, that they are "arrivals at another frontier, one of social conflict." Communist-led strikes and oppressive strategies on the part of the Associated Farmers have turned the fields into a war zone. "The future of the refugees," therefore, "is hardly likely to be tranquil. They will be caught in whatever rural labor struggles arise." Predicting imminent crises, when some will find stability but others "will mill incessantly through the harvests" and live in deplorable conditions, the article returns readers, finally, to the border at Yuma, where "the refugees are straggling west," and, after crossing "the Tehachapi and view[ing] the wild flowers of the southern San Joaquin Valley," the migrants find that "California 'looks like Paradise compared to what it was there.'"[69] "Again the Covered Wagon" ends by wondering how long that vision will sustain this massive migration if all are denied a part of California's culture, if "the grandchildren of the emigrants of 1935" are not allowed to place "grandmother's cookstove" next to "the gold-seeker's pan." History is a continuum, and the migrant's place in the historical process that created and continues to create California is clear.

Taylor, who wrote the majority of the text from both his and Lange's records, understood the migrant "problem," as the government called it, in ways quite similar to the understanding of John Steinbeck, whose attempts to lift the Dust Bowl refugees out of the social place to which they had been flung equaled Taylor's. Both men seemed to understand that widespread rejection of the Dust Bowl refugees was linked to California's ability to treat them as if they were of a different race. And, in strictly social terms, they were. While the sudden influx of white families was new to California's economy and society, westerners soon learned to see the white migrants as simply another cog in the wheel of imported farm labor. Californians adopted several policies—both public and private—whose goal was to treat the Dust Bowl migrants as their parents and grandparents had treated the numerous ethnic field workers and laborers who had come and gone over the years, exoticizing their religious practices, their appearance, even their living conditions—forced though they were—and insisting on isolating and fetishizing them. They were of the ethnic migratory worker class, no matter what the color of their skin, and their identity was being rapidly constructed in terms of a popular mythos that lumped all migratory workers under the aegis of the happy "harvest gypsy." It was the myth of the "harvest gypsies" that allowed Californians, who would not have tolerated the living conditions of the migrants for their pets, to go beyond simple tolerance to acceptance. Steinbeck, who seemed as genuinely distraught as Taylor over the situation and who traveled extensively with federal employee Tom Collins to government and squatter camps in order to see what was really happening, attempted to counter that obstinate myth by emphasizing the whiteness of the Okies as a means to virtually de-exoticize them. "The Harvest Gypsies," his 1936 *San Francisco News* series, was published by the Simon J. Lubin Society in 1938 under the title *Their Blood Is Strong.* A vivid collection of articles that was the seed for *The Grapes of Wrath,* it emphasizes not simply how crucial the migrants' work is to the state, but how different from their predecessors the migrants are ethnically:

> The earlier foreign migrants have invariably been drawn from a peon class. This is not the case with the new migrants. They are small farmers who have lost their farms, or farm hands who have lived with the family in the old American way. They are men who have worked hard on their own farms and have felt the pride of possessing and living in close touch with the land. They are resourceful and intelligent Americans who have gone through the

hell of the drought, have seen their lands wither and die and the top soil blow away; and this, to a man who has owned his land, is a curious and terrible pain.

And then they have made the crossing and have seen often the death of their children on the way. Their cars have been broken down and been repaired with the ingenuity of the land man. Often they patched the worn-out tires every few miles. They have weathered the thing, and they can weather much more for their blood is strong.

They are descendants of men who crossed into the middle west, who won their lands by fighting, who cultivated the prairies and stayed with them until they went back to desert. And because of their tradition and their training, they are not migrants by nature. They are gypsies by force of circumstance.[70]

Steinbeck's travels with Tom Collins brought him to the same conclusion that Taylor and Lange reached: that government-sponsored camps were the answer to California's migrant problem.[71] Much of the tragedy in *The Grapes of Wrath* hinges on the Joad family's having to leave Weedpatch Camp: Jim Casy is murdered, Tom Joad commits his second murder, and the disintegration of the Joad family accelerates. Steinbeck makes it clear that the family cannot stay at the safe, clean camp and that the stability it offers is the last they will see in the novel, beyond the future that Tom predicts to his mother.

For both Steinbeck and Taylor, the distinction between the "new migrants" and their migrant predecessors is located rhetorically in homemaking, a quintessentially American quality that Steinbeck takes great pains to illustrate in order to separate the "Okies" from the European gypsies. The "gypsies by force of circumstance" desire a settled stability in a shifting landscape. For Taylor, the right to make homes, denied to migrant farm workers in ways it had never been either in the Midwest or the pioneer West, would indeed settle the land. His papers note a title by Henry Wallace, "The Migrant of Today Would, Seventy-Five Years Ago, Have Been a Pioneer," which refers as much to the perception of the migrants as to their actual experience. The migrants would have been seen as pioneers, the title suggests; their trek west was a crucial aspect of American history, one that led to the population and development of this last frontier.

The economic and political difference between early western pioneers and those of the 1930s was their difficulty in securing land for a home. California provided no footing from which a worker might make that first step up the agricultural ladder at the heart of Jeffersonian homesteading, a Populist and Progressive urge that Taylor shared with so many of his New Deal colleagues. No matter how hard field laborers worked, they would almost certainly be unable to buy the land they "improved" or even establish themselves on it as tenant farmers, because the size and scale of California's farms worked best with industrial farming methods that were supplemented by seasonal hand labor. As James Gregory describes it, California farming demanded a "reliable pool of temporary workers who could move about the state with the rhythms of the growing season, descending upon particular crop areas at key periods to perform the cultivation, thinning, pruning, and, most important, harvesting tasks needed to bring the diverse agricultural products to market."[72] Taylor recognized that the migrants' association with this homeless "pool" had articulated them in the public's imagination in certain ways, and it *wasn't* as pioneers. Kept at arm's length, they were marginalized members of society, separated both physically and socially from the California dream.

The complex attempt to exonerate the public's abhorrence of

migrant workers in the abstract and condemn the denigration of *these* specific migrants explains why Steinbeck sought to emphasize their European whiteness. Taylor, conversely, attempted to redefine the status of migratory workers altogether, wrapping them in the abstract but patriotic blanket of the pioneer, for, aside from a handful of popular images of gold-rush prospectors and "cowboys and Indians," the westward pioneers are intimately and intrinsically associated with farming. "Staking a claim" referred to homesteading long before and long after it explained the rights of placer miners, and provided idealized images of Conestoga wagons laboring across literally golden fields of grain. In establishing a context for the migratory workers of the 1930s within this long tradition of American agriculture, Taylor associated them with an entire history of patriotic reform and protest, from Thomas Jefferson through the 1892 Populist Party platform.

But he differed from this tradition by situating them in a distinctively Californian context, emphasizing the racial lineage of farm work in the state and its economic impact and implications. He took none of the precautions Steinbeck took with his audience, the planned evocation of an imagined heritage, a non-raced history that exoticized and marginalized people of color. While Taylor calls on the trope of "Americans of old stock" in "Again the Covered Wagon," he is at most able to say that they "predominate among the emigrants." There are with them, "a few Mexicans, mestizos with many children; occasionally Negroes: all are crossing over into California."[73] He is aware of race but locates California's problems not in its mixture of race and ethnicity but in the long tradition of racism that has characterized farm work in the state. He believed, mistakenly, that labor racism, like many other problems, was the kind of social and moral wrong that people could correct. He never seemed to question whether or not they *would*.

As Taylor explained in his oral history, his entrance into California's culture, despite his physical arrival much earlier, actually occurred when he began studying Mexican migrant labor and learned of Mexican workers' inability to buy homes in the state. Over the years, the nearly complete absence of home ownership would come up again and again, disturbing him personally as much as it troubled his Progressive ideology of labor—urban or rural—and the destructive results of exploitation and oppression. The kinds of homes he saw were a direct result of the state's unwillingness to provide real estate opportunities for its workers and its willingness to bankroll large-acreage growers who kept their workers and their conditions sequestered from public view. Exposing the conditions could not be a simple task, for many Californians clung tenaciously to prejudices and stereotypes that insisted that the very conditions into which the migrants were forced defined them. In one remarkable speech, Taylor attempted to describe the migrants as he assumed others saw them and then to refute that perception.

> Are these people Riff-Raff? Are they the unmitigated "moochers" that some declare? Are they an "invading horde of idle," as the newspapers call them? After having seen hundreds of them all the way from Yuma to Marysville, I cannot subscribe to this view. These people are victims of dust storms, of drought which preceded the dust, of protracted depression which preceded the drought. "It seems like God has forsaken us back there in Arkan-

sas," said a former farm-owner at a San Luis Obispo pea-pickers' camp. "The cotton is burned up" is their common story. They are largely farmers who have been carrying on agriculture on the family pattern which has been so long regarded as the great source of stability in our nation. One of them, recently picking fruit with his family in the Sacramento Valley, told succinctly this story of his decline from farmer to farm laborer: 1927—made $7,000 as a cotton farmer in Texas; 1928—broke even; 1929—went in the hole; 1930—deeper; 1931—lost everything; 1932—hit the road; 1935—serving the farmers of California as a "fruit tramp."[74]

The rhetorical attempt to contextualize the migrants within this historical trajectory while singling them out within the particular moment in time worked to separate them from some of the bloody agricultural history being written at the time. One of the greatest problems government workers faced in providing physical space for a concentration of workers was the public's willingness to assume that any grouping would inevitably lead to unrest, dissent, and violence. A February 1934 statement by W. B. Hughes, a SERA employee, claimed that the growers resented the presence of relief workers. "Several growers wanted to beat me up and I almost got punched in the face once." Noting that all relief for strikers came from federal sources, Hughes recalled that there were accusations that "food was given to unworthy people," admitting that they doubtless "did make mistakes." But people there "were hungry and starving."[75] Growers feared, Taylor himself claimed, "that if you brought migrants together in government camps, that they would agitate, organize and strike. *That* they did not want."[76] John Steinbeck would find that out only a year later, when he published *In Dubious Battle,* his roundly criticized fictional story of labor strife and communist agitation within the migrant camps. In February

1938, prolonged rains flooded a camp near Visalia, and for several days Steinbeck joined relief efforts there, moving families and caring for the sick. People were dying from cholera or starvation, often simply dropping dead in their tracks, and Steinbeck would later say the experience hurt inside, "clear to the back of my head."[77] He wrote to his agent, Elizabeth Otis: "Do you know what they are afraid of? They think that if these people are allowed to live in camps with proper sanitary facilities, they will organize and that is the bugbear of the large landowner and the corporate farmer."[78]

Taylor's attitude toward the migrants' organizational capacities was less romantic than Steinbeck's, whose novels focusing on the "phalanx" theory suggested an inevitable surge of communal will that would move far beyond the individual. Taylor had seen group theories at work in the self-help cooperatives, and he knew that there was little inevitable about their will, that men and women tended to break down under conditions of stress, hunger, persecution, and illness—all of which threatened the migrants of California. The tendency of county officials, growers, and local citizens to see the migrants as a featureless group was at the heart of their problem because few of the actual difficulties they faced came to light. The rural rehabilitation that provided the name for the government agency Taylor worked for was real to him; the rehabilitative mechanism would begin with clean camps, built with government funds.

In June, Taylor had received a letter from Lowry Nelson,[79] director of the newly formed Resettlement Administration, saying he had just arrived in Washington, D.C., and found himself "a part of the maelstrom [and] trying to get myself oriented in the new Resettlement Administration." Nelson believed that the work Taylor was doing, "should help greatly in our working out the final decisions [on camps]."[80] Ultimately, it would be Nelson himself who, in Taylor's memory, secured the camps: "The way those two camps got started was, that Dorothea and I took Lowry Nelson into the field with us. . . . We took him and his wife with us in my station wagon down as far as Yuma, Arizona, east of the Imperial Valley, an entrance to California for many thousands of families. So for the length of the state, except for the Sacramento Valley, he saw first-hand what the actual condition was. By that time we also knew what our camp program was for."[81]

Nelson knew of twenty thousand dollars that had been allotted to a project that was no longer active and recommended that the money go to California SERA for two camps, one in Marysville and another in Arvin, in Kern County. Washington agreed, although apparently with some reluctance, as later Taylor conceded that "there was unease over the camp program in Washington; there was grower opposition. There were precedents for state and city public housing, but never yet for federal."[82] Local opposition among growers and residents made California an inhospitable venue for such programs, and it was, Taylor always thought, the fact of the emergency decision, "rather than a thoroughly considered one," that started the camps. The Rural Rehabilitation division was about to be transferred into the Relief Administration, an emergency administration headed by Rexford Tugwell, one of FDR's braintrusters. Taylor notes that "Tugwell assembled a staff of young liberals who wanted to do something in the emergency," but there were still bureaucratic issues to be negotiated.

> They had all kinds of questions to put to me. If I answered one way, why the answer might stop the whole project. I was asked, for example, "After all, hadn't this condition of misery among the migrant workers existed for a long, long time?"

When I answered, "Well, yes, it had," then I was confronted with the assertion, "But the Relief Administration is an 'emergency' administration, and this isn't a new emergency."[83]

Taylor used his wit to declare the migrant workers' condition to be an emergency "because it was magnified extremely beyond anything before in volume and pervasiveness on the agricultural landscape." Once more, he put the migrants within the scope of history while still separating the Dust Bowl exodus from the traditional narrative, the "conditions of misery" that had indeed "existed for a long, long time."

Taylor's belief in the kinds of housing he and Lange secured that spring would come into full play when they authored another article for *Survey Graphic,* "From the Ground Up" (September 1936). The essay's text and photographs focus clearly on the good that government camps do, carefully creating a scenario in which the dispossessed are shown to have fallen, and would be raised by the government camps that must be built. It begins with the Texas farmer whom Taylor met the spring before and who appears repeatedly in Taylor's rhetoric:

A dispossessed Texas farmer last fall told his story succinctly:
1927—made $7000 in cotton
1928—broke even
1929—went in the hole.
1930—still deeper.
1931—lost everything.
1932—hit the road.

The article ends by noting, "In 1935 he was working with his family as a fruit tramp in the Sacramento Valley."[84] In this structure, readers can see the man's fall from a productive and profitable farmer all the way down; at the end of his six-year slide is rock bottom: a life of transiency signified by "the road." The road represents everything from which the migrant must be raised—not just transiency, but also a lack of productivity, an inability to partake in the American system, and a loss of identity. Housing, in its remediation of transience and homelessness, becomes the de facto means by which to redeem migrants from their fall.

The essay looks to governmental involvement as a means to redeem and rescue migrants from their condition, and in that sense it is "a kind of sequel," writes Cara Finnegan, to "Again the Covered Wagon." Published a year later, "From the Ground Up" has a history nearly as long as the article itself. The article was submitted in May, but correspondence between Taylor and the editorial staff at *Survey Graphic* indicates concerns and revisions that extended the publication date to September.[85] Doubtless, some of those decisions revolved around the unusual placement of two photographs by Lange, each taking a full page, as frontispieces to the article, for *Survey Graphic*'s standard approach to photography was as an illustrative component or as a feature in and of itself.[86] Thus, Lange's two full-page photographs, appearing separately from Taylor's article under the title "Draggin'-Around People," are a departure, since additional photographs she created follow the more traditional format, appearing within the article itself as illustrations of the text.

To what extent do the two photographs, one of which, "Migrant Mother," would become Lange's most famous, belong to the article? Finnegan's thorough discussion hinges on the great disparity between the photographs within the article, which she calls "flat, prescriptive, dull,"[87] and those that preface it, both of which resonate with a "curious dialectic of universality and individual anxiety"—a quality that Lawrence Levine would also note and that most people observe when looking at Migrant Mother.[88] The internal photographs, Finnegan concludes, "visualize and uphold the ideals of carefully planned social order," an impersonality that "contrasts sharply" with the "frontality and intimacy" of the frontispieces. To some degree, such a critique holds true, although it does not seem to constitute the "fundamental blindness in rhetorical practice" that Finnegan alleges.[89]

Certainly, there is a disparity between the two types of photographs, but acknowledging that disparity urges us to ask why, to push for an explanation, and to find it in the "gap" between the two opening photographs and the photos within the essay that follow. Specifically, that gap is closed by the idea of the essay as an *actual* sequel to "Again the Covered Wagon." The two photographs, both of which focus on dislocation and the unsettled life of migrants, act as a bridge between "Again the Covered Wagon" and "From the Ground Up," becoming the second article in a sequence of three, all of which, when taken together, construct the narrative pattern of fall and redemption. What would become the "Migrant Mother" photograph is called "Draggin'-Around People"; the other is entitled "California Field Hand." Both are indicated as Resettlement Administration photographs by Dorothea Lange, emphasizing the fact that the agency is involved in documenting the conditions of migrants and finding solutions to their problems. "Draggin'-Around People" is captioned, "A blighted pea crop in California in 1935 left the pickers without work. This family sold their tent to get food."[90] The brief caption emphasizes the plight of homelessness by focusing on unemployment and its result—transiency. The family in the photograph is composed of the woman and three visible children, one a baby, and there is no mention of the woman's husband.[91] As some have complained since, there is no mention of Florence Thompson's Native American ethnicity, her long years spent in California, or her complete circumstances. In this context, Thompson is not even identified as a "mother," but as a *kind* of "people." Thus, in this deliberate lack of personal detail, the woman is indeed presented as a representative of the many "draggin'-around people" described so vividly in "Again the Covered Wagon," people whose inability to put down the roots they once had—and expected to establish again when they arrived in California—victimizes them; it makes their lives "hardly . . . tranquil" and makes them vulnerable to outside agitation. It is the pairing of the photographic text of Lange's article and the text of Taylor's ongoing argument that creates a coherent narrative: the fall and, through camps and housing, the redemption. These are the second-wave pioneers, writ large, capable of rising "from the ground up."

Just as significantly for the narrative Taylor and Lange were building,[92] the second photograph identifies the subject as a "gaunt Mexican in Imperial Valley." He says to the audience, "I have worked hard all my life and all I have now is my old body." Like the first photograph, this one emphasizes place, despite the absence of any landscape or, as in the photographs that follow, identifiable place markers. Still, their captioning insists that they are California photographs, and their separate titles create in the magazine a table of contents that features two articles on California out of the magazine's total of twelve.[93] In short, *Survey Graphic* was not simply a national but an international magazine, now with more than 10 percent of its edition dedicated to the Far West's farthest-out inhabitants. These two "companion" articles on California suggest Taylor's growing understanding of California's impact on the Great Depression.

For Taylor, the Great Depression began not with the image of the falling ticker tape but with the image of the dispossessed, whom he first saw in his years of studying Mexican migrant labor in California. Since that time, Taylor's work had shown him more clearly the state's unique situation in the nation. Increasingly, California was the point of convergence for the Great Depression's rural problems, and as those problems deepened, California's place in the country's economy, as well as its imagination, expanded. The "factories in the fields" were not a western problem; nor were they a local one. The great westward movement of American poor indicated that many of the major problems of the Great Depression were playing out in the fields of California.

"Shanty Town," c. 1935. Dorothea Lange, American, 1895–1965.
© The Dorothea Lange Collection, Oakland Museum of California,
City of Oakland. Gift of Paul S. Taylor.

CHAPTER 5

A New Social Order

And the worlds were built in the evening. The people, moving
in from the highways, made them with their tents and their
hearts and their brains.

John Steinbeck, *The Grapes of Wrath*

In mid-March 1935, when Taylor's crew was visiting some fruit
pickers in the Sacramento Valley, Taylor recalls, "On that trip, I
was there, and both Maynard Dixon and Dorothea were there;
that was before Dorothea's and my marriage."[1] Whatever feeling
Taylor had about Lange he kept under wraps, even many years
later. After the long trip in March, he and Lange worked at least
once more together, in the town of Winters, late in May. Then,
in June, Taylor, his students, and Lange set out for a long trip
once again. Their field notes begin at Sacramento, on June 10,
when Lange recorded a comment that would in a few years be
echoed in Steinbeck's *The Grapes of Wrath*, when the Joads meet
their first family whose failure to find work in California has sent
them back home (189). "I'm like the rest of them in Okl.," her

notes say. "[Indecipherable] the money grew on bushes out here. Now I know and I write them back the difference." Hard-earned knowledge juxtaposed itself against biblical faith two days later in Visalia, when a migrant told her, "I have that hope that I'll have a better home—if not on this Earth then on the next."

It is this core of religiosity within the migrant community— many were Pentecostal, and nearly all were Protestant[2]—that allowed them to fit so easily into what critics would recognize in *The Grapes of Wrath* as a distinct narrative: a sweeping, nearly panoramic epic of an exile from the original Eden and the subsequent journey into the wilderness in search of a new Eden. Less focused on the migrants' ability to transform the wilderness, however, than was the errand that critic Perry Miller identified as the mission of early Puritans, this journey followed the path of the traditional American jeremiad but left its "pilgrims" unable to make their way through the desert wilderness to a new Eden. That inability, for Steinbeck, signaled an ideological failure, one that required the slow growth of an entirely new social order and protested the current one. But for Taylor, the failure was social,[3] the protest immediate, leveled not against the entire structure but against people—growers who exploited their workers, citizens who refused to help their brothers and sisters. It was "less a sense of idealized community, more [of] resentment that great benefits were going to the big growers," Clark Kerr said about him.[4] Human greed and apathy led to these conditions, and it would take a sustained effort to show others the necessity and desirability of these pilgrims' redemption. To both Lange and Taylor, the long-term goal and its benefit were clear. Camps, while necessary, were only an immediate response; permanent homes on plots of land where families could build and grow into communities that would transform the West—that was the real solution.

On this point, the White House would agree and was at the same moment marshaling its forces to move into housing the country's poorest and hardest-hit farm families. That spring, a separate agency was created, apart from the emergency-based FERA, the purpose of which was to concentrate on, among much else, resettlement and the attendant issue of housing.[5] Signed into effect by Executive Order 7027, which designated liberal agricultural reformer and current Under Secretary of Agriculture Rexford Tugwell as its head, the Resettlement Administration (RA) was charged with three areas of activity: land use; loans and grants to help small farmers purchase land, equipment, and livestock; and resettlement of destitute families and construction of model communities.[6] The government was going into the construction business, and in case it needed some public relations work to be successful, Tugwell hired his former student Roy Stryker for the kind of publicity that would create public goodwill toward what was bound to be a controversial program.

FROM DREAM TO DOCUMENTARY

Back in California, Taylor and Lange were gathering exactly the kind of evidence and documents that Roy Stryker would need. They found destitute families whose rural lives had been blasted apart by poverty but who retained a tight-knit core: "100% families,"[7] Taylor had written in his notes during the March trip. While growers complained that the children could not work, women worried about their children's inability to attend school, and men shook their heads and mused that they themselves had been raised "better." Some families expressed a loyalty to and hope in the president, but most expressed their isolation, as if California were experiencing a different Great Depression than the rest of the nation. The dream the state had once sustained had soured. North of Salinas, a worker told Taylor, "People's always been moving west. That's the way the country was settled. People looking for something better. Now the east [sic] is filled up—Pretty soon if people keep coming west it'll be so you might as well stay where you are."[8] In the squatter camps, Frederick Turner Jackson was right: the frontier was closed.

With the migrants' disillusionment and hope confronting them in equal measure, the crew headed south into the Imperial Valley to follow the long, snaking band of Highway 99. On June 13, near Bakersfield, Taylor juxtaposed two quotations in his notebook. A migrant told him, "I'm not used to this kind of life. It's kind of hard to take it—sleeping and eating on the ground." Across from that he quoted a local official: "I believe they really like this. After a few years they get to like it."[9] Sometime after Bakersfield, Lange's notes record a migrant woman's frustration: "This kind of life drives a woman crazy—you get so disgusted with no place to stop and no place to go. They went to school when we was stopped, but not the last two-three years. Six children 14–12–10–7–4–2."[10] They worked continuously south: San Bernardino, Indio, Coachella, then Westmorland, and Escalera, slightly east of Brawley. After Brawly they went farther south to the border town of El Centro and then to Calexico, where Taylor's notes are in Spanish, and Lange's, with none of his language background, recorded a sort of chant: "Gracias Adios/A dios/Gracias Adios."[11] Slowly, at the geographical bottom of the state, they turned around and headed up: El Centro, Calipatria, Hemet. June 23 brought the crew to San Bernardino, and on June 25 they were heading up into the Tehachapi mountain range.

Here they encountered a brilliant crest of sky and clouds, and it was wildflower season.[12] They stopped the car and got out, and, leaving the others behind, they waded out into an endless horizon of purple lupine. There they finally admitted what both must have known for months. They loved each other. It happened, as many intimate moments would over the next thirty years, quickly and quietly, sandwiched between work and the many other people whom work involved. Then they got back into the car and drove to a migrant auto camp, a dismal collection of bald tires and tents on the outskirts of Tulare.

The story of Lange and Taylor among the lupine is one that Daniel Dixon tells with intimate and knowledgeable familiarity; it's one that the large circle of Lange/Taylor/Dixon offspring and friends, many of whom are still in the Berkeley, California, area, all know, too. To nearly all, that trip was a turning point, a point at which Lange and Taylor began their unprecedented partnership. Either before or on that trip, Lange had written in her notebook, "June, Imperial Valley—last trip with Chapparito."[13] The Spanish term translates, literally, to "little man," but its connotation is spousal; it is a word lovers use, a familiar term, an expression of endearment, intimacy, and love. A few months later, when he wrote to Lange from Washington, Taylor signed off on his first letter back to Lange, "Muy buenas noches, mi chaparrita, Pablo."

Working together over the course of nearly twelve months, they had come to understand what they could do together. Taylor gave Lange a respect for her work and offered a security that she had long craved. In exchange, she gave Taylor what Daniel Dixon called "justification." In a 2003 interview, Dixon mused that as an adult, he could now understand that his stepfather was

> a romantic about American justice, [and] the injustice of what was happening. And all of this connected and filtered through his profound loyalty to the agricultural society, [or] dream of society, [or] ideal—and the progressive movement in the Midwest. . . . He took some breathtaking risks to preserve that ideal, but he was still an academic. And [his initial question was] was this woman going to be able to give him the material he needed to advance this purpose, which he perceived as being the country's purpose? So he and Dorothea took off. And he said within almost the first day, he was confident that she was going to be able to justify; I believe justify was his phrase.[14]

It remained only for them to figure out the actual way, as opposed to the ideological way, to translate their passions, both personal and professional, into something workable. What they agreed upon methodologically was, in Clark Kerr's words, "absolute accuracy," an idea that Kerr insists was indeed a "passion" for Taylor: "no interviews with set questions in logical order but a friendly conversation that covered all the points, no posed photographs but snapshots of people in the ordinary conduct of their lives."[15] What Lange brought to that passion was her desire "to get the truth about those people. Their truth. She was totally honest," her son says. Like Taylor, she wanted a new style of portrait, a snapshot of real life. Dixon believes that to some extent, it was his mother's insistence on using a large-format camera that enabled that truth, or perhaps it was because of the truth it brought that she insisted on using her Graflex long after 35mm cameras were available: "She never went anywhere without the Graflex, a great big old cumbersome thing. They [her subjects] wouldn't notice until it made a sound like a bomb explosion; the shutter was like the slamming of a garage door. People really had a chance to prepare themselves, gather themselves, to make sure that the person she was photographing was the person that they felt themselves to be. That's what gives them their integrity. It isn't that she *gives* them integrity; it's that they *claim* it for themselves."[16]

The exact chronology of how they did it, however, is more elusive. For Taylor, the road may have been clearest. The Taylor/Whiteside "open marriage" experiment had been a failure for him. Despite his wife's absolutely earnest efforts to stay open and honest and, within her own definition, loving, Taylor could not function in anything but a monogamous relationship, and Katharine was simply unable to provide him with that. When Taylor returned from the June trip, as Katharine remembers it, he "came home full of joy and explained he had developed a deep love for Dorothea Lange, who had been along as his photographer on his trips." Katharine recalls that she "really rejoiced and congratulated him," and assumed that her husband would keep going along with the open marriage plan that had directed their marriage for so long; but Taylor was done with open marriage. "Gradually," Katharine realized "that being conventional as he was he wanted [Lange] to divorce her husband and marry him."[17]

Since both Taylor's and Lange's field notes end in late June, Taylor's return home and his declaration to Katharine of his desire to marry Lange may have occurred early in July. Events are more difficult to pinpoint in Lange's home life. At some point between her return from the field and early September, Lange called Imogen Cunningham to ask if she could bring Taylor and his daughter to dinner. "But it's after five," Cunningham said, "and all I have is a small leg of lamb." "That's all right," Lange replied, "let Paul carve it and it will come out all right." Cunningham remembers not only the leg of lamb turning out "all right," but Lange taking her down into the basement to tell her that she was going to marry Taylor. "But you're married to Maynard!" Cunningham gasped, to which Lange replied, "Yes, he's a good man, and strong enough to take it; he helped me come to this decision."[18]

Dixon did not, however, seem to take it well. In his autobiographical notes, the entry reads, "Tragic interlude: divorce."[19] Speculation surrounded the shared circumstances of the Nevada residency Maynard and Katharine agreed to for the divorces, and a penciled note in Katharine's autobiography suggests that an affair occurred in Nevada while she and Dixon were there.[20] But, undoubtedly, it was the children for whom the tragedy reverberated loudest and longest. Years later, Daniel's memory of it remained clear. He went early one morning into his parents' bedroom, and they told him they were going to be divorced. Daniel told biographer Milton Meltzer that he remembered hearing the words "and fixing his attention on the three moles on his father's head, just visible under the fine dark hair. He ran out on the street and excitedly told all the children that his folks were going to be divorced."[21] Mary Edwards, who worked as Lange's darkroom assistant at the time, gave Willard Van Dyke a different version. "Mary was working for [Lange] at the time that she decided that she was going to leave Maynard. She reported that she tucked Danny into bed that night. She explained as quietly and as nonemotionally as she was able to do what she was about to do. And Danny said, 'Well, you got what you wanted again, didn't you?'" Kathy, the oldest of the Taylor children, says, "Paul and Dorothea took me and my brother and sister to the top of Mount Tamalpais and she took a picture just after we received the news. My brother Ross is central and is throwing with all his might, a stone or ball, perhaps in anger at the news. My little sister Margot is in the background. I am not in it."[22]

Kathy, who remained distant from her father until Lange died, locates what was for the children a long-standing problem with their step-parental relations—the emphasis on work. "She took a picture just after we received the news," Kathy remembers, in the same way that Milton Meltzer would comment on Lange's famous photograph of her three-year-old son, John, handing her a bouquet of daisies. "Only the arm, hand, and flowers are in the frame. It is a sweet offering, yet when her three-year-old son made the gesture, she obviously reached for a camera and photographed it."[23] The fact is that Lange and Taylor fell in love over what they could do together, over the strength that her photography, so long unrecognized as a central and unique power, gave to his work. Paul Taylor recognized that Dorothea Lange's photographs would change things, and in that recognition they saw each other in ways that few couples do.

In September, Taylor traveled to Washington. From there, he wrote a series of letters to Lange, the first of which described a meeting with Lawrence Hewes, now in the Washington Resettlement Administration office. Taylor left Hewes feeling upbeat about a number of developments, especially Hewes's information that Lange's assignment as regional field investigator-photographer in the Resettlement Administration had been arranged. After dinner, Taylor wrote, "Dorothea my dear," describing Lange's new position to her and warning that she would have less freedom in

"Ross Taylor at Ten Years Old—Driven and Angry," c. 1935.
Dorothea Lange, American, 1895–1965. © The Dorothea Lange
Collection, Oakland Museum of California, City of Oakland.
Gift of Paul S. Taylor.

the RA than she did with Rural Rehabilitation and would have to
attend more carefully to administrative regulation. The majority
of his letter finds him engrossed in the work before him, hoping
he has "laid the groundwork for a favorable decision when Tugwell comes to California," and wondering if he is "really getting
anywhere."[24]

The next day, Taylor met with Roy Stryker for the second time. While Taylor would later recollect that Lange's official tenure with the Resettlement Administration began in August, at his September meetings in Washington it seems clear that he was still working out the details to insure that she would attain a stable position. He knew Stryker's first response to Lange's work had been positive.[25] The second meeting with Stryker apparently went just as well. That evening Taylor wrote to Lange, noting that it was "Thursday night—or really, Friday morning, after most folks have gone to bed." Obviously keyed up, he wrote excitedly, "Dorothea, my beloved—Your letter reached me just after a long conference with Mr. Stryker—His ideas are as nearly ours as can be imagined." Covering the basic requirements for RA photographic work, including having "some assignments," Stryker had then asked Taylor if he would oversee Lange's work "along those lines? Yes, I will, says I, thinking of the advantages of continuing as your boss—retaining a prestige I had thot [sic] lost. He (Stryker) thinks your work is great," Taylor continued. "That you and Ward Evans [sic], a man he's just sent into the south are in a class alone."[26] His ebullience is such that it is not until the letter's end that he comes to what he terms "our changed relationship," and he introduces the matter professionally. Telling Lange that he will find out before he leaves if it will "have an adverse effect on the job," he mentions that family members have previously had government jobs, although not in the same division, but thinks "it probably will be O.K. since we're already on the job & my apptment [sic] is temporary anyway."[27] Finally, he responds to some concern Lange has expressed in her letter to him. "I sent the wire partly so you'd feel easy 'financially' about sending the boys to Ojai," he tells her. "I do have full confidence in your judgment.

Send them now if it's best." He tells her he can arrange use of a darkroom at the university and adds, "won't you have decided . . . whether or when you'll marry Pablo?"[28] The next day he wrote to Lange, telling her that as soon as she got news of her official appointment, or even before, she should "go to Mr. Macarthur's office" to take the required oath of office, assuring him that she had "information straight from Mr. Tugwell's office" that her appointment "has been made." All those changes should be made before any change in marital status, he adds. Then, toward the end of the letter, he tells Lange of Stryker's "real" plan:

> to do a 4 volume photographic History of American agricul-
> ture—So, very quietly—without telling why all this work you
> & the others are to do—you see what's in mind—Documentary
> history—the archives of Library of Congress—or maybe U of C.
> for region #9 [their designated region]—50 years hence—see
> what Brady did during the Civil War, etc—Isn't that a prospect
> for you? I'm more than half ready to chuck my job, if necessary
> for you to retain yours—Would you let me go on field trips with
> you—I think our lives would be enriched by it![29]

THE RESETTLEMENT ADMINISTRATION

The man who proposed this history came into the Resettlement Administration for a specific reason, something far shorter in term than his "real" plan. Many articles and books tell the story of the RA/FSA, but nearly all agree that more than anything else, it was the "resettlement" aspect of the agency's mission—the movement of families from cities to farms and the settling of workers in government-administered camps—that called forth the Historical Division, whose purpose was, essentially, a public relations effort.[30] For that division's director, Roy Stryker, the mandate was more about education than anything else. "We succeeded in doing exactly what Rex Tugwell said we should do: *We introduced Americans to America.*"[31]

As Stryker's professor at Columbia University, Tugwell had taken a liking to the thoroughly midwestern World War I veteran, who left the war, Stryker's friend Nancy Wood writes, with an "astounding—if not original—set of expletives, a distinction which . . . marked him all his days."[32] Wood's essay also recounts Tugwell's introducing Stryker to the work of Lewis Hine and Jacob Riis, the photographers whose pictures of industrial hardships and city slums had already brought about changes in social and political thought in the country. Stryker worked as a teaching assistant in Columbia's Department of Economics, and his belief in the power of photography shaped his teaching. Taking his classes on field trips to let his students "see things for themselves," Stryker also began to dig up pictures "to show city boys things that every farm boy knows about. Everywhere I went," he remembered, "I kept a pocket full of notes about my ideas for pictures. I wanted there to be a file on the things we were seeing, but of course there wasn't."[33] Although his unorthodox approach to teaching economics convinced Columbia not to grant Stryker his Ph.D., it convinced Tugwell to bring him on as coauthor of Tugwell's massive text, *American Economic Life,* to supply all the text's illustrations. And when Tugwell went to Washington, appointed by FDR as assistant secretary of agriculture, he summoned Stryker to head the division that would collect pictures of America's rural areas and their problems. Stryker says, "But

I didn't know how to go about doing the job he wanted me to do—and he sensed it. One day he brought me into the office and said to me, 'Roy, a man may have holes in his shoes, and you may see the holes when you take the picture. But maybe your sense of the human being will teach you there's a lot more to that man than the holes in his shoes, and you ought to try and get that idea across.'"[34]

Although Lange was the fourth photographer Stryker hired—Arthur Rothstein, Carl Mydans, and Walker Evans preceded her—it is easy to see why she fit in so immediately, considering how closely Tugwell's philosophical maxim mirrored her own revelation when she turned from the studio to take that early photograph of a man "as he stood in his world," including "his back against the wall, with his livelihood, like the wheelbarrow, overturned."[35]

Her arrival marked the moment at which the tremendous efforts, skills, and energy of the three men hired before her finally coalesced. Rothstein, the first and for some time the only RA photographer, had worked with Stryker as a student at Columbia. In 1934, when Tugwell and Stryker were working on a book of photographs illustrating American agriculture, Rothstein had come onto the project via a National Youth Administration grant.[36] A yearbook photographer and science major with a love for the technical side of photography, Rothstein followed Stryker back to Washington in the summer of 1935, this time to make much more than a book. Carl Mydans had begun as a college reporter and then, after graduating, became a financial reporter for *American Banker,* a Wall Street newspaper. Working with a 35mm camera, he sought photographs that captured the spontaneous moment, snapshots of real life. After working for a time in the Suburban

Resettlement Agency, he came to the RA when it incorporated his agency. Walker Evans, hired at roughly the same time as Mydans, was in many ways his opposite. In France, Evans had studied with the avant garde portraitist Nadar, and had studied many of the Parisian street photographs of Eugène Atget. By the time he joined the RA, he was two years into what would become a lifelong relationship with the New York Museum of Modern Art, producing the museum's first one-man show in 1938. Slow, deliberate, confident, and extraordinarily gifted, Evans relied on a large-format view camera, waiting until he found the one photograph that represented everything he was seeing.[37]

Everyone involved in the initial days of the project profoundly influenced the shaping of the Resettlement Administration, but for years only Lange would produce a consistent number of photographs in the West that got across Tugwell's belief that "there's a lot more to that man than the holes in his shoes." Her work with Taylor had for months been seeking to tell the story of how those holes got there and what caused them. Working with Taylor's graduate students had shown her how to—and perhaps how *not* to—discover the stories of those who stood in front of her camera, equipping her with more than technical skill, more than a quick and natural approach, more than artistry—but she had all those, too.[38] Simultaneously, as her field notes show, the technique she was developing was teaching her about the conditions she was facing in California. Although her camera was a visual witness to deplorable living conditions, she also heard and likely felt the fierce pride of migrants who preferred not to accept relief, the desperation of those who could not find work, and the anger of those who found themselves ostracized and marginalized. In addition, she had by the summer of 1935 an abiding and intensely personal passion for her subject matter, for she had by then learned to see it not only through the compassionate and questioning lens that had guided her through the San Francisco streets and breadlines, but through the informed and idealistic eyes of a man she loved. As Chris Gardner said, "They influenced one another, but they knew from the beginning that they underwrote each other's viewpoints. And I think they knew that from the beginning before they were emotionally involved, from what Dorie always told me."[39]

Before Lange's hiring by Stryker, Taylor asked her to put together a third document, *Notes from the Field,* that she would submit to the government entirely on her own. The document is a compilation of notes, quotations, and photographs that Taylor called an "interim report." As Taylor recalled, "The style was to carry a small notation in words (by myself), perhaps a paragraph, perhaps a page, and opposite the text to carry a relevant photograph."[40] *Notes from the Field* was submitted to Harry Drobish on June 4, 1935. Years later Taylor told Suzanne Reiss, "This report is Dorothea's. I wanted to build her up in the mind of the bureaucracy, so I told her to sign this one." Conceding that he had written the text, he said, "but, you see, I didn't do the photographs on the other reports, though I signed them."[41]

In both theme and method, *Notes from the Field* anticipates their book, *An American Exodus: A Record of Human Erosion,* with its mix of quotations, commentary, newspaper clippings, and photos. *Notes* is, as Paul Strand would say of *An American Exodus,* in a "complex" form, patterned in the style of a documentary film, with a plot or narrative direction, relevant text, and photographs of individuals and events.[42] It begins with two photographs taken in Marysville: one of an encampment "without proper water and sanitary facilities," and another of a worthless pump—more like an exclamation point than evidence—resting on rotted wooden boards. They are followed by a photo taken May 25 of a "fruit tramp who owns a garden acre in Tulare County." He and his son are camped 250 miles from home, on the banks of Putah Creek, having come to pick fruit; his wife and daughter remain in Tulare County. The last caption speaks to the point Lange and Taylor had been making for half a year: "These people are as anxious to settle down as others are to have them."[43] The implied summary statement is clear; broken-down camps and facilities become a corollary of broken-up families and lives.

The page that follows is entitled "What the Migrants Say—" and to Lange, what they said was "We have to get out in the whole state to make a living. We try so we can't get any help. The judge who distributes relief said, 'You work in Solano County, but spend your money in Winters (in Yolo County).' But my boys are American citizens. If war was declared, they'd have to fight, no matter where they was. I don't see why we can't be citizens because we move around with the fruit trying to make a living." Pictures from the UXA in Oroville follow, a coda to the photographs from the year before, stressing the improved conditions. Then, quotations from migrants who have experienced a downward trajectory, economically and materially, precede those that speak to the genesis of the problem: "refugees from drought in the Southwest find themselves migrant laborers in California." What happens when they arrive? Lange answers the question in a photograph that predicts that of Florence Thompson, the migrant mother who came to represent the Great Depression and who would a year later appear in *Survey Graphic* as "draggin'-

"Drought Refugee from Oklahoma." 1935. Dorothea Lange,
American, 1895–1965. From *Notes from the Field*. © The Dorothea
Lange Collection, Oakland Museum of California, City of Oakland.
Gift of Paul S. Taylor.

around people." A young "mother of five children," eyes cast
to an uncertain future, says, "We're getting along as good as us
draggin'-around people can expect—if you call it a livin.'"[44]

Notes from the Field ends with a brief photo essay, which starts
with a full-page photograph of a Hooverville near the conflu-
ence of the Sacramento and American Rivers. There, near a "rag
house," stands a man, under whom the caption reads: "They
have built homes here out of nothing. They have planted trees
and flowers. These flimsy shacks represent many a last stand to

maintain self-respect." From there, a photograph of a home "dismantled in obedience to eviction orders" serves as prelude to the last photograph, a full-page image of a man and his young child. He says, "How can we go when we ain't got no place to go to?" It is a powerful, moving sequence of photographs, the new social order that Steinbeck would predict residing quietly and firmly within the homes built "out of nothing." At its heart is the direct question the father asks of anyone, everyone, a question that turns the audience into judge, jury, and witness.

A "DIFFERENT AND PECULIAR" STATE

In September of that year, only a week or so before he left for Washington, Taylor was invited to speak at the California Commonwealth Club, at the opulent Palace Hotel in San Francisco. He titled his speech "The Migrants and California's Future: The Trek to California and the Trek in California," highlighting the dual immigrant/migrant status that the Dust Bowlers claimed in their transient lives and all that such lives meant. His opening remarks addressed all that the general public seemed to think that transience meant, quoting headlines that referred to the menace to California from an "influx of indigents" that "leaves one appalled." Immediately picking up the problem of propaganda, an important theme in *The Grapes of Wrath,* Taylor then cited magazines that were berating California's propensity to broadcast its beauty, the seeming cause of the migrant influx: "All this migration of the unemployed is a part of [our] reward for all the milk-and-honey-ballyhoo [we] had been broadcasting for years." Against these two perspectives, Taylor turned his listeners to a visual account:

Stand today at the highway portals of California, particularly at the southeastern border. See the shiny cars of tourists, the huge trucks of commerce, the equipment of campers, as they roll by. And at intervals the slow-moving and conspicuous cars loaded with the refugees from drought and depression in other states. They travel in old automobiles and light trucks, some of them homemade, and frequently with trailers behind. All their worldly possessions are piled on the car and covered with old canvas or ragged bedding, with perhaps bedsprings atop, a small iron cook-stove on the running board, a battered trunk, lantern, and galvanized iron washtub tied on behind. Children, aunts, grandmothers and a dog are jammed into the car, stretching its capacity incredibly. A neighbor boy sprawls on top of the loaded trailer.[45]

The paragraph demonstrated Taylor's intimate familiarity with the migrants—his knowledge of their belongings and their character, and his innate ability to create a visual image through words. Throughout the speech, he relied on all this knowledge to make the migrants real and to make himself credible, a recording witness with visual evidence. He quoted them frequently, allowing their voices to come in and counteract the social construction of migrants as "moochers" or "riff raff": he said, "It is not only despair, but hope that draws the refugees to California, hope of finding work, of keeping off or getting off relief. . . . 'We haven't had to have no help yet. Lots of 'em have, but we haven't,' said Oklahoma pea pickers on El Camino Real at Mission San Jose." Taylor's irony was rich as he invoked starving pea pickers on "The King's Highway." He provided a concise explanation of the economic conditions leading to the present "dislocated" society of migrant workers, and then turned to the solution: Resettlement Administration camps to counteract the dreadful squalor in the squatters' camps. His message, ultimately, was that the people were here, and they would live somewhere, and for everyone's benefit, it should be somewhere decent. But the underlying message was that they were, indeed, people.

Despite its controversial stance, Taylor's speech went over well with the mainly liberal audience. Fifteen thousand copies were mimeographed and distributed. The next day he received a letter:

> Dear Dr. Taylor
>
> As I told you yesterday, your address was one of the most genuinely appreciated talks we have had in some time. Our members like the able way in which you told them what you had seen and they liked your delivery. One of them said, "That talk's worth a dozen propaganda speeches."
>
> So, for the Club, the Luncheon Committee, and myself, I want to tender our sincere thanks.
>
> Yours very truly,
> William L. Hudson
> Asst. Executive Secretary
> Commonwealth Club of San Francisco[46]

Lange's praise was more intimate. In 1924, the club began broadcasting its speeches on a statewide band, so Lange was able to hear Taylor's September 13 speech despite her inability to attend. "Of its kind, Unsurpassed," she telegraphed him, referring to an earlier photograph she had taken while they were in the field together, a shot of a homemade privy, with screening by Standard Oil saying "Unsurpassed." "That was a joke," Taylor recalled, a means by which an evening apart still held a shared moment.[47] It spoke to an already deep intimacy that his letters from Washington, written only a week later, confirm.

When Taylor returned from Washington, he and Lange headed to Marysville for a Resettlement Administration conference. He spoke on behalf of his research, outlining the "factories in the field" scenario that Carey McWilliams would make famous a few years later in his book of the same name: underpaid, uninvested, unprotected workers exploited by owners who rarely showed up at the location on which their employees toiled were charged with the labor of "food products in open air factories."[48] Intensive crops requiring hand labor for only brief periods of time had created an agricultural system unlike any other, he argued, one marked by racial diversity, enforced mobility, and indecent living conditions. All those he had met, he claimed, longed for stability, for even the smallest patch of land. In closing, he presented the group with what he called a human document. A man said to him, " 'Here is my story: 1927, made $7,000 in cotton, a farmer. 1928, broke even. 1929, went in the hole. 1930, deeper. 1931, lost everything. 1932, hit the road' and in 1935 he was serving the farmers of California in the fruit. So," Taylor concluded, " the problem of agriculture and industry merge and the problem of the farm laborer and the farmer are largely one."[49]

When he was asked about the racial composition of laborers in regard to the repatriation of Mexicans, a government program in full swing at the time, Taylor insisted that no major changes had occurred in the south of the state; Mexican workers had been in charge of harvests for as long as he had been in the state. "North of the Tehachapi," however, he claimed, "I have never seen so many whites in California agriculture in my life as this year from Kern County up. There are considerable numbers of them. I can't give you a percentage."

MARRIAGE:
"OUR WORK WENT ON FROM THEN, TOGETHER"

In Lange's September–October notebook, a note written in near haiku form provides a year-by-year account of the downward spiral she was recognizing again and again:

1927 7000
Even
Hole
Still deeper.

The recording of the "human document" Taylor turned to again and again reinforces how closely the two worked, their observations literally becoming one. Soon after, her photographs and notes thin; there are five photographs from late November taken in San Luis Obispo County, another trip to Nipomo, and little else recorded. Yet much was happening in her life and in Taylor's. After the required six weeks in Nevada, Katharine Whiteside Taylor had relocated to New York, and in December 1935 she received a letter from Taylor. Opening it, she recalled, "The first words were, 'Dorothea and I were married a few days ago.' That knowledge shot through me like a sharp pain, and I wept as I had not since leaving Berkeley. . . . I had not fully realized what this final break would mean to me." Along with this pain was also a "keen-cutting" realization that Taylor's new wife was someone wholly outside of Katharine's current frame of reference. Admitting that while married, even while fulfilling the role of a professor's wife and directing a successful cooperative preschool, she could never bring herself to spend more than "ten or twelve dollars" for a suit, Katharine wrote with vivid recollection,

"I remember how shocked I was when Kathy told me Dorothea spent $50 for a suit."[50]

Actually, Lange spent more, according to Milton Meltzer: "$60 to have a beige gabardine suit tailor-made for her wedding—an extravagance that shocked friends."[51] But the beautiful wedding suit was perhaps the only extravagance Lange, whose first wedding had been marked by candlelight and peach blossoms, allowed herself. She was, after all, a woman who had for fifteen years been ridiculed by her husband for her love of fine things. While she had clearly not lost it, she had long since learned to do without such things, and the careful attention to detail she brought to her studio wedding in 1920 would not characterize her wedding to Paul Taylor, which seems to have come unannounced. Lange said in an interview conducted late in her life, "The next thing I knew, I was married to the man who was the head of the team."[52] She seems to have recounted the day in more detail, earlier in her life, to Chris Gardner, who gave Theresa Heyman the following account: "They were married in some hideous place that [Dorothea] really didn't want to be, you know in some place and they'd been out photographing all day. The ceremony was sort of just an after thought. She was damn tired, she never did things that way, ceremonial things, . . . but they were so poor by the work that they had to do, the fact that they were on this job and the fact that there was no money coming through from Stryker, he hadn't been able to get the money flowing yet."[53]

Gardner implies that Taylor felt social concerns, that they may not have intended to get married so soon, "but Paul thought it would be a good idea if they did. . . . They were going to be out in the field for awhile and there were other people traveling with them, there were researchers, there always were."[54] So without knowing exactly why Taylor and Lange got married on that particular day, she speculated that "it seems that Paul, in his methodical way, just went ahead and got her down there and got a license and they were all ready to be married." A justice of the peace performed the ceremony, and, while their separate hotel rooms confirm the spontaneous character of the ceremony, by the time they returned to the hotel, "Paul had already had his bags moved into her room." Gardner, knowing Lange was a woman who liked to "get ready" for an "historic occasion," thinks she "felt emotionally about Paul that it had come too suddenly, too fast. She was not a woman who liked sudden ruptures, . . . yet after they were married, they probably immediately . . . worked out the relationship that they worked with from then on."[55]

Taylor says simply, "Our marriage . . . took place on December 6, 1935. When Dorothea and I went to Albuquerque in early December, we were married there. On the afternoon of the same day she went out and photographed. And our work went on from then, together."[56] Yet, as Taylor was the first to acknowledge, his work was going to materialize in a different way than hers, in spite of his unrelenting faith in her ability. "There were family situations to face," he told Suzanne Reiss. "There were the children of two families. . . . It competed, of course, with her work. That is, she was not free to do nothing but her work in photography."[57] Taylor and Lange bought a large house on Virginia Street, one big enough for all five children, but initially, the children came only on the weekends. Dan remembers with displeasure having to live for a year in El Cerrito: "By the time John and I got there, Ross had already been there for six months or so. He'd organized the kids in the neighborhood to repel us. He was devious about it."[58] Kathy's memories are no happier. She writes, "The first year after the divorce was the hardest for me. My mother went alone to New York City to get her Ed.D. (Doctor of Education) at Columbia University Teacher's College. That year was the hardest for me. Paul and Dorothea at first had me live with them which didn't work out, and so I was farmed out to live with a Berkeley family who lived below the hills. The people were nice, but it was a hard, dreary year for me. Painful."[59]

Painful. Painful for the children; painful for Katharine, emotionally at sea in New York, certainly; and to some extent painful for Taylor, who admits, "It wasn't altogether easy to pull up stakes of two families and recreate relationships, but on the whole, it was done."[60] In the end, however, the burden of creating a harmonious home life fell squarely on Lange. Dan's memories of Paul remain "rather dim." He says, "I remember his figure, I can remember everything he said, I remember his presence was steady, quiet, and it was only when we actually tried to live together and I began to have trouble with school that he became more immediate, and he would try to help me with my homework."[61] Ron Partridge, who soon began working with Lange as her field assistant, vividly remembers Taylor in the Virginia Street house. With all three boys playing instruments or "basketball in the living room," Taylor could still sit in the same room and work. "NO problem writing a report," Partridge recalls, or taking a nap, which to him was thirty minutes. "At the end of thirty minutes he would get up and say, 'Well, well, now, now, ahem, my my'—he was always doubling everything—and off he'd go sit at his desk and start working again, refreshed."[62]

Lange was in charge simply because she was, despite a new job, the most involved with the children. She kept the house, Betsy Partridge reports, "immaculate, the wooden floors shining with fresh wax, dishes put away, beds made every morning."[63] Dan believes that because her desire to give her photographic subjects complete control of their own image took away her professional control, she counteracted with a need to completely control her own home and those in it. "She never cursed, she never yelled. But she could exert pressure!" he says, and when pressed for an example, he could only reply, "I don't think of it in terms of an incident. I think of it in terms of an environment." Her son's theory is that when she came back from the field, relieved from the self-imposed "inhibitions and disciplines" of her job, "she turned the house into a work of art. And she attempted to create an environment, and she attempted to control her children because she could not control her subjects [in the field]. And all those instincts came rushing out of her. I was in my early teens, but everybody felt it. Paul was crazy in love with her. But not so crazy—he went off to the university every day."[64]

Lange faced a dilemma that many women faced—one with which the decade struggled in new ways. Fisher writes, "The social crisis of the 1930s consisted not only in economic collapse, but equally in an uncertainty surrounding personal identity," an uncertainty that housed "fractures and change in prevailing notions of the masculine and feminine." Those fractures, she argues, produced "insistent efforts to fix the identity of the woman photographer."[65] Working mother, charged with home and career—she had negotiated the role for many years with Dixon, but there were crucial changes now, not simply those based on the fact that her marriage to Paul Taylor was, as Chris Gardner called it, "the one." Up until the time she took her camera into the streets of San Francisco, Lange's photographic work as a married woman had supported a life that, socially and financially, was mostly de-

"Squatter camp. California." 1936. Library of Congress, Prints and
Photographs Division, FSA-OWI Collection, LC-USF34-009995-C
(LC-DIG fsa 8b29941).

fined by her husband; now, as part of a small and groundbreaking
crew of government workers, her work in the agricultural fields
of California presented new demands, technically and physically.
It was also rapidly posing a myriad of new questions about her
identity and those of the women in front her camera.

Domestic identity became a theme Lange not only experienced
but witnessed in the lives of those whom she photographed, and
her sense of homemaking practices and their role in establishing a new social order grew more complicated in the years following her marriage. In a photograph of an anonymous squatter

camp, the sense of community inherent to any cluster of homes is both established and interrogated by the groupings of cardboard shacks that may or may not include more beyond the limits of the photograph. Within the details of the photograph exists a distorted mirror of home life: symmetry in the patchwork of shacks, shrubs lining the ditch, a peaceful stretch of shady branches, even a tricycle tilting haphazardly, as if dropped from play. In the photograph's center, home and community are distilled into a single image of mother and child. The mother's simple gesture, reaching down to steady her daughter's steps, is intimate, familiar. It locates the heart of community within the mundane practices of domesticity, and in that gesture the photograph transcends the moment and the time while also, in its specificity and the conditions it decries, insisting on both. It is precisely the familiarity of such a pose that collides with the reality of the physical situation the camera documents. Lange had begun to recognize in the physical circumstances before her a secondary story, something beyond poverty and hunger, something that could not be remedied by government camps, something that went even deeper than tule shacks and cardboard walls. A new narrative had begun to emerge.

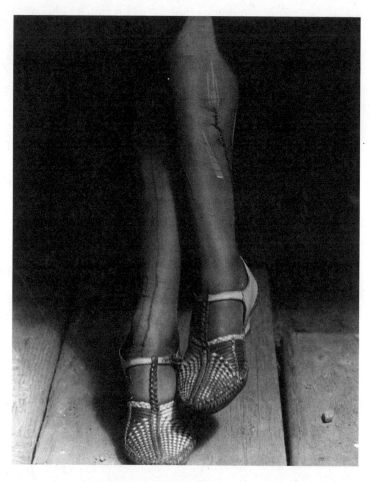

"A Sign of the Times—Depression—Mended Stockings—
Stenographer," c. 1934. Dorothea Lange, American, 1895–1965.
© The Dorothea Lange Collection, Oakland Museum of California,
City of Oakland. Gift of Paul S. Taylor.

CHAPTER 6

Women on the Breadlines

When Lange first stepped out of her studio, she took her camera onto a street that was predominantly male. Breadlines and social agencies, while staffing women, employed more men and served more men, making women a minority in the visual landscape.[1] As a woman on the street, Lange was forced to work within a context historically shaped by social stereotypes, none of which looked favorably at women on the street. Despite the constructs she faced, some of her first photographs articulated the Great Depression through a distinctively female vernacular, protesting conditions through feminine signifiers rather than strike signs. Recognizing early on that women suffered a double onus, even at the very onset of the Depression, Lange recorded in one of her earliest street photographs a simple testimony to the expectation that, despite economic conditions, women must conform to socially constructed behaviors, including visual markers: good women still "looked" a certain way. In her photograph of a woman's legs, the rent hosiery, the intricate and even arduous process, repeated again and again, of stitching up stockings when it proved too costly either to buy new or to forego altogether—all are conveyed in the hard focus and crystalline detail. Lange's photograph of mended hosiery insists on the difficulty a woman faced when she was not provided the means to meet the expectations society held for her.

Those expectations carried deep and volatile meanings when it came to public assistance, and before Lange headed into the fields, she produced a remarkable series of photographs taken at a government relief line. Unlike her photograph "White Angel Breadline," which would become famous, these photographs document women lining up for food. The differences in the photographs reveal much of what Lange recorded socially. "White Angel Breadline," with its distant range, suggests the photographic subject as one of many; he is outside, a man among many men in a crowded, open-air forum. The photographs Lange took of women are inside a building, capturing a darkened, interior aspect suggesting a very different kind of breadline. Eight are intimate portraits, taken from close range, suggesting some level of acceptance or even participation from the women. One woman hunts through her brown paper bag. Another stares, a pained expression on her face, at a block of cheese or butter. Three more women accept brown bags, all looking grim or unhappy. In one, a young Asian American woman stands at the front of the line, waiting, her face in neutral composition. None of the women looks happy except for one, a woman in a beret and tattered fur collar, a clutch purse tucked beneath her arm, looking pleased . . . or perhaps looking as she thinks she should.[2]

Lange's photographs are in many ways a mirror of Meridel Le Sueur's article "Women on the Breadlines," published in the

Untitled, c. 1933. Dorothea Lange, American, 1895–1965.
© The Dorothea Lange Collection, Oakland Museum of California,
City of Oakland. Gift of Paul S. Taylor.

journal *New Masses* (1926–1948), the leading Communist mouth-
piece.[3] Considering the differences in the women's backgrounds
and the path each took to confronting women on the breadlines,
it is remarkable that they would produce such similar texts. Born
five years after Lange, Le Sueur took an indirect and often difficult route from her Anglo, middle-class origins to "red" writing.[4] She was raised by a grandmother who lectured on temperance and a mother who made money by lecturing on women's
issues. After leaving her first husband (Meridel's father, William
Wharton), Marian Wharton married Arthur Le Sueur, an active
socialist, when Meridel was seventeen. Taking her stepfather's last
name, Le Sueur herself joined the Communist Party (CP) in 1924,
writing regularly for the *Daily Worker,* and in 1927 went to jail for
protesting the Sacco and Vanzetti executions. After the birth of
her second daughter, she divorced her husband in 1930, but continued her work for the CP, amid some controversy. It was, one
member recalled, "generally felt that it was not only foolish but
even wrong to have a child . . . because you couldn't feed it [and]
because you wouldn't be able to do what you should be doing." As
a single mother, Le Sueur's life could be economically marginal,
allowing her to write of the conditions of working-class women
with empathy, not as a "Party emissary but as one who, to a certain extent, shared their fate."[5] Indeed, despite her active involvement with the CP and the sense of personal community it provided her, Le Sueur was at best ambivalent, resisting (as a writer)
its heavy-handed aesthetics and (as a woman) the contradictory
attitudes toward women that marked this male-dominated organization. Her work, Constance Coiner writes, was "variously
straining toward and away from Party tenets and attitudes."[6]

That tension is perhaps clearest in "Women on the Breadlines," which documents the lives of the women Le Sueur met at a Minneapolis unemployment bureau. The piece, written in the first person, employs an active, present-tense narrative, insisting that readers join her: "I am sitting in the city free employment bureau." The immediacy of Le Sueur's narrative voice lends urgency to the problems the women face, as if they are, while readers watch, being denied work, running out of food, going "into hysterics" because they cannot "eat sometimes and [have] nightmares at night." Le Sueur places herself squarely among those seeking work, avoiding an anthropological stance: when a woman with a tumor "that she will die of" comes in, Le Sueur writes, "We cannot meet her eyes. When she looks at any of us we look away." When the woman "goes down decently," Le Sueur includes herself when she says, "And we all look away" (5, 7).

Le Sueur tells each story carefully and in detail, starting with the thirty-five-year-old Bernice, who came to the city as a girl, learned to mistrust all she heard from the "men in the park," and now can make it a whole winter on only twenty-five dollars by living in a condemned house. Another girl who has not worked for eight months flies into a rage at not receiving a job and receives, in turn, a similar rage from the dispatcher. And then there are Ellen and her friend, who last saw Ellen "back of a café . . . kicking, showing her legs for tossed coins." This friend is "unbelievably jaunty," and although Le Sueur knows she has not had work for months, she "has a flare of life," and "the runs in her stockings are neatly mended clear down her flat shank" (6). To emphasize the degradation of her subjects, Le Sueur ends on a note of female solidarity: "So we wait in this room like cattle . . . worse than beasts at a slaughter" (7). The inclusive pronoun of the conclusion emphasizes the wide range of Le Sueur's text, its insistence on overall female subjectivity. Not all of the women are married; nor are they mothers. They are, however, living distinctively codified female lives, and much of the horror of their lives is tied to the home—or, more precisely, to the woman's life and social identity in a substandard home, or no home at all. The women in the narrative assume that Ellen, whose unforgettable back-door exchange provides her with breakfast, will now "go on the street" (6). Bernice lives "alone in little rooms" (5), even after the house in which she rents a room has been condemned. Taken as a whole, the portraits provide a searing glimpse into the lives of all women, not only those who struggle to maintain families but also those who are single, widowed, or abandoned by husbands who have left them. The men, who go out looking for jobs, drift away, and the women struggle "alone to feed the many mouths."

"Women on the Breadlines" ran with a brief disclaimer from the editors of *New Masses,* indicting it for its "defeatist attitude" and pointing out that as "able . . . and informative" as its depictions might be, they lacked the "revolutionary spirit and direction which characterize the usual contribution to *New Masses*" (7). It is true that Le Sueur's relationship to the women about whom she writes was not that of Party emissary, and the editors at *New Masses* were likely right in their complaint that few who read "Women on the Breadlines" would be converted to the Communist Party. Instead, as would Lange, she turns away from the reform narrative when faced with those whom she understands best and finds herself able to help least. As compassionate witnesses and sisterly comrades, both Le Sueur and Lange were able to recognize a specifically female condition within the Great Depression, one far less able to respond to the conversion narrative that both women could understand on a larger scale.

As Le Sueur argued, the difficulty for women seeking relief was equaled only by the public's difficulty in knowing what to do with, how to perceive, women who had ventured out of the home and onto the streets, for whatever reason. The relief agencies that Le Sueur and Lange chronicled were not anomalous,[7] and the women within them were not uncharacteristic. Unemployed single women faced starvation while cramped into tiny quarters, nibbling at crumbs; widows without pensions could not feed themselves on jewelry or furs they had managed to retain, and worried wives whose husbands could stop off at a soup kitchen while looking for a job had no such recourse. But the public preferred to sustain the myth that while in the home, a woman was somehow safe, her identity intact.

In challenging the public mythos, Lange and Le Sueur both highlighted two pervasive fears many women faced during the Great Depression: hunger and homelessness. Le Sueur, as would Lange increasingly, fashions her "documentary" of the situation into a protest against it. Within its objective stance, "Women on the Breadlines" houses a protest against both the CP and the Hoover-era limits of state and municipal efforts, neither of which had in 1932 managed to remedy the living conditions of these women. This level of protest would become a growing element in Lange's work. Her exploration of the conditions and expectations domestic ideologies placed on migrant women would lead her to create a counternarrative to the jeremiadic structure she worked on with her husband, and this narrative focused on the absence of any viable path "up" for women to take. Additionally, just as Le Sueur situated herself within the room to which she bore witness, Lange began to work on an "exchange" basis, an implied relationship of the writer/photographer who presents the story to the reader/audience to whom it is presented. That relationship is mediated by the subject's own role, for it is her image, her story, and, often, her voice that determine the way it is read. In that exchange, Lange's photographs, as did Le Sueur's piece, insist on a female subjectivity within the New Deal narrative—the story of how the country was surviving the Great Depression. The great difference between the two women, however, lies in location. In Minneapolis, homeless women were forced to walk the street or to cower, hidden and invisible, within condemned structures. In California, migrant women were denied domestic structures of any kind, the very fact of their relentless transiency and public conditions insisting that they would remain unable to set up housekeeping, and this at a historical moment in which women's social identity was more closely identified with domesticity and the homesite than it had been in decades. Working with her husband to place migrant women within a pioneer ideology that would redeem them, Lange faced a dilemma within California's fields, the social imperative to locate in women the redemptive quality of domesticity in a physical environment that denied them the opportunity to be domestic.

THE DOMESTIC DILEMMA

Dust Bowl women's domestic dilemma in California revealed new complications in what had been for many years the contentious and conflicted position of domesticity in the United States. While women and their writing frequently sought to establish the feminine ideals, often Christian, that underlay much of nineteenth-century culture, they also produced critiques and openly contested the often repressive social and economic position they inhabited. Idealized as the Victorian "angels of the house," women simultaneously explored the privilege and oppression that role entailed. By the time Lange was at work during the Great Depression, issues of women's place in society—including questions of domestic worth, professional value, and sociopolitical status—had been openly raging for one hundred years, with each shift in the cultural temperament bringing about increasingly diverse, even antagonistic, social practices and messages. The expectations Lange's audience had of how women should act and behave, and, indeed, the expectations of Dust Bowl women about their own appearance and behavior, all factor into a full understanding of Lange's work. Her exploration of the migrant woman's role in California's Depression-era landscape relied on a traditional understanding of the woman's "place" in the home and built on decades of domestic ideology formed by a variety of political and cultural influences.

During the early nineteenth century, the home acquired a specific identity as a result of its separation from the public, or market, world—a separation most often articulated as the "separate sphere" ideology. Leading up to that moment, the importance of domestic labor had given housekeeping a ritualistic quality, but that quality, and its near magical resonances, disappeared by the end of the industrial revolution. Constance Classen argues that the change in view had direct consequences for traditional women's work. "For one, as it was no longer considered infused with the magical forces of nature, much of women's work, from child-rearing to cooking, lost its mythical dimensions and began to be portrayed as banal, simply a matter of good (or bad) housekeeping."⁸ Industrialization removed any number of productive activities from the home and put them on the market, thereby reducing the value of domestic production while paradoxically increasing the ideological value of domesticity. The home became an idea "whose worth was measured by standards of morality and propriety."[9] Industrialization and consumerism worked hand in hand, for as home goods moved into factory production, homemakers began purchasing the very articles they had formerly produced at home. Thus, as industry expanded, the home itself became a "necessary complement to a market economy."[10] Robbed of its productive capacity, gendered, sentimentalized, and etherealized, the domestic sphere grew to symbolize a corrective to the "evils" of the wildly expanding market economy, and "the home provided a touchstone of values for reforming the entire society."[11] In the pervasive concerns about the social ramifications of the new economy, Americans embraced the idea of the home and the security it continued to suggest as something that could and should "compensate for or ameliorate the market's destabilizing, undemocratic, or hierarchical effects."[12] Images of homemaking were able to represent nation-building, because of the home's symbolic relationship to the American citizen's individual (and mass) identity, and to suggest a safe haven from the troubling market economy on which the country was being built.

The subsequent "cult of domesticity" found its way into nearly every venue of social and cultural life, including publishing, with "literate, well-educated, white, middle-class women" beginning to conceive of themselves "in relation to work that they began to write of as 'theirs.'"[13] Often sentimental in nature, domestic cultural production nonetheless established firmly the link between idealized American citizenship and domesticity; at the same time, its very existence signified a growing sense of a female subjectivity both created by women and controlled by society. Glenna Matthews sums up the socio-historical moment when she refers to the home's "heightened emotional role" as stabilizer of the Jacksonian Age's turmoil and instability. Middle-class women had more time "and a greater profusion of utensils and other artifacts with which to create the good home," and in response, "novels, advice books, and periodicals all began to reflect a highly positive image of the 'notable housewife' in action."[14] By the midpoint of the century, domestic novels depicting the pleasures of homemaking and housekeeping proliferated. Indeed, she argues, by 1850 the home "acquired so diverse and expanded a set of roles . . . it ceased to be automatically taken for granted by men" and became "a mainstay of the national culture."[15] Significantly, the home's richly heightened symbolic capacity was at that time being utilized as a site for literary protest. In *Uncle Tom's Cabin,* Harriet Beecher Stowe drew on the domestic site's prominence in the American imagination, positioning domesticity "at the very heart of American democracy."[16] The novel's kitchen and hearth settings and sentimental tones created safe signifiers through which Stowe's middle-class readers could empathize and sympathize with the unsafe stance of abolition, bringing the unstable, tumultuous reality of slave life into the stabilizing, domestic sphere. In so doing, the novel established a means of domestic protest that would inform the work of, among others, women such as Lange and Le Sueur, who were looking once more at the domestic spaces within their culture as a means of understanding it.

By the turn of the century, the "cult" had shifted, as the "new woman" gained social and economic capital. "Women's work" came to include a host of political efforts while also, increasingly, referring to employment outside of the home. Some traditional women's work, such as home canning and gardening, became associated with rural societies, where it contributed in crucial ways to the family's income. In much of the popular imagination, however, the cult of domesticity was giving way to new ideas of technology and science, increasingly secularized ideas of life, and the relentlessly forward movement of the Progressive era. "The prevailing social ethos shifted from an emphasis on a superior, feminized otherworldliness and sentimentality to one that espoused the values of science, objectivity, and progress."[17] Social workers studied the home conditions of the poor, drawing parallels between public health and morals in ways that blamed poverty and depravity on what essentially constituted bad housekeeping.[18]

Homemaking and housekeeping were not less important; they had simply shifted in social meaning. During this time the move to "professionalize" domestic work was great, with Zona Gale's kitchenless homes, Charlotte Perkins Gilman's heroine in *Diantha* (1912) starting a hot meal delivery service, Edward Bellamy's cooperative kitchen in *Looking Backward,* and the Jane Clubs, which offered cooperative boardinghouses and cooperative laundries to woman workers. Prior to that, Christine McGaffey Frederick, a former suffragist, developed an entire domestic system based on the theories of Frederick Winslow Taylor's scientific management system. Frederick's "scientific housekeeping promised women more control over the household finances, acknowledged the complexities of women's work in the home, and validated women's work."[19] Even here, however, the obsession with efficiency that defined her "new housekeeping" was serving essentially domestic, even sentimental purposes, as Frederick's explanation of how she came to "invent" her system makes clear: "Indeed, I was often without much energy to 'dress up' in the evening . . . and when my husband came home, I was generally too spiritless to enjoy listening to his story of the day's work."[20]

The *Ladies Home Journal,* in which Frederick's explanation appeared, is a good case in point. Jennifer Scanlon's study of the journal shows that "while the *Journal* of 1924 appears at first glance to be more supportive of women's political work," closer study of articles that focus on, for example, women's political participation, shows that they actually emphasize political activities that "complement women's traditional roles as wives and mothers."[21] Stories and articles in the *Journal* focus on "the social world of women, the world of kitchen, husbands and children," because such concerns are "already familiar to the people who chose to read them."[22] Indeed, any number of books, magazines, and movies suggest that women never escaped from their primary identification with the home; it was just articulated in different ways. Patricia Raub contends that despite the "renegotiation" women's roles were undergoing, the best-selling novels of the era depicted "flappers whose deepest desire was to marry and raise a family, women who sacrificed their happiness for the men they loved, young matrons who strove to save their marriage regardless of personal cost, and frontierswomen who battled wild animals, drought, blizzards, and despair for the sake of their family." Raub's study concludes that with only a few exceptions, best-selling women novelists of the twenties and thirties "assumed women's work was home work."[23]

The change, then, was not so much within the domestic sphere itself, but in the *perception* of the domestic space, which was, by the 1930s, increasingly unstable. Matthews wonders if, because by the 1920s the home had become "sufficiently devalued so as to lose some of its ability to be an emotional haven,"[24] that was the moment at which the phrase "just a housewife" came into common usage. Scanlon's reading of fiction published in the

Ladies Home Journal finds that beneath the traditional plot lines of these stories, "female protagonists, to arrive at the happy endings, have to struggle with men, with children, with gender roles, with themselves."[25] Nicola Humble, writing about the "feminine middlebrow novel" that came into existence in the interwar period that includes the Great Depression, explains this increasing destabilization, contrasting the role of the Victorian home in "sooth[ing] and soften[ing] the culture's aggressive materialism" with the middlebrow home's "process of disintegration."[26]

The Great Depression affected nearly every aspect of life in mainstream society, and in the face of social and economic turbulence, much of that society struggled to increase women's identification with family and home—perhaps as a desperate attempt to recapture a solid image of strength in the national imagination by invoking the nineteenth-century idealization of the domestic sanctuary. Susan Ware's study of women during the Great Depression contends that "the typical woman in the 1930s had a husband who was still employed, although he probably had taken a pay cut to keep his job," and that even if the husband lost his job entirely, "the family often had enough resources to survive without going on relief or losing its possessions.[27] Widespread destitution was, according to most reports, not prevalent (although destitution was by no means absent); instead, a new socially sanctioned frugality was the order of the day, one best achieved, in the view of many, by sending women back into the home. Thus, the old saying "Use it up. Wear it out, make it do, or do without," which provided the title for an oral history by Jeane Westin, articulated a significant, if not major, shift in domestic ideology. Rather than moving away from home-based skills, women recovered the "small economies" of their sisters in decades past: "sheets were split down the middle and resewn to equalize wear; adult clothing was cut down to child size; broken crockery, string, and old rags were saved in case they might come in handy some day."[28]

For those within family structures, their main "contribution" came from their ability to embrace homemaking—to pick up practices recently put aside: canning, baking from scratch, and, both metaphorically and realistically, working *with* scratch. Perhaps more than anything, the "back to the home" movement, which included a variety of political and social strictures against working women, extolled the virtues of women who were skilled at staying home. The economic and cultural concern over family stability, and the hostility many women encountered in seeking employment outside the home (thereby "stealing" jobs from unemployed men), resulted in a reaffirmation of the separate spheres that had divided men's lives from women's in the nineteenth century. Laura Hapke charges that "working women, especially married ones, became the scapegoats of a movement to reassert the separate sphere thinking of past decades," with "working women . . . carrying the baggage of a lingering Victorianism concerning their physical and moral fitness for work."[29] As Le Sueur's "Women on the Breadlines" made clear, women without husbands suffered disproportionately, both economically and socially, with little recourse for their plight, but all women suffered. They were denied equal pay for equal work under provisions of the NRA and, if married, were forbidden to work in government and other employment venues. Perhaps most pernicious, a widespread public program put forth a clear anti-employment agenda for women, publishing pamphlets entitled "Do You Need Your Job?" As Hapke argues, "They were accused of emasculation, promiscuity, or both if they resisted these constraints but praised if they complied with the dictates of the back-to-the-home movement."[30] Indeed, public attempts aimed at defending the home front brought women ridicule, simply because they were public: "Women Picket Butcher Shops in Detroit Suburb," one headline trumpeted in 1935. "Slap. Scratch. Pull Hair. Men Are Chief Victims."[31] The home space had become sacrosanct in the public imagination, a site from which the good wife would not, during bad times, venture. In the public arena, women were invisible.

"WITH A COFFEE POT AND SKILLET"

Among the poems ethnomusicologist Charles Todd collected in his survey of Okie songs and poems is one by Flora Robertson, "Why We Come to California."

> California, California,
> Here I come too
> With a coffee pot and skillet,
> And I'm a coming to you.[32]

The idea that the West was shaped at least in part by this valiant attempt to domesticate it was long accepted as part of its history, particularly California's. For many years, it remained an unchallenged master narrative, a notion that spanned the migratory route of the early pioneer women from east to west, the nineteenth-century voyages of the many imported or "picture" brides for whom California was an eastern port, the journey up from Mexico following the Spanish mission era, and the second "pioneer" wave from the Midwest and South during the 1930s. When Anglo women began moving into California following the Gold Rush, they brought with them domestic weaponry with which to tame the wilderness.[33] Citing, as just one example, miners' wives who took from mine to mine "a few cherished belongings" that would secure, at least symbolically, "the domestic stability their peripatetic lives so clearly lacked," Robert Griswold points to the underlying need such domestic efforts fulfilled: "Domestic ideology—in particular the valorization of motherhood and the emphasis on women's moral responsibilities to their families and communities—was central to the world view of Anglo women in the West. Although the spheres may have overlapped, the cultural values of domestic ideology had a powerful appeal to female settlers: they gave meaning to women's domestic work, made the blurring of sex roles culturally intelligible, helped confirm women's self-worth, offered a sense of stability in an inherently unstable world, and fostered bonds of friendship with other women."[34]

Thus, domesticity took on qualitatively and quantitatively different characteristics in the nineteenth-century West. While the same ideology was at work, western women were charged with the additional task of physically settling the landscape into which they had migrated, and tales of double-decked Conestoga wagons teetering along the passes filled not only with the kitchen sink but with iron beds and upright pianos go back as far as the Donner party mythology. Just as their pioneering predecessors had, Dust Bowl women brought with them entire domestic structures, including beds, kitchen wares, and even ornaments— objects with which they had constructed the interiors of homes left behind. Woman after woman crossed California's borders with pots, pans, and brooms tied onto jalopies, expecting their Midwestern skills to translate into a stable settlement in which they would exercise some level of command over their families, expecting the Golden West's promise of fresh starts and fortune to extend to them as much as it had to prospectors and entrepreneurs. In this "manifestly destined" push west, the physical claim made by home*staking* was reified by home*making,* both an actual process that transpired *upon* the land and a cultural concept that brought validation *to* the land.

Settling increased the economic and social values of land by bringing it into the growing market system and stabilizing it within the culture that system produced. As the verbs within the words *homemaker* and *housekeeping* imply, certain domestic skills occlude the possibility of transiency by their very dependence on ritual and routine. Indeed, in a traditional understanding of the term, *housekeeping* assumes longevity—a kept house is not simply neat, well-maintained and appointed; it is a house actually kept in the family. The house is something passed on to children, so that housekeeping practices must guard against the potential ravages of time. In this sense, housekeeping assumes a long period of attachment to a finite piece of land. That attachment was something that Paul Taylor certainly recognized, and it influenced his belief that the successful steward of the land needed to own land, not subsist on it as a sharecropper or tenant farmer. Pioneers had by and large come west to claim land; thus, articulating the migrants in those terms was a way to put them into a cultural landscape in which they could ultimately own land.

Many of Lange's photographs show women attempting to recreate domesticity in the ways pioneer women had, thus linking them to California's mythologized first U.S. citizens, the pioneers.[35] Thus, at some level, her photographs document the ongoing domestic attempt to tame the western landscape: women wash clothes, in both government-sponsored camps and ditchside squatter camps; a woman sweeps dirt in front of a tent; women hang cast-iron pots and pans on cardboard or bamboo walls; and in one remarkable series, Lange photographed an iron bedstead brought west and set up whole outside a tent, bedding and all. The photographs, taken together, seem to argue that these basic chores of housekeeping—cooking, doing laundry, cleaning, sewing—are both ritualized and necessary: necessary not simply as a pattern of survival, but necessary *to society*. And at the metaphorical center of each photograph is the kitchen, often signified by the pervasive stovepipe that juts out of even the flimsiest tent. The hearth, no matter what the circumstances, suggests to the audience stability, even decency.

Thus, from tent doorways and within the patched kitchens of shanties, women stand calmly, sweeping, stirring pots, or hanging laundry on the line, their familiar postures suggesting a similarity to other, nonmigrant women engaged in the same tasks. Their domestic work, photographed in this way, functions in the same way as did the kitchen scenes in Stowe's novel. By highlighting a venerable tradition of domesticity, the photographs perform what critic John Seelye called a "crucial function" that sentimental literature can perform as protest literature: after it creates a hearth, it "redeems what have been considered marginal persons by bringing them into the domestic center," warmed by the light of that home fire.[36]

However, the fact that none of the domestic work depicted in the photographs goes on within an actual house is highly significant; the photograph forces this anomaly on the viewers, who must in turn reassess traditional expectations of homemaking and homemakers. As Paula Geyh has shown, readers face a similar reassessment in Marilynne Robinson's 1980 novel, *Housekeeping,* which examines the extent to which women are allowed to establish a social identity when they are not contained within an

"In a carrot pullers' camp near Holtville, California." February 1939.
Library of Congress, Prints and Photographs Division, FSA-OWI
Collection (LC-DIG fsa 8b33359).

acceptable house. Geyh's work is useful in approaching Lange's work by providing clearer insight into the subtext that exists in Lange's photographs of women attempting to "keep" houses that literally refused to stay still. As Geyh points out, the main characters in *Housekeeping* are keeping house in a nontraditional space, a cluttered house into which leaves and water come at will, challenging the boundary between "within" and "without." In Lange's photographs, that traditional boundary between outside and inside is apparent only in its absence—flimsy walls attempt but fail to enclose an identifiable space. Moreover, the women within are not stable. Just as the protagonists of *Housekeeping* will, eventually, ride the rails, so do the subjects of Lange's photographs live in perpetual motion; the automobiles that serve as kitchen sites are constant reminders that within days, the family will move yet again. The traditionally female domestic space of the home, which provides what Geyh calls a "settled subjectivity," is put into tension with a transient subjectivity, an "unhousing . . . which encompasses not just the movement across boundaries but an apparent denial of them altogether."[37] Just as Robinson's novel contests the definition of a woman as defined *only* by her home, and by extension her homemaking/housekeeping, so do Lange's photographs challenge a female subjectivity that is defined spatially *only* in terms of the structure. While the text of many of these photographs is indeed the pioneer myth—the argument of the migrants' redemptive move west and the associated call to action on their behalf—the subtext is far more conflicted, for it contains the narrative of shifting domestic identity.

Unlike the fictional characters in Robinson's novel, Lange's housekeepers are not transients by choice, for even though many made the conscious decision to pack up and head west, few expected anything less than the home with the white picket fence that John Steinbeck's Ma Joad believes is waiting for her in California. The strength of that belief, the attempts to pursue it despite circumstances, and the impossibility of doing so—all illuminate a photograph Lange took soon after her marriage, entitled "Blue Monday in a California migratory camp." Like so many others, it focuses on a basic homemaking task as a means to clearly question and challenge the then widespread view that Dust Bowl migrants had little social stability or integrity. At the same time, it struggles with the very notion of stability and integrity it seeks to establish. Beneath its rather straightforward, documentary façade, the major focal points of the photograph—a woman, her back to the camera, bent over a washtub perched on the bumper of an old jalopy, and a bucket of water placed directly below a spare tire mounted above the bumper—begin to contest certain notions of female subjectivity in the West.

"Blue Monday in a California migratory camp" documents the process of wash day, traditionally a Monday, and bluing, a reference to a whitening agent.[38] But beyond this simple text, we can read the photograph at a number of levels. The physical difficulty the woman encounters in upholding the traditional wash day ritual is visually apparent in the washtub, balanced on the car's bumper. Anyone familiar with the bluing process would know that the absence of any obvious source of water nearby would greatly increase the woman's difficulty, for a "blue" Monday would entail at least four tubs of water.[39] In this sense, the contradiction between the woman's domestic efforts and the environmental conditions that she, as a migrant, experiences forms a protest against those conditions. Beyond even that, however, is the irony of the term *migratory,* for the domestic ritual in which the woman is engaged is *anything* but migratory, having become so settled within the domestic tradition that it has become part of a lexicon: Blue Monday. Thus, in this sense, the photograph reveals a highly political protest, arguing for the nontransient identity of this class of people, the "harvest gypsies," who are being thrust

"Blue Monday in a California migratory camp." February 1936.
Library of Congress, Prints and Photographs Division, FSA-OWI
Collection, LC-USF34-002483-E (LC-DIG fsa 8b27274).

into a transient and therefore dispossessed social position. Additionally, Lange's own identity comes into play. There is, of course, no bottle of Mrs. Stewart's Bluing evident anywhere in the photograph. There is not, as in so many of Lange's photographs, a quotation from the photographed subject or a comment based on observation. Instead, Lange has provided the title, informed by her own knowledge of domestic ritual, giving the photograph that sense of equality and egalitarian exchange distinctive to "Women on the Breadlines" that Lange later attempted to capture in the photographic event of "Migrant Mother."

Taken as a whole, the photograph moves beyond simple points of protest, however, and contests the entire idea of the western myth of homesteading, of moving into the golden land of dreams and settling down. The woman's efforts, which are simultaneously futile and in accord with the expectations for women, directly contradict the likelihood of domesticity's valorization in the large-scale western mythos, despite the mythical idea that it would "tame" the West. In essence, as the woman stands, doing exactly what she has been socially conditioned to do in order to settle the West, she has no effect on her own condition or the overall condition of California. The entire visual scenario begs the question of one of the West's most popular ideas—the domestication accomplished through the efforts of its pioneer women. In putting the migratory woman into the visual trope of that domestic ideology, Lange's photograph challenges the value of that fiction. In short, the photograph forces a contested reading: it challenges the anti-Okie hostility and stereotypes of Depression-era California by putting the photographed woman within the pioneer fiction of the West, thereby offering her an authenticity both historical and cultural. At the same time, by showing how worthless the California fields showed that myth to be in reality, Lange challenges the cultural and historical value of the very fiction itself. The woman's dogged washing of clothes in the dust-ridden space she inhabits is an ironic tagline to the way that women were valorized for "taming" western domestic spaces in the same way that men "tamed" the landscape.

For nearly one hundred years, California had been the migratory dream of the United States, its "manifest destiny," and the homestake or homestead in which pioneer women settled the West had been its symbol. Increasingly, when Lange walked into the squatter and roadside camps of recent arrivals to a state to which she too had migrated, she saw a specific California story. Cars overloaded with furniture that families either believed they would need on arriving or simply could not bear to leave behind; women attempting to somehow reestablish themselves as capable, competent homemakers and housekeepers, even in the face of constant transience. As early as her first spring working with Taylor, Lange had identified in her notebook the genesis of the western problem, commenting that "refugees from drought in the Southwest find themselves migrant laborers in California." It was not simply, as Lange would soon write to Stryker from the South, that she understood that the California refugees were southern and midwestern "tractor refugees" on a futile western errand; she understood that for women that errand contained specific futilities. Within this singularly domestic reading of social trauma, Lange recognized that the trauma was identifiably different for women than it was for men, even the men to whom they were married and with whom they experienced that trauma. In the spring of 1935, she took down a woman's lament that the life she lived "broke" her up: "I want to have furniture." Another verbalized her "shame" in "these [sic] house."[40] Concerns about homemaking were as real as concerns about children's education (the latter often voiced by men as well), but women's inability to establish themselves as mothers, wives, and homemakers created a deeper rift between them and their husbands. "Good God only knows why we come here," one said to Lange, " 'cept he's in a movin' mood——."[41] A different sort of "fall" was emerging, a loss of domestic and maternal abilities, an identity that had functioned in the Midwest or South but did not transport to the West. "I came to this country when I was 14 years old," one woman said to Lange. "I have 11 children and always a struggle to et *[sic]* enough food. Nothing but to suffer. Now I have told my husband to go away because I don't want anymore children."[42] In response, Lange's photographs began to document not simply the struggle that migrant farm workers faced to live and eat, but the struggle that women increasingly faced in those early years of California's Great Depression to secure a workable identity in an unworkable situation.

Throughout *The Grapes of Wrath,* John Steinbeck placed in the hands of women much, if not all, of the hope of a new order that would rise from the failed Eden of California. Pa takes it calmly when Ma becomes the leader of the family, and Steinbeck's romanticizing of matriarchal strength is most intense when, at the novel's end, Rose of Sharon, the heir apparent of this new matriarchal structure, is called upon to breastfeed the heart of mankind. But in Lange's photos, no such romantic vision exists. Breastfeeding mothers look tired, worried, and hungry, just as motherhood in general is fraught with care and hovering on the edge of exhaustion. In setting out to document this period, Lange recognized that in the highly agricultural social landscape before her, women faced a California paradox. Their entrance into "Eden" was not denied simply because they were Okies; instead, the past on which the western promise had been built was a lie; for Paradise to fail, it must have existed. Taking photographs of hundreds of women whose dispossessed lives contradicted the dream of a Golden State and the entire idea of the western dream, Lange presented a silent critique of California's failure—not simply its well-documented failure to be the land of plenty for three hundred and fifty thousand migrants, but its social failure and the tension between men and women that failure had created.

EXCHANGE LABOR

Increasingly, Lange would attempt to define and document this highly destabilized idea of motherhood and female subjectivity, and she would succeed in March 1936, when she returned to Nipomo to take a seven-photograph sequence documenting a worn-out mother in the pea fields.[43] In the most famous of them, three of the woman's seven children cluster around her, two turning their faces into her thin shoulder, while the baby is positioned to nurse—one of a handful of images of breastfeeding mothers Lange took. The mother herself, looking at least ten years older than her thirty-two years, stares worriedly out into a vacant future. She is a mother who has been stripped of traditionally maternal qualities—fertility, amplitude, abundance. Instead, her bony arms and wizened breast suggest the futility of her attempt to feed her child, Lange's tight framing of the woman forcing the photograph beyond the basic fact of hard conditions and into the story of a woman bereft of her basic identity, a mother forced out of motherhood. Lange sought to photograph a mother who, despite her label of "migrant" and the host of pejorative connotations attached to such a term, was attempting against great odds to build a home and to establish a fixed identity within the migratory wilderness called the Great Central Valley, and whose attempts to do so were denied.

Lange's description of the moment that produced the photograph "Migrant Mother" is well documented. After describing the fatigue she felt, the rains that were urging her homeward, she passed a sign reading "Peapicker's Camp." Of course, she had been in the same area photographing pea pickers the year before, so the "voice" she says she heard may have been more pragmatic than her explanation, which gives it a near magical resonance, suggests. Still, the moment of the photograph itself remains extraordinary:

> I saw and approached the hungry and desperate mother, as if drawn by a magnet. I do not remember how I explained my presence or my camera to her, but I do remember she asked me no questions. I made five exposures, working closer and closer from the same direction. I did not ask her name or her history. She told me her age, that she was 32. She said that they had been living on frozen vegetables from the surrounding fields, and birds that the children killed. She had just sold the tires from her car to buy food. There she sat in that lean-to tent with her children huddled around her, and seemed to know that my pictures might help her, and so she helped me. There was a sort of equality about it.[44]

At the heart of Lange's recollection is the question of the extent to which photography can work as an exchange system. Her son says, "She never described herself as an artist, and the kind of work she was doing made it impossible for her to function as one. She had to be the servant of the people and the work she did. They [her photographic subjects] were the ones who were speaking, not she. That was the importance of it to her, that's why it was so important for her to write down their words."[45] Certainly, Lange herself was insistent that the minute she moved out from the studio to the street, her work sought to do as much (if not much more) for her subjects as it did for her.[46] Along with many socially minded writers, photographers, journalists, and WPA oral historians of the decade, she set out to document those whom she was observing as part of a broad program to help them. Many worked on the ideological premise that drove Taylor's writing— the idea that the poor could be represented as not simply sympathetic but worthy of and entitled to relief. The mechanisms for pulling them "up" may have varied from farm to factory, but at heart was a similar urge.

Currently, we understand Depression-era documentary photography, overall, as an objective system that was produced by subjective means. The relationship of photographer to photographed is as important as the photograph itself, and one of the questions becomes who was "in charge" of the representation, a concept Lange, herself, sought to explain at various points in her oral history. It is not just *what* Lange's photographs presented, but *how* it was *represented.* Carol Schloss, in attempting to address the general idea of literary and visual representation in the work of the Depression-era photographers and journalists, articulated this puzzle as "the problem of coming-upon, of approach, of the politics enacted in and through art—not as something that precedes creativity or that stands to the side of it, but as something enacted through the creation of a text and something that remains embodied in it."[47] The crux of that problem exists in the basics of power relations. "How can one," she asks, "come upon poverty, pain or deprivation?"[48] The omitted ending of the sentence, "when one is not poor, or in pain, or deprived," is assumed.

The question looms largest, perhaps, over "Migrant Mother," whom Lange describes literally in terms of her approach, her "coming upon" the woman and the photograph; but it resonates in all of her photographs, particularly those of domestic sites and women maintaining them, for Lange, as a female homemaker, both shared and did not share significant qualities with the women she approached. Untangling such a relationship requires a better understanding not simply of the photographer and the photograph, but a third element—namely, those for whom the photograph was produced. What can we understand about those for whom the photograph was created? Lawrence Levine posed this question about Lange's "Migrant Mother." Knowing the cultural context in which the photograph was created and received reinforces Levine's argument that understanding popular culture, especially the popular culture of the Great Depression, requires "a clearer perception of audience behavior," for "the audience remains the missing link, the forgotten element, in cultural history."[49] As Levine points out, people in the Great Depression "did not passively accept whatever popular culture was thrown their way"; they read movie and book reviews, chose radio programs— all of which resulted in, predictably, popular movies, radio shows, and books being tailored to audience responses.[50] From Levine's work on the Great Depression as a trove of "industrial folklore," an opportunity to understand ordinary people's reception of and influence on cultural production, we gain a broad understanding of contemporary "reader response," or reception theory, which works from the premise that texts—of any type—harbor multiple meanings, all of which engage with audiences that are, in Levine's words, "more than monolithic assemblies of compliant people."[51] The active role of audiences in constructing meaning constitutes a "filling in of gaps" that Levine sees at the heart of understanding cultural production; it is made possible in movies, photographs, and literatures that insist, by some means, on an absence of information: "This is what stimulates the reader into filling the blanks with projections. He is drawn into the events and made to supply what is meant from what is not said."[52]

Lange's understanding of this process was quite clear toward the end of her life, when she explained captioning: "I don't like the kind of written material that tells a person what to look for," she said, "or that explains the photograph. I like the kind of material that gives more background, that fortifies it without directing the person's mind."[53] Lange's use of textual cues to the audience "just gives [the audience] more with which to look at the picture";[54] moreover, her inclusion, whenever possible, of the subject's words provides cues that make her own visual narrative all the more complicated because so much occurs off camera. For example, in captions that identify where people came from and why they left, the audience must fill in the gap of an entire former life: "The cotton burned up," says one, and "We got blowed out in Oklahoma," says another. The journey west is reduced to a few verbal signifiers and must be recreated by an audience that is relied upon to supply images of drought, wind storms, and erosion. "I'm a havin' trouble with my bearin's" reads the caption for a photo of a man with his hands on his hips, the linguistic play on the word *bearings* (both the automobile's worn part and the man's sense of literal and figurative direction in life) alluding to miles of travel without ever naming it. Within each photograph, a story exists beyond the photograph, something that continues to happen outside of the frame, comparable to a film's blind field—the place just outside of the screen from which characters will emerge or to which they will retreat.[55] In a real sense, the subjects in Lange's photographs emerge from a past the audience must actively create based on the subjects' spare, but evocative, words.

This framing device, to go back to Carol Schloss's original

question, provides a dynamic understanding of photography, if we understand the meaning of the term "frame" in its wide cultural and ideological suggestiveness. Lange, who creates the physical and contextual frame, creates also an exchange with the subject of the photograph, who is within that frame. The photographed subject participates in creating that frame by setting up, both visually and verbally, its parameters; but that subject is also perceived (a different way of framing) by the audience, whose members bring their own conceptions to the photograph. What viewers note beyond their anticipation of what should be in that frame is the point at which the photograph, no matter what its purpose, can animate within them a response that may create an entirely different "frame" of mind. Indeed, discussions of Lange's "Migrant Mother" often revolve around this very idea. "After all these years," Roy Stryker said in 1972, "I still get that picture out and look at it. The quietness and stillness of it. . . . Was that woman calm or not? I've never known. I cannot account for that woman. So many times I've asked myself what is she thinking?"[56]

Certainly, the photograph carries a unique strength, an ability to move the audience that persists through time. Cara Finnegan is persuasive in demonstrating that writing about the photograph "necessitates engagement with an ongoing interpretive controversy over the social, political, and ethical meanings"[57] of the image. As part of her own "engagement," she cites Andrea Fisher, Milton Meltzer, Robert Coles, Robert Hariman and John L. Lucaittes, and Paula Rabinowitz. To those, add Theresa Heyman, Lawrence Levine, Richard Steven Street, Linda Gordon—indeed, most works about Lange, some of which display extraordinary and original insight, discuss "Migrant Mother" at some point. It has achieved an iconic position within our social memory and our current understanding because of the nearly Madonna-like posture of the mother with children, its repeated exhibition for different causes and in different eras, and, most recently, the photograph's refusal to acknowledge the reality of its subject, the migrant woman Florence Thompson. It is a photograph with intensity, with Levine's "gap," with, as well, a profoundly human sensibility, a "restraint and strange courage," Stryker would say, summarizing nearly everything about the photograph when he added, "You can see anything you want to in her."[58]

It is also, significantly, only one of the photographs Lange took that day. Lange's own description of the process by which she came to that photograph includes her physical journey to the woman. "Coming upon" her, to use Carol Schloss's phrase, slowly, the photographs bear witness to Lange's actual approach, each becoming physically closer and increasingly intimate—from the tent and its camp surroundings, to just the tent, to just the interior of the tent, to, finally, just the woman and the three children. Lined up, the photographs allow the audience to walk with Lange toward the family. Thompson's own memory of the event appears online at the Web site of Wessels Living History Farm: "Well, [in 1936] we started from L.A. to Watsonville. And the timing chain broke on my car. And I had a guy to pull into this pea camp in Nipomo. I started to cook dinner for my kids, and all the little kids around the camp came in. 'Can I have a bite? Can I have a bite?' And they was hungry, them people was. And I got my car fixed, and I was just getting ready to pull out when she [Dorothea Lange] come back and snapped my picture."[59] Thompson's memory of fixing a meal begged for by those who had been starving prior to her arrival emphasizes the element that the only famous photograph of the series seems to omit: the domestic practices in which she was engaged. The other photographs, which contextualize Thompson and her children within their living space, include numerous domestic accoutrements that emphasize the domestic practices of a woman actively engaged in homemaking, and, because of the tentative physical circumstances—lean-to tent, frozen fields, absent vehicle—dramatize the transient conditions that prevented her from home*making* and thereby realizing the social identity such practices should have offered to her.

Those tools acted in many of Lange's photographs as deeply imbedded signifiers, symbols that allowed a continuum of readings, from the pioneer ideologies that had placed women at the heart of the closing western frontier to a more contemporary interrogation of social masculinity that had too long ignored the contributions of domestic and interior spaces and, in so doing, never provided to women in the West the opportunities for settlement it promised. In the final version of "Migrant Mother," however, Lange moved much closer, stepping beyond even Le Sueur's protest against the New Deal's broad discrimination against women, and encapsulating in the last photograph she took of Thompson the raw historical moment of the Great Depression in the burden it placed on mothers. "The Depression hit just about the time them girls' dad died," Thompson told Bill Ganzel. "I was twenty-eight years old, and I had five kids and one on the way. You couldn't *get* no work and what you could, it was very hard and cheap." Her daughter remembers, "Women, especially, would give to their children and they would do without. When we were growing up, if mother weighed one hundred pounds, she was fat." [60]

"Was that woman calm or not . . . what is she thinking?" Stryker mused. According to Thompson's account, she was

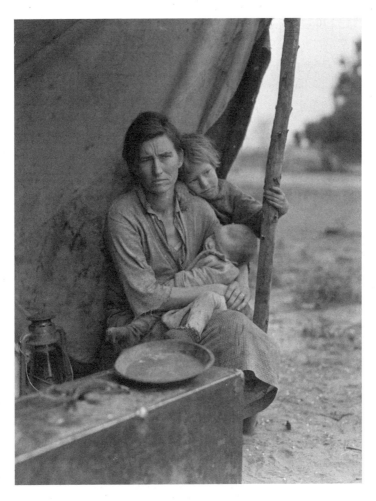

"Migrant agricultural worker's family. Seven children without food. Mother aged thirty-two. Father is a native Californian. Nipomo, California." February or March 1936. Library of Congress, Prints and Photographs Division, FSA-OWI Collection, LC-USF34-009095-C (LC-DIG fsa 8b29525).

"thinking," along the same lines as Ma Joad when she talks, early in *The Grapes of Wrath,* about "how soon they gonna wanta eat some more pork bones" (124) and, more precisely, where any food might be had. Steinbeck may not even have known how accurate his portrait of migrant women in California was, focused as his vision was on the larger issue of new societies, new orders. But, just as his Joads represented the larger picture indicated in the intercalary, or general, chapters of nameless families whose lives blended into an overriding and all-encompassing narrative of migration, the "Migrant Mother" produced by this photograph represents a tangible quality, the large vision of perseverance and strength, as well as a dream deferred or altogether denied. At the same time, however, it is both a disservice to Thompson and to Lange and a misrepresentation of the photograph itself to ignore the fact that in this image of Thompson's life, however much her own identity is reduced, however much, like Ma Joad, she is asked to represent a larger group of people, there is the fact of her experience as a mother who does not know where she will find the next meal for the children she bore—that is her own story. It is a story to which she testified. Lange's understanding of the photograph's power was clear years later, when she discussed with Suzanne Reiss the nature of documentary work. Holding up to Reiss a photograph of Patrice Lumumba's widow taken less than two weeks after the official announcement of his murder, Lange pointed to the mourning woman and said, "Isn't that marvelous? Now if one were documenting the Congo crisis and one could do it in such elemental terms, that would be a great documentary series, you see."[61] The strength of "Migrant Mother" lies in the fact that Lange was able to achieve that intensely personal moment in a way that revealed the Great Depression in "elemental terms."

BREAKING BOUNDARIES

"Migrant Mother" made it clear that as Lange was documenting the general plight of the migrants and their claim to a pioneer status, she was simultaneously documenting its gendered difficulties, even impossibilities. In so doing, her photographs contested the long-standing boundary that society had constructed and sentimentalized between public and private spaces, a boundary that denied migrant women, in their relentlessly public lives, domestic standing. But that boundary was not the only line migrant women attempted to cross, as a small handful of photographs within Lange's inventory indicate. A 1938 photograph insists on the same contested reading as the "Blue Monday" photograph, displaying at first glance all the basic evidence for reform that Taylor and Lange set out to document: a tattered tent and car full of belongings testify to the transitory lives the harvesters must lead, while a family gathered around the table signifies a "normality" and stability that protest the enforced migratory conditions in which the people must live. In the foreground, a water bucket does more than simply attest to the lack of a nearby water supply; it also protests the political reality of western farming and irrigation, and the dual issues of acreage limitation and federally subsidized water, all of which were squarely at the heart of California's war between small, family-sized and community-oriented farms and the impersonal, mechanized corporate farm.

But there is more. Among the visual details, which by now seem almost commonplace in the archive of RA/FSA photography, the woman nearest the camera stands out. Her white dress, red lips, and pincurled hair suggest an afternoon bridge game; her loose posture and relaxed arm evoke the languor of a cigarette break.

"Potato harvesters, Kern County, California." June 1935. Library of Congress, Prints and Photographs Division, FSA-OWI Collection, LC-USF34-003807-ZE-B (LC-DIG fsa 8b13866).

She looks directly at the camera over her shoulder, as if to invite the person behind the camera into her circle, and at the same time, to suggest she does not care too much whether that person will accept her invitation. There is something jaunty, even saucy about her, enough so that for a moment, the crate she sits on, the water bucket beside her, the skinny child behind her, and, even further beyond, the dilapidated car and clustered tents—all are lost. There is simply a glamorous woman slouched carelessly in a white dress. Visually, she displays the style of a Hollywood starlet, her face and general appearance suggesting her association with the burgeoning Hollywood cinema and the wealth of magazine advertisements that had begun to saturate the lives of American women, even in rural counties, by the 1930s. Similarly, a photograph Lange took in a carrot pickers' camp in the Imperial Valley seems at first glance to be merely a frontal portrait of a woman. The caption is not long: "In a carrot pickers' camp, Imperial Valley, California. Woman from Broken Bow, Oklahoma. 'Are you going to take my picture, wait till I get my hair combed.'" The woman is neither beautiful nor glamorous; indeed, she squints directly into the sun, a visual angle that emphasizes the number of harsh lines and deep furrows on her face, and her hair is parted plainly in the middle. Her clothing, also washed out by the sun's harsh light, looks clean, if old, and the body beneath the blouse and skirt looks no more or less cared for than the clothing on top of it. Yet, the position of the woman's arms, one upswept and outstretched arm, turned slightly behind her with her hand holding lightly the top of the tent, and the other tucked back behind her hips—serves to put her breasts out prominently: it is a classic Hollywood pose that Lange photographs with no apparent irony. That pose might not be as striking were it not for Lange's accompanying caption: "Are you going to take my picture, wait till I get my hair combed."

When looking at the photograph, the audience comes into contact with the woman herself and all the social and personal responses she brings to the event. The combination of Lange's identifying caption, providing only enough information to draw the audience in, with the woman's image and her words, interjected into the photographer/audience dynamic, carries the audience not simply to the woman's birthplace and back to California but into her life *as* a woman, her awareness of beauty standards and her ability to invoke them despite her "migrant" condition. That trajectory is much longer, and is something to which the

"In a carrot pickers' camp, Imperial Valley, California. Woman from Broken Bow, Oklahoma. 'Are you going to take my picture, wait till I get my hair combed.'" February 1939. Library of Congress, Prints and Photographs Division, FSA-OWI Collection, LC-USF34-019333-E (LC-DIG fsa 8b33365).

audience must respond, something beyond the photograph, which demands the audience's involved mediation.

"The movies—with their highly made-up stars, glamorous lighting, and close-ups—particularly influenced the way American women and men looked at women,"[62] writes historian Kathy

Peiss in *Hope in a Jar,* an exploration of America's development of a beauty industry and a bona fide beauty "culture" to go with it. The wealth of cultural signifiers associated with American beauty, because they are both powerful and contradictory, allowed Lange's photographs to present migrant women as both different from and the same as other women. Those signifiers show up again and again in her documentary photographs, acting as a sort of translating device, taking the unfamiliar—the migrant woman's life—and putting it into terms that American culture could easily understand. Working her way through California's fields and encountering not simply rural communities, but makeshift, roadside complexes that tried to function as communities, Lange noted that a woman's familiarity with the basic markers of the beauty culture could easily connote both her similarity to and affiliation with other, "normal" women, and her independence, her willingness and ability to construct her self: the premise on which the West was built. Thus her photographs of women in seemingly anomalous representations could protest the exclusion of migrant women from California's cultural landscape by arguing that their lives were essentially the same as the lives of the audience. But the "gap" the photographs present simultaneously invites the audience into a far more complicated and permanent involvement with these women who are presented in various stages of "dressing up."

The prevailing idea of the 1930s, for good reason, often oscillates between the back-to-the-home movement, with the social and political strictures it put on women, and their "retrenchment" as they sought to cling to some of the freedoms gained during suffrage and through, at least iconographically, the image of the flapper. Recent scholarship, however, explores a less polarized view. One such study, by Sarah Berry,[63] analyzes the rapid changes in the fashion industry as a means to locate women's attempts at autonomy within the social sphere and their transgression across class and social lines. Berry sets out an engrossing argument, tracing the shift of fashion from the elitist haute couture available only to the wealthiest and most "aristocratic" of American women to ready-made wear and patterns copied from the costumes worn in Hollywood movies. Women's desire to dress like the heroines of their favorite movies was as much responsible for the shift in fashion as were advances in manufacturing and textiles; clothing was indeed less expensive, but fashion was now populist, available to the masses, and, more significantly, unanchored from its European/Fifth Avenue moorings. The emergence of California in the fashion industry led magazines to feature countless movie stars in their advertisements for hygiene, beauty, and, more directly, clothing.

The screen star's emergence as a fashion icon represented a decidedly new transgression of class as well as social boundaries. In both real and reel life, costume acted "as a catalyst for new kinds of social behavior . . . in a range of films that focus[ed] on women's ability to act with authority and ability in new or intimidating situations."[64] Grounded in the decade's tenacious belief in transformation—born from the idea that a sudden shift in fortunes like the Crash could lead to its reversal—1930s movies cherished rapid and "radical transformations into a totally altered existence,"[65] most famously articulated in *The Wizard of Oz,* when Dorothy Gale opens her front door to a brightly colored terrain. To explain the process by which such "magic" occurred, Berry follows Bourdieu's wide-ranging analysis of class, taste, and "distinction" in order to understand this mechanism of class transgression. "American films of the 1930s certainly promoted specific kinds of gender, racial, and class stereotypes, but they also drew attention to the ways that dress and performance increasingly functioned to define social identity,"[66] she writes. Bourdieu's explanation of consumer culture as self-referential, promoting "seeming" over "being," explores the role of the symbolic within a system of difference, whereby each strata of class defines its step up in terms of the level below it. "Whereas the working classes, reduced to 'essential' good and virtues, demand cleanness and practicality, the middle classes, relatively freer from necessity, look for . . . a fashionable and original garment."[67]

Stepping up socially provided yet another translation of the American jeremiad, and Lea Jacobs writes that "the downward trajectory of the fall was replaced by a rise in class . . . dubbed the 'Cinderella story' within the industry." Because of the widespread hope it entailed, social mobility became a popular and, more importantly, an easily signified theme. That is, the story is less the story of Cinderella's "happy ending" than it is an exploration into the night she successfully passes herself off as royalty. "A shimmering gown or a top hat enable characters to move at will into or out of upper-class settings," Jacobs writes, suggesting that the struggle to "appropriate distinctive signs" of the class higher up simultaneously conserves and subverts the entire class system. What Jacobs calls "transformation scenes" rely on "boundaries of class difference, often quite marked at the beginning" of the movie, being "crossed repeatedly and ultimately transcended without any hint of work, struggle, or resentment between classes."[68] Like Dorothy Gale's opened front door, women magically ascended the social ladder by donning new garments, and in so doing, subverted the strict demarcations between the upper and lower classes. Clothing works to corrode older social systems, the kinds of "naturalized hierarchies" in which the rich, who are born into wealth, remain naturally. Instead of accepting a rigid hierarchical system, the movies argue that such systems can be passed—transgressed—through fashion.

(CROSS) DRESS THE PART

Significantly, stories of racial passing worked to protest the social construction of race, arguing for a nonessentialist understanding of color while at the same time acknowledging the results, both negative and positive, of codified race. For instance, Nella Larson's *Passing* (1929) further complicated the color line by its insistence that gender also worked to construct categories, including freedoms and limitations, which have no biological basis. The radical urge of that argument, when eugenics flourished in the country, is clear. Thus, the argument of "passing," whether related to race, class, gender, or all three, emphasizes the subjects' attempts to represent themselves, to take control of a system that has defined and often oppressed them. Passing, crossing, "bluff—if it succeeds . . . [are ways] of escaping the limits of social condition by playing on the relative autonomy of the symbolic . . . in order to impose a self-representation normally associated with a higher condition and to win for it the acceptance and recognition which make it a legitimate, objective representation."[69] Lange's photographs of migrant women participating in beauty culture play out in California specifically because the state both helped to create that culture and worked to deny migrant women access to it and to any broader establishment of lives and identities. Just as John Ford's film of *The Grapes of Wrath* has Ma Joad save and then hand over her earrings to Rose of Sharon for a dance, just as the women in the San Francisco food lines retained their fur collars, the migrant women in these photographs literally insist on creating their own identities through one of the most powerful ways available to women of the time: dressing the part.[70] Like their urban sisters, the migrants are attempting to transcend the "naturalized hierarchies" of society through costume, a form of cross-dressing, or passing. Just as in the many domestic photographs that subtly contested women's "settled subjectivity" with a transient subjectivity, these photographs' class transgressions encompass "not just the movement across boundaries but an apparent denial of them altogether."[71] And, just as in Lange's photographs of sweeping or cooking, the women are making this attempt with the barest of resources. Because the audience for these photographs is directed as much by the subject of the photographs as any other elements, they create a unique system of exchange, further complicating the terms of female subjectivity. The photographs become a dialogic exchange that includes the photographer, the audience, and the subject *in* (not *of*) the photograph. Actively participating in the cultural processes in which the audience *and* the photographer are engaged, the women are not represented by or for a distant subject, but assume their own subjectivity by becoming part of the event, and in no moment more so than when a woman whose clothing and hair style represent her as impoverished says, directly to the audience, "Let me comb my hair." Lange's recording of this woman's claim to the physical standards of Hollywood's highest-paid female film stars forces the subject into the actual moment the photograph is created and into a second moment, at which the audience views the photograph. It puts the female voice in the "gap" and creates an exchange among the photographer who recorded the moment, the always "speaking" subject of the photograph, and the audience, which is, in Roland Barthes's words, "animated" by the entire event.

Lange had learned the technique of posing and photographing women before she ever arrived in California. Of the mentors and teachers she had worked with, Arnold Genthe may have taught her the most. Despite her memory of Genthe as "an old roué," she was quick to explain that she knew "he wasn't at all a vulgar man; he loved women. He understood them. He could make the plainest woman an illuminated woman."[72] Once in San Francisco, her understanding of women would determine her ability to become really involved with them and to take successful portraits of them. As the Depression progressed, Lange recognized that a woman's fashioning of herself, as her earlier studio portraiture experience had shown her, was ongoing, despite radically different economic and social conditions. Women were, in the California fields, attempting to control their identity through various attempts at self-presentation.

Lange's photographs of women keeping house in temporary environments protested not only the migrant oppression taking place in California in the 1930s, but also the entire western mythos. They argued against the populist urge to return to a better past by showing that such a past never, in fact, existed for women. As Geyh points out, they also suggested that the dissolution of the boundaries that defined housekeeping could signify a dissolution of larger social boundaries.[73] But the "unhousing" that takes place in these photographs is only one of the ways that Lange's photographs narrativize a growing rupture within the social system that the migrant problem, as it was called, pulled into focus in California. Some of her photographs create a narrative not simply distinctively western, but wholly contemporary, giving contemporary

Americans a different way to envision this highly marginalized segment of society, a narrative based on the radical changes resulting from the growing class instability in California. The women in these photographs seem unaware that they were not, despite their impoverished living conditions, a part of the mainstream ideology of what women should look like, an ideology being changed permanently by the California film industry. Caught without planning or expectation on Lange's part, these women were able to interject themselves into Lange's vision, assuming the visual iconography of a class and status to which their circumstances denied them access. In these photographs, Lange records the pivotal moment at which women in American society, including rural, impoverished, and marginalized women, are actively engaged in concerns of the changing modern female identity.

Both the many photographs of women attempting to "keep" house in transient conditions and the photographs in which women attempt to identify themselves within current trends in fashion record the difficult and often bold means women adopted to establish an identity in a hostile West. It is tempting to think of what Lange might have produced had she limited herself for the remainder of the decade to California. Her work with Taylor at this point drew heavily on the pioneer ideology while at the same time contesting it, opening up the way, potentially, for a new narrative in which pioneer women are figured under very different terms. But the western ideology and the simple route of trying to "get on" in the Golden State had begun to shift radically for both Lange and Taylor and would result in their reconception of California not simply as the end result of a difficult and hostile journey, but as the locus of the entire Great Depression. It would begin for them in the summer of 1936, when they took their first trip through the South.

"In Farm Security Administration (FSA) migrant labor camp during pea harvest. Family from Oklahoma with eleven children. Father, eldest daughter and eldest son working. She: 'I want to go back to where we can live happy, live decent, and grow what we eat.' He: 'I've made my mistake and now we can't go back. I've got nothing to farm with.' Brawley, Imperial County, California." 1939. Library of Congress, Prints & Photographs Division, FSA-OWI Collection, LC-USF34-021049-C (LC-DIG fsa 8b34905).

CHAPTER 7

An American Exodus

In 1939, a couple at philosophical odds, their eleven children literally spilling out of a ragged tent, seemed to encompass all Lange was seeing in terms of the broken dream the West offered, particularly for women who had been unable to construct a new domestic identity. The highly gendered experiences of the Dust Bowl refugees created tensions between husbands and wives who could seem unable to understand each other, tensions Steinbeck attempted to dramatize in *The Grapes of Wrath*.

Late in novel, after complaining that the "man ain't got no say no more,"[1] Pa lapses into a nostalgic wish for home. Ma locates the differences between her attitude and her husband's in gender, telling him of the adaptability of women, whose lives are "all one flow, like a stream, little eddies, little waterfalls, but the river . . . goes right on."[2] For Steinbeck, the fluidity of an imagined feminine principle could metaphorically convert into the kind of adaptability that the new social order he sought to create would require. In this sense, Ma's exhortation to "jus' try to live the day, jus' the day," converts domesticity into a broad redemptive hope.

However, much earlier in *The Grapes of Wrath,* a response Ma makes to her son Al unveils a different portrayal of women's experience in the Dust Bowl West. Driving out of Oklahoma, Al asks Ma if she is "thinkin' what's it gonna be like when we get there?" "'No,' she said quickly. 'No, I ain't. . . . You got to live ahead 'cause you're so young, but—it's jus' the road goin' by for me. An' it's jus' how soon they gonna wanta eat some more pork bones.' Her face tightened. 'That's all I can do. I can't do no more. All the rest'd get upset if I done any more'n that. They all depen' on me jus' thinkin' about that.'"[3] Ma's response points out the difficulty women encountered in constructing a life that meshed with the familial expectations they faced. Juxtaposed against the reality of migrant conditions, the repetitive nature of domestic labor—the meals to be cooked, served, and cleaned up after again and again—highlights the futility of the jeremiadic structure, which relies on trajectory, not circularity. Constant travel and migration made the already ephemeral goals of the domestic sphere seem more distant, exposing the fact that no markers existed by which a woman might stake a claim that indicated she had, once and for all, accomplished her goals. The photograph Lange took in Brawley (page 230) reflects the tension that deferred dream created: the wife wants to return to the place that offered a better chance of creating the domestic life by which her identity would be constructed, and the husband's difficult role as breadwinner leaves him with no recourse.

Additionally, the photograph is significant because it attempts to bypass any metaphoric qualities and instead hinges only on the migrants themselves, for it is their words that create the conflict. Unable to carry the weight of any new social orders, the family members struggle instead with the burden of their past, and they indicate that struggle in a verbal element that fixes the photograph's meaning. Anne Whiston Spirn's recent study of Lange's work with grouping photographs and providing extended general captions, all a means of telling the "big story," sets 1939 as the hallmark year. She sees Lange's budding work with general captioning as "a key step linking her experiments with words and images in the mid-1930s to her photo essays for *Life* magazine in the 1950s and her work of the 1960s, which freely combined photographs with spare prose."[4] Whiston Spirn looks, rightly, at the five photographs Lange took of this couple and their children, providing the entire general caption that Lange crafted, which includes a deep history of their wages, hometown, time on the road, and the twenty miles they would have to travel in order to find fieldwork.[5] Yet the core of the photograph remains in the couple's words. Lange did indeed find a new way of working in 1939; the deep contextualizing of her photographic fieldwork was aided by her own growing familiarity with and understanding of the times and reinforced by the stories she took down from those whom she photographed. All would allow her and Taylor to craft their tour de force, *An American Exodus: A Record of Human Erosion,* the book that most demonstrates their full understanding of the migration west. That understanding was dramatically shaped by a series of summer trips through the South that changed the way both thought about the "exodus" of dispossessed and dislocated refugees from the Dust Bowl to California.

The first trip, and perhaps the most dramatic, came in the summer of 1936. That year, Roosevelt was contending for a second term against the Kansan Alfred Landon, and the president demanded reports from every program that had sprung into existence since he first catalyzed the country in the hundred days following his oath of office. It was a mixed year. Despite the fact that crop losses exceeded one hundred million dollars and uprooted Dust Bowl families were streaming into California, the total cash income of farmers had risen from its low of four billion dollars in 1932 to seven billion dollars.[6] Still, the main recovery seemed to be in the urban industrial sector, where, Burns writes, "at least six million jobs had been created."[7] In the South, flaws in the Agricultural Adjustment Act, the Social Security Act,[8] and the distribution channels of the Resettlement Administration were exacerbating poverty.

In 1936, Tom Blaisdell, who, having received his Ph.D. from Columbia four years earlier, maintained the Columbia lineage of many of those brought into the sphere of the New Deal, was appointed as head of the Research Division of the new Social Security agency. On April 21, 1936, he sent a telegram to Taylor: "WOULD YOU CONSIDER UNDERTAKING FOR SOCIAL SECURITY BOARD STUDY OF GENERAL PROBLEM OF MIGRATORY LABOR AND ITS RELATIONSHIP TO SOCIAL SECURITY STOP FEEL THIS IS OF TREMENDOUS IMPORTANCE IN DEVELOPMENT OF POLICY AND PROGRAM STOP THERE IS NO SECOND CHOICE STOP."[9] Taylor recalls, "Farm labor was excluded from all Social Security Programs," and so "Congress specifically instructed the Board to make studies of the excluded occupations." When asked if he would do those studies, his answer was "Yes, I would. So I transferred to the Social Security Board on or about June 1st, 1936."[10] Although Lange and Taylor were now no longer working in the same agency, Taylor recalls their two chiefs, Blaisdell and Stryker, as being "in perfect harmony," and the couple headed south in the summer of 1936. Through Tennessee, Arkansas, Louisiana, Mississippi, and, if Taylor's memory is right, Texas and Oklahoma as well, Lange's photographs run rich, from plantations overhung with darkly fecund vines to stark field laborers in the relentless sun.

Representations of southern culture in the 1930s permeate American literature, music, and art. The Federal Writers' Project set out to record life in America: oral histories of former slaves along with guidebook descriptions (done for all states) and contemporary testimonials articulated post-plantation agricultural life in the South. One, entitled "Get Out and Hoe," captures the personal repercussions felt by landless "croppers" unable to rise above the furnish system, in which those working the land mortgaged a share of their harvest for advances of food and supplies. It recounts the history, as told by its subjects, of a woman and the husband who deserts her when the couple's youngest child dies, the second they had lost. The woman speaks calmly of her husband's return, which comes after he has fathered a child with another woman. The wife takes back her husband because they need "to get out and hoe in the tobacco tomorrow," she says. She concludes on what she seems to believe is a positive note: "The landlord gives us five-sixths of what we raise, so we get along pretty good when the crops are fair. Of course we have to furnish the fertilizer and livestock. This year we had seven barns of tobacco and four acres of corn. Wheat turned out pretty good, too. We raised forty-three bushels, and I hear the price is going to be fair at the roller mill. I canned about all our extra fruits and vegetables. I reckon we will get about a hundred cans in the pantry."[11]

The shares the landlord gives and the "fertilizer and livestock" the narrator and her husband must furnish on their own are features of an economic system that found its predecessor in the postbellum crop-lien system, in which farmers' entire crops were put up as "credit" so that they could purchase seed, tools, and food to get them through the year, at the end of which they more often than not found themselves still owing the "furnishing merchant" money. Of the crop-lien system, Goodwyn writes, "[It] defined with brutalizing finality not only the day-to-day existence of most Southerners who worked the land, but also the narrowed possibilities of their entire lives. Both the literal meaning and the ultimate dimension of the crop lien were visible in simple scenes occurring daily, year after year, decade after decade, in every village of every Southern state."[12] The Great Depression exacerbated the system's firm hold in the South; as early as 1934, Washington had recognized the growing issue of rural tenant farming in the South, which had climbed to nearly 50 percent by 1930, with "70 percent of the farm operators . . . working someone else's land" in Mississippi.[13] Lack of land tenure and chronic poverty were seen as inextricably linked in the South, and bills such as the Bankhead-Jones Farm Tenant Act were already under discussion. Along with Blaisdell's Research Division, Rexford Tugwell proposed that same summer a special citizens' committee to study how the Resettlement Administration could address the problem, and after the November election, Roosevelt would appoint a full-fledged President's Committee on Farm Tenancy.[14]

In Georgia, Lange and Taylor heard firsthand from tenant farmers about rural tenancy and the furnish system, its "3rds and 4ths, and teams and tools, and feed." A month later, a South Carolinian farmer provided more details, telling them that on thirds, "he furnished [his own] teams and tools and 1/3 fertilizer. No prospect this year of a crop."[15] Government programs designed to help the poor did not always do so, sometimes simply replicating the conditions of systemic southern poverty. Early in July, Lange and Taylor visited a Resettlement Administration project called Dixie Plantation, a government project run so badly and exploiting its enrollees so shamelessly that one told Lange it was as "bad as on a plantation." Another complained, "They've had us in their power so long they think they own us," and told her of being threatened with whipping. In Mississippi, she noted a "negro—Fleming—threatened with lynching."[16] Southern poverty was different—entrenched, stable, the condition of an indelible caste, with none of the transiency or mobility that was both the hallmark and strange hope of western agricultural poverty. In contrast to such rooted, beaten-down acceptance of poverty, the western migrant worker's mobility took on another shade, an increased "westernness," something unique both to the life and character of the California migrant.

The South was not the only eye-opener the couple experienced that summer. Heading back to California, they made stops in the Midwest, all of which confirmed Taylor's growing understanding of the entire geographical, sociological, and economic system, in which conditions in the Midwest were part of a domino effect that started in the South and ended in California. As an Oklahoman told Lange on August 4, "If I could pull out I'd go somewhere, too. Most every day you hear them say of someone went to Calif. Here there ain't nothing. Ain't worked a days work in 4 mos."[17] Lange wrote back to her supervisor, "I understand much more now about our drought refugees in California. A lot of them were also tractor refugees."[18] For both Lange and Taylor, agricultural dislocation was no longer a strictly Californian problem but a national crisis. They returned that summer with a deepened perspective, seeing those in their own state as more connected to a wider problem.

OUT OF THE FRYING PAN . . .

After their return, they continued traveling in California, making the most of their time before school began for Taylor and the children. Taylor's notebooks show that the couple went from Oklahoma, on August 10, to Indio, California, on August 16, and then they headed to Berkeley. There, according to Lange's biographer, Milton Meltzer, "with seventeen thousand miles of travel behind her, Dorothea had two concerns. One was to develop the vast batch of cross-country negatives and send them with proof prints to Stryker. The other was to get back out on the road again for the good working months of autumn."[19] Realistically, of course, she had far more than two concerns. The boys had been boarded out all summer, and their hostility, particularly Dan's, was beginning to show. In addition, Taylor's three children had decided to go back east with their mother in September. First, however, their mother would have to leave Lange and Taylor's house, for Lange and Taylor had invited Katharine to stay in their home with the children while they were gone. Recognizing that the divorce had come upon her at a time when she was entirely incapable of making decisions, Katharine Whiteside Taylor had used the time in her ex-husband's home to come into a fury. She had left some of her things in the home, and could feel Lange's presence in them— mostly the "kitchen things." She writes that "it was when I saw my own grandmother's pancake-turner" that the "volcanic fire buried deep below" erupted.[20] The homecoming scene is hard to imagine, with the genuinely outraged ex-wife, the exhausted current wife and husband, and somewhere in the house the children. Katharine threatened to try to annul Lange and Taylor's marriage. "This," she writes dryly, "was of course profoundly upsetting to them."[21]

Whatever the actual response of the moment, Katharine's memoir accounts its long-term result as a "coldness and distance" that never left, lasting even beyond Lange's death, when "loyalty to her memory" made forgiveness of his first wife impossible for Taylor. Certainly, the rupture within the family was lasting, although we can only speculate about Taylor's feelings. His grandson told a family story, one set years later, in the 1970s. By then, Katharine Whiteside Taylor had returned to San Francisco, to the upper Haight-Ashbury district, and had garnered both respect and a following for her Jungian work. She was still, her grandson says, "not conservative," and even "flamboyant," with much younger boyfriends. At a cocktail party, she began talking with Taylor. He said, "Do I know you?" and she replied, "Yes, we were married once." His grandson offers, "He did have glaucoma."[22]

While Lange and Taylor were sorting out their home scene, a furor of another sort had taken place over the RA photographic unit and its work. After a year together, the photographers on Stryker's "team" were all working for a purpose, a common good with which Stryker himself imbued their assignments. That was certainly the case with Arthur Rothstein, whose fieldwork had produced the now famous photograph "Dust Storm, Cimarron Co., 1936," used enough to have worn out the original negative.[23] Then, in North Dakota, Rothstein erred. Coming upon a patch of cracked earth and a nearby steer skull, Rothstein made a number of photographs, shifting the position of the skull, "looking for good lighting effects and angles."[24] Initially, the movement of the skull seemed innocuous, and Rothstein's photographs were released to the press and used by newspapers all over the country. Everyone seemed to like the shots.[25] Not everyone, however, and not for long. By August, Rothstein's photographs had been politicized into an issue. Drought on the high plains had moved into election-year rhetoric, and Roosevelt assigned a task force to tour Oklahoma, Kansas, Nebraska, and the Dakotas on a fact-finding mission. Roosevelt himself was scheduled to appear toward the end of the trip, in Bismarck, North Dakota. Not far from there, in Fargo, the editor of *The Forum,* a Republican newspaper, ran a front-page story about the now infamous skull pictures, headlined "It's a Fake." Hundreds of copies were distributed to the press that met the president upon his arrival, and East Coast papers picked up the story immediately, from which point it went out on the newswires to countless smaller papers all over the country.[26]

The Republican hope, clearly, was to discredit the massive Roosevelt machine, under which Alf Landon was already steamrolled. Hope is just that, however, and when the *New Republic,* in the fall of 1936, offered five dollars "for the name of an American of either sex, of recognized intellectual distinction and progressive outlook, who is willing to admit publicly that he intends to vote for Landon,"[27] few takers cashed in on the deal. Instead, the Resettlement Administration became the fodder, and the press went on a feeding frenzy.

> The Revelation that Dr. Rexford Tugwell's "Resettlement Administration," the principal socialistic experiment of the New Deal, has been guilty [of] . . . flagrantly faked "drought" pictures, designed to give the public an exaggerated idea of the amount of damage done by the lack of rainfall, is a highly instructive, but not especially surprising development.
>
> The whole resettlement program is a ghastly fake, based on fake ideas, and what is more natural than that it should be promoted by fake methods similar to those used by ordinary confidence men.[28]

Lange would remember the episode as a "hard time we had." Recalling the congressional involvement and the many questions about the intent and methods of their small unit, she said, "People laugh at it now. We laugh at it when we get together, but it wasn't funny then."[29]

Rothstein's long-term reputation did not suffer, but the agency did. It is hard to say whether or not the "skull issue" factored into the next chapter of the Resettlement Administration, but in the fall, Stryker was told to pare down the size of his photographic staff. Out in California, Lange received the news: as of October, the Resettlement Administration would have only two photographers on payroll, neither of them Lange. Many critics offer explanations for Lange's first dismissal—and those that followed—from the government agency that ultimately made her famous, and to which she dedicated her middle years. She was fired because she was "difficult" about her negatives; she was fired because she was the farthest from Washington; she was fired because she was the oldest; she was fired but Stryker anguished over the decision; she was fired to Stryker's great relief. She was indeed fired; that much is uncontestable, although she was immediately offered a per diem arrangement to continue, which she accepted. From November 5 to 14, she worked in the Sacramento area with Rondal Partridge as her assistant. There, she continued to record the voices of those who demanded to set the terms of their own documentation: "You've heard them pronounce it—nobody will go hungry," one said scornfully. "Now take a look at this and take the picture. That baby's been sucking sugar and water. Can't get milk for her."[30]

"THAT'S WHAT IT IS GOING TO TAKE"

On December 12, 1935, Frederick Soule, an RA regional information advisor, wrote to John Franklin Carter, director of the RA Division of Information, "I wonder if the Resettlement Administration has considered the educational possibilities at the San Diego exposition, which will reopen in January and run until Armistice Day, 1936."[31] That March, Soule responded to Roy

Stryker thanking him for a letter, indicating he liked the idea of using "some of Miss Lange's pictures to localize the exhibit."[32] Then, in May, Lange wrote to Soule about the work she had been doing in preparation for that summer: "Have been making an effort to get together for our region an exhibit of photographs showing the work of Resettlement, for the use of speaker, etc, but it's hard going. To get such a group together, mounted, and captioned means getting clearance through an exhibit division, etc etc, no end of running around. So—I'm going to steal a print here, and steal a print there, pick up the prints that fall behind the desk—and we'll have some photographs yet!"[33] Soule wanted exhibits at the large fairs—San Diego and the State Fair in Sacramento; he also suggested, if possible, the Pacific Slope Dairy Show in Oakland, and district fairs in Stockton, Fresno, and Riverside, all important agricultural centers. By June 24, he had stretched the list of county fairs to eleven and included the huge San Francisco Livestock Exposition, annually held at the Cow Palace, while also mentioning to his Washington contact, Grace Falke, a June 26 "tryout" exhibit sponsored by Dr. Lillien J. Martin, for the Women's City Club in San Francisco. "Doubtless you know Dr. Martin and recognize the significance of her sponsorship," Soule wrote. "If not take advantage of 'Who's Who.'"[34]

In the remaining months of 1936, exhibits traveled to fairs and gatherings whenever possible. When negotiations for a display in Portland fell through, Charles Pain of the State Fair was contacted. The same month, Soule committed to exhibitions at the Los Angeles County fair and in San Diego. The urgency for public support drove Soule, and likely Lange. In a letter, Soule wrote of the drought's resulting in "budgetary revisions" and urged that the public be made aware of "the good that has been accom-

plished by our program so far," so much that even in the face of
a crisis such as the drought, the Resettlement program continued
to receive congressional funding. "In other words," he concluded,
"that's what it is going to take. Public support of our program
reflected in legislation—and we should try to get the idea across
to the public, always staying within strict factual limits."[35]

When January 1937 arrived, Grace Falke sent out a memo to
all regional directors of the RA indicating that they should put in
writing what they would need in order to best utilize the funds
available for exhibits, and RA Western Regional Director Jonathan Garst repeated an October memo calling for better display
space and "a display assembled in the region directed toward
focusing attention on western problems." To Will Alexander, he
wrote the following: "Miss Lange has probably explained to you
how she arranged the photographs. In the first place, she made
selections from prints which both our office and she had available, mounted them, captioned them and got them up on short
notice. There were four panels and it gave a very comprehensive
presentation of the problem."[36]

Thus, the interchange between Lange's fieldwork, intense
and isolated, and the public consumption of that fieldwork—in
highly trafficked venues—was becoming more and more organized. Garst's memo refers to a number of significant points in
Lange's growing awareness of her own work: the clear fact that
she "arranged" her photographs, that she selected them, that she
had prints of her own, and that she was continuing to develop
methods of presenting her photographs with captions in ways that
"gave a very comprehensive presentation of the problem."[37] She
seems quite autonomous, working to organize the equivalent of
an artistic show, controlling the way her work communicated to

a mass audience. She was ready to take on something of her own, for her own purposes, and she would soon get the opportunity.

Lange was reinstated by Stryker early in 1937, and she continued working with Taylor on a Senate report, submitted in early April 1937, that revolved around one essential idea: "Erosion of the soil has its counterpart in the erosion of our society." That essential metaphoric relationship, which Lange and Taylor had used two years earlier in their first government report and never dropped, provided the central idea for a proposal she sent to *Life* magazine.[38] Ultimately, *Life* did not run the piece, but the coalescence of photographs and ideas under the metaphor of erosion would ultimately serve Lange and Taylor well as they began to confront the growing public interest in Lange's photographs.

In the meantime, they headed south once again, for the summer of 1937. Both were plunged into a full-scale realization of what the summer before had just begun to hint to them: the South was the cradle of poverty from which three hundred and fifty thousand migrants had descended upon California. On June 8, Taylor sent a letter to Blaisdell, describing a shack he and Lange had visited. Upon knocking, they watched seven men file out and onto the porch; there they told their tale, in Taylor's words, "the tragedy of an 'enclosure movement' founded on tractors and large-scale farming operations, with the displacement of tenants, abandonment of houses, reduction to wage labor, dependence on WPA, and flight to California among its results."[39] Less than a week later, pathos compounding daily within this tragic southern narrative, the normally restrained Taylor burst forth to Blaisdell: "More displacement of cotton tenants by tractors and large-scale farming methods! If this sort of thing is going on in the Delta, too, why O why wasn't it stressed in the tenancy report. This puts dynamite

behind a tenancy program. It vastly enlarges the *labor* aspect of
rural social security! We can't wait for the mechanical picker. The
ground is being cut from under the feet of tenants, croppers and
even laborers. Tenancy is on the way out as a mode of life."[40] "This
sort of thing" was indeed "going on in the Delta, too." Lange took
one of her most famous photographs in Mississippi that June.[41]

Frequently anthologized and analyzed, the photograph points
to the shock Lange experienced as she faced, again and again, the
disenfranchised sharecroppers of the South. As is so often the case,
the interchange between photograph and text indicates a deeper
understanding that Lange hopes the image will convey—that the
agricultural conditions before her were indicative not simply of a
means of subsistence, but of an entire culture—social, systemic,
ingrained. This is the landscape Lange and her camera faced,
a system with a history longer than California's statehood and
more pervasive in its stranglehold on culture, economy, and even
psychology. The San Francisco streets had proposed to Lange
the challenge of taking a picture of man *in his environment*—her
work in the Delta fulfilled her earlier attempts and went beyond
them. There she encountered both the conditions for telling the
story and a physical environment that presented a perfect simile
of those stories: the decayed, ensnared, rundown remnants of a
former grandeur, bred by and based on a system that was not simply unraveling but may never have worked. In this environment,
black and white tenant farmers and sharecroppers stood among
the social, ecological, and personal ruins of their lives.

When the massive Bankhead-Jones Farm Tenant Act—a rescue from the southern system so long in the making[42]—finally
alighted on President Roosevelt's desk on July 22, 1937, its passage
shifted the Resettlement Administration into the Department of

"Hoe Culture. Alabama tenant farmer near Anniston." 1937. Library of Congress, Prints and Photographs Division, FSA-OWI Collection, LC-USF34-009328-C (LC-DIG fsa 8b29603/cph 3a00975).

Agriculture, changed its name to the Farm Security Administration, and charged it with carrying out the functions of the tenancy act.[43] Among the many programs of the FSA was a Migratory Farm Labor Section, housed within the FSA's Resettlement Division, and charged with the responsibility of administrating a labor camp program.[44] In June 1937, Will Alexander listed eight camps in California; by 1942, the FSA had completed ninety-five camps in the country, accommodating more than seventy-five thousand people. Thus, the creation of the FSA signaled a legitimizing of the migrant farm labor problem via a bona fide government agency dedicated to solving it. The division both acknowledged and furthered the public's interest, an interest that a number of artistic and documentary publications had addressed and would continue to spotlight. There was Erskine Caldwell's and Margaret Bourke-White's collaboration of photograph and text, *You Have Seen Their Faces,* published in early 1937, and *Land of the Free,* Archibald MacLeish's epic poem of unemployment paired with RA/FSA file photographs, a majority of which were Lange's. Soon after, Herman C. Nixon studied southern tenancy in *Forty Acres and Steel Mules,* using FSA photographs, and there would come, in 1940, writer James Agee's and photographer Walker Evans's stunning *Let Us Now Praise Famous Men* and Richard Wright's *Twelve Million Black Voices,* with FSA employee Russell Lee's photographs and Washington staffer Ed Rosskam's editorial expertise.[45]

Despite this interest, so much of it visual, the FSA meant a shift in budget, and Stryker once again declared he was able to retain only two photographers. Lange was told she would have to go. This time, however, her "layoff" lasted for nearly one year. Her photographs during that time include, as they had the year before, fall and early spring work in California and then, in 1938, a third summer in the South.[46] As the year drew to a close, Lange put her most intense effort into a project that would "spread information of a current condition, and the need to do something about it now."[47]

In its experimental form and visual intensity, the book that she and Taylor created during this time, *An American Exodus: A Record of Human Erosion,* sets out to document the conditions behind the pattern of movement leading to the arrival of the now nearly three hundred and fifty thousand Americans in California, tying their "exodus" from their homes to the tenancy and sharecropping failures of southern and midwestern farming. Building on their work to date and going far beyond the photo-textual books that preceded theirs, Lange and Taylor attempted to incorporate not only photographs and written text, but the voices—including reportorial voices in local and historical newspapers—of those in the regions they were documenting. Paul Strand accurately identified the "complex nature" of the completed project as similar to that of a documentary film. A variety of approaches, visual and aural, create a sense of movement in the book, all seeking to compel the audience in a similar direction, west. And the unified end point is not simply geographical. The "different elements" of the text, as Strand recognized, seek to "achieve a basic unity of statement whose sum would be 'a record of human erosion.'"[48]

Coming out the in the same year as both McWilliams's *Factories in the Field* and Steinbeck's *The Grapes of Wrath,* Lange and Taylor's *An American Exodus,* like the other two books, protests the conditions of western migratory workers by identifying the historical and current causes of their conditions and making their stories "real." Like McWilliams's, the text points to the appalling labor practices that dehumanize western agricultural workers—

and those who employ them; like Steinbeck's, it narrates the story
of the tidal wave of migrants in biblical proportions, pointing to
the exiled as capable of developing "other patterns . . . new patterns," envisioning a new West that would become "an anchor of
stability to families, and the foundation of a better community
life."[49] The themes are primary, a continuation of the discoveries
Lange and Taylor made in five years of working together; they
are also richly metaphorical. The cotton gin is set out as the sig-
nifier for all dehumanizing agricultural practices; the stampede
west is a conversion experience that transformed the nation;
the agricultural ladder a broken remnant of a better chance at
prosperity. The exodus—its genesis in soil erosion, its outcome a
human erosion that has dispersed like soil but is much wider and
greater in magnitude and history—creates the core of the book.
In this stance, drawing on earlier ideas, themes, and arguments
from their articles and reports, Taylor and Lange created their
greatest protest, exposing the diasporic conditions inherent to the
lives of the "refugees," an outcast tribe whose wilderness provides
them with no manna, from heaven or elsewhere.

At the same time, their errand, cast finally in these explicitly
jeremiadic terms, is not that of William Bradford or even Lewis
and Clark. At the book's onset, Taylor sets out his terms: "Exodus from the land is not new." Citing European migrations from
the Portuguese on, Taylor identifies their two "streams": those
who migrated to the industrial and urban portions of the United
States, and those "described a century ago by the Frenchman
de Tocqueville, [who] moved westward with 'the solemnity of
a providential event . . . like a deluge of men rising unabatedly,
and daily driven onward by the hand of God'" (5). It is to those
"driven onward by the hand of God" that Taylor and Lange turn

in this book, the destiny of their providential lives manifest not in finding or making an earthly paradise, but in its dramatic confrontation with "the end of the western frontier of free land" (5).

In this opening, the text seems as if it will be built on the successful invocation of a conservative appeal, placing the migrants within the now familiar guise of the American pioneer, but also aligning each with foundational ideologies and myths of the country as a whole. The text asserts boldly that the country exists because of migration, that each wave of migrants pushed "off the soil" has, in fact, remained within the American lexicon of freedom and liberty. This latest "deluge of men," like their forebears, is a "tide of people which moves to the Pacific Coast. But this time the cities and towns are already burdened with unemployed, and opportunity upon the land is sharply restricted" (5). Throughout *An American Exodus,* this theme carries on from much of Taylor and Lange's earlier work, from their invocation of both the pioneer myth and its dramatic collision with Frederick Turner Jackson's "closing" of the frontier. The tragedy of this migration, would, as in *The Grapes of Wrath,* put the sociology of America within its geographical limits. When the West was won, America apparently ran out of the land it takes to make Americans.

But *An American Exodus* turns from the trajectory Taylor and Lange had followed together for the past five years. Part of that shift is due to Lange's own ideas about how to present her work, to her increased understanding of California's culpability in both creating and shattering dreams and, as her work with female subjects had shown her, to its long-standing ability to slip free, as a trickster, from the very myth it had created. The "regional movement" of the text was, according to Henry Mayer,[50] Lange's idea, and it provides narrative containment for the ideas Taylor was struggling to bring to some kind of conclusion about migrants in California. Meltzer mentions that the two face "honestly and unsentimentally the implications of their findings," which show among other things that despite all their own work, "needy migrants were still entering California at a rate of six thousand a month. And no one had yet counted the large numbers going elsewhere."[51] What drives the text's movement is the entrance to California, which functions textually as both a mythological construct and an actual geography—but one that had by then been shaped and, too often, malformed by its own mythos.

After three summers in the South, both understood that the move to the machine, which had transformed the South, starting with the gin, constituted the new manifest destiny, the effects of agricultural mechanization not simply affecting the West but bound to it. They make that clear with the opening photograph entitled "The Empire of Cotton," which "now stretches from the Atlantic to the Pacific" (9). The trail of wreckage that cotton created is the subject of many if not all of the photographs of the South, with southern sociologist Rupert Vance, local newspaper articles, state officials, and the southerners themselves adding their voices to Taylor's to tell the tale. At midpoint, the book moves to the Midwest and the plains, a historic photograph of the "race for claims at the opening of the Cherokee outlet"(45) leading migrants through the Midwest and a landscape in which "mechanization is a process without end. Tractors replace mules" (73), while, in the following photograph, "Tractors replace not only mules, but people," leaving "the treeless landscape . . . strewn with empty houses" (74). The result? A "tractored out" farmer who "can count 23 farmers in the west half of this county that have had to leave the farms to give three men more land" (82).

Finally, the book heads west, with those whose lives it documents, where "a carrot-tying invention" gives a man "no more chance than a one-legged man in a foot race" (114) and "machinery prepares the ground, plants, and cultivates sugar beets," leaving only hand labor for "mobile gangs" (132). Machines are a constant throughout *An American Exodus*. Far more than a subtext, they constitute a vast system that both propels and pulls migrants from their homes and to the West.

Machinery acted in many ways as the entry point to the South for both Lange and Taylor; indeed, a close look at Taylor's vast accumulation of field notes shows that he seems to have actually begun the text of *An American Exodus* in 1938 in Arkansas.[52] That Taylor had found the core of his argument in the South was clear from his distraught telegram to Tom Blaisdell. He and Lange spent the first month of the 1938 trip in Texas with Taylor, preparing a report on tenancy for the Social Security agency. In the report, he outlines the process by which large-scale tractor farming, such as he has already witnessed in California, is rapidly taking over in the South, an area that formerly supported many small farms and tenant farmers. "Hordes of migratory laborers" characterize harvest time in this system, and the current exodus of tenant farmers will likely, he says, "be permanent. Perhaps it should be." Without either land or employment available to them, tenant farmers' future came to a grim conclusion in Taylor's eyes: "relief at home, or . . . refuge elsewhere. Whether the drought continues or the rains come, the westward stream of the distressed will continue to be fed by victims of enclosure by mechanization."[53]

Submitted in June, Taylor's report argues openly against the social ravages of agricultural mechanization, which is responsible for the rapid displacement of tenant families. "The misery entailed by cutting the ground from under these families is enormous," Taylor writes in conclusion.[54] On the same trip, Lange recorded, on one sheet of paper, nine quotations. The first seven are all variations on how the tractor is to blame for the problems people face. The last two put the problem of mechanization into the spare yet far-reaching language she was so adept at culling: "I'm a wonderin' if this is happening all over the U.S.," one says. The next: "I know one thing, it's hurting our schools and hurting our homes. You can't have a country without you've got home owners. It's no good for the country."[55] The machine, displacement, western exodus—all create a link between the South and the West, Taylor would write in *An American Exodus,* that "is literally human" (148). All, finally, came together under the rubric that Taylor and Lange had been working to articulate in both shared and individual terms: homemaking.

As had Henry Adams, Lange and Taylor had experienced an American education, a drawing back of a curtain, and behind it stood, in both its promise and its destruction, a dynamo: the shift to a technological society that would encompass farming and agricultural society. And, just as Adams's revelation of the power of technological progress had contained his awareness of its opposition—the "virgin" of religion—for Lange and Taylor, the "virgin" was homemaking. Much more than a simple process, homemaking was a nearly religious practice that had once been at the heart of the pioneer movement, the women whose kitchen tools and linens loaded down the Conestoga wagons acting as both actual participants in the process of Anglo-European western settlement and highly charged symbols of its progress. But *An American Exodus* recognizes the passing of that time, recognizes that, again, as with Adams's dynamo and the society in which it throbs, people believe in technology; they desire the advances they believe technology will bring. Technology replaces the "church" of the sacred home: "Industrial expansion alone offers hope of permanently raising agricultural income to high levels and of employing at good standards the population produced but unneeded on the farms," Taylor argued, insisting that California must provide decent housing for agricultural workers while it waits for the "industrial expansion" that will employ those who will never be able to buy land and whose permanent migrant status ostracizes them from the communities in which they live and work. Housing, Taylor reminded his readers, "is not only shelter, but . . . an anchor of stability to families, and the foundation of a better community life" (155). Thus, while Steinbeck would, in the final scene of *The Grapes of Wrath,* put Ma Joad and Rose of Sharon at the heart of the "new order" that the migrants are hoping to build in the West, *An American Exodus* recognizes the power of the machine to shape the future of agricultural communities. The protest they put forth in their book's final chapter is not against the machine but against the *misuse* of the machine, the colonialist mentality that breeds plantations under the machine and turns technology into an imperialist weapon. "The advance of the machine," he asserts, "should not, and probably cannot be halted," but its exploitation can: "We do not favor denying participation in the advantages of a machine-produced standard of living to more farmers for subsistence" (153–54).

PARABLES OF EROSION

"And another wonderful parable for children is the story of erosion. We don't have any good examples of erosion here; so we show them photographs of what has happened in . . . all the places where greedy, stupid people have tried to take without giving, to exploit without love or understanding. Treat Nature well, and Nature will treat you well. Hurt or destroy Nature, and Nature will soon destroy you. In a Dust Bowl, 'Do as you would be done by' is self-evident."[56]

Principal Narayan, head of the educational system in the fictional Pala, in Aldous Huxley's utopian novel *Island,* explains to wandering cynic Will Farnaby this lesson on ecology; one of several in a text bursting with explanations of how to live a self-actualized life through nonconsumerism, egalitarian cooperatives, and the yoga of love. Is the Taylor-Lange version of "associations of tenants and small farmers for joint purchase of machinery, large-scale corporate farms under competent management with the working farmers for stockholders, and cooperative farms" (155) a Utopian vision, something as easily vaporized as Huxley's Island, Hawthorne's Blithedale, Perkins Gilman's Herland? *An American Exodus* is a multivalent book; its composite narratives force readers to see different voices wedded harmoniously together. The textual insistence on collectivity is rhetorically inscribed and, like many utopian narratives, which look to the future by understanding the route to the present, the book's historical narrative eventually looks forward, its emphasis on land as an active participant in the story of the migrant culture acting as a prelude to Taylor's lifelong battle to enforce the 160-acre limitation. Taylor would come to believe that if enforced, the limitation could lead to small-acreage farming and increased opportunities for migrant farm families to buy land and begin homesteading, a legal and social change in migrants' status that would restructure California's culture for the better. Understanding the extent of large-acreage exploitation of land was the first step to his own awareness of the relation between land and water in California, and *An American Exodus* seeks to inform readers of that exploitation as much as it seeks to inform them of the migrants' suffering. Photographs in the "Last West" section of the book document continued unrest, articulated in strikes, as if to prove to readers that the "problem" was not going away, that changes must occur. Unfortunately, as many have pointed out, those changes came about not socially but politically, when Hitler invaded Poland, and California offered jobs to the migrants as the country mobilized for war.

Already in press when that occurred, *An American Exodus* was only able to take into account the changes America *might* see, but it is still a hugely ambitious book that covers vast territory in a collage of forms. While acknowledged today as a masterpiece, the book struggled for publication and was almost immediately remaindered due to poor sales. Yet it stands as a testament not simply to the distress Lange and Taylor witnessed but to the strength of their commitment to their protest and ideas of reform. In their zealous focus on the conditions of the moment, neither could predict how far-ranging their influence would be. They set out as a team to establish a common ground with those whom they believed they could help, but that ground, like the entire landscape of the country, continued to shift between them, producing results neither could have projected nor created alone. Perhaps more than any book of that time, it explains California— its culture, its history, its practices, its role in the nation. Taylor and Lange published *An American Exodus* as a culmination of their research, something they thought would start, not end, the discussion of "what to do" with the migrants. While the war ended the migrant problem, *An American Exodus* did indeed help to start the discussion about California.

Lange and Taylor sought for five years to let their subjects tell their own stories. Rather than the creation of vernacular dialogue, for which *The Grapes of Wrath* was both criticized and remembered, or the third-person historical voice of *Factories in the Fields* that McWilliams occasionally modulated up to outrage or down to despair, *An American Exodus* built on the insistence of its authors during their work in California that the migrants themselves were best equipped to tell their stories in their own words. Lange and Taylor, in recording those stories, attempted to be no more than a "sort of a channel for other people."[57] The cultural shift such an insistence signals is with us today in various narratives, in critical studies, in departments and scholarly fields devoted to exploring and articulating the position of the "other." When revisionist and new social historians seek counternarratives of the Great Depression through oral histories, as do Devra Weber and Andrew J. Dunar and Dennis McBride,[58] they are working within the framework Taylor and Lange helped to pioneer. To an even greater extent, Taylor and Lange's recording and presenting of the unmediated voices of those whose role in history had been previously ignored finds its way into much later work. When George Sánchez explores the processes of assimilation through the voice of a Mexican American teenager who explains "Ambivalent Americanism," it becomes clear that "immigrants played their own part in this drama."[59] And in *California Uncovered: Stories for the Twenty-first Century,* the vast array of Chinese, Vietnamese, Japanese, Lebanese, Afghani, Mexican American, African American, Anglo, and Miwok narratives is a tribute to the voices of the marginalized, the invisible, the immigrants.[60]

"An 'Arkansas Hoosier' born in 1855. Conway, Arkansas." June 1938. Library of Congress, Prints and Photographs Division, FSA-OWI Collection, LC-USF34-018289-C (LC-DIG fsa 8b32429).

That idea was at the heart of Lange and Taylor's efforts to make sure that fieldworkers speak rather than being spoken for. Their insistence on textualizing the voices of those whose lives they sought to represent, placing those voices at the heart of a reform narrative crafted to reach the American public, continues to affect our current understanding of who shapes and who narrates the stories that explain our lives.

Ma Burnham

My father was a Confederate soldier. He give his age a year older than what it was to get into the army. After the war he bought 280 acres from the railroad and cleared it. We never had a mortgage on it.

In 19 and 20 the land was sold and the money divided. Now none of the children own their land. It's all done gone, but it raised a family. I've done my duty—I feel like I have. I've raised 12 children—6 dead, 6 alive, and 2 orphans. . . .

Then all owned their farms. The land was good and there was free range. We made all we ate and wore. We had a loom and wheel. The old settlers had the cream. Now this hill land has washed. And we don't get anything for what we sell. We had two teams when this depression hit us. We sold one team—we had to get by—and we sold 4 cows. . . .

Folks from this part has left for California in just the last year or so. My two grandsons—they were renters here and no more—went to California to hunt work. . . .

If you see my grandsons in California tell 'em you met up with Ma Burnham of Conroy, Arkansas.

June 28, 1938[61]

"Stalled on the desert, facing a future in California. No money, ten children. From Chickasaw, Oklahoma. Southern California." March 1937. Library of Congress, Prints and Photographs Division, FSA-OWI Collection, LC-USF34-016312-E (LC-DIG fsa 8b31796).

Can the Subaltern Speak?

> In the situations which we describe are living participants who can speak. . . . So far as possible we have let them speak to you face to face.
>
> Dorothea Lange and Paul Taylor,
> *An American Exodus: A Record of Human Erosion*

Eighty years before the second great western exodus, and a continent away, Marx wrote of a similar group of agricultural workers: "In so far as millions of families live under economic conditions that separate their mode of life, their interests and their culture from those of the other classes, and that place them in an attitude hostile toward the latter, they constitute a class."[1] Marx's description of the French agricultural peasantry—"the allotted patch of land, the farmer and his family; alongside that of another allotted patch of land, another farmer and another family"—could have served as a caption for Lange's photographs or an inscription above Taylor's writing. Like the French farmers before them, the Dust Bowl migrants' existence in California was disorganized, dislocated, disenfranchised, and lacking, as Lange once said of the Oroville UXA, "anything to hand," yet they were seen by others as a coherent if inferior class.

Despite that perception, Depression-era field-workers were, like their French predecessors, drawn together only by locality and proximity to one another, "much as a bag with potatoes constitutes a potato-bag," Marx wrote. Without any historical sense of political or social unity, without any articulated program of organization, the "Okie class" lacked the collective voice of a class, and they could not effectively work or act in their own interest. Like the peasantry Marx analyzed, they were unable to "assert their class interests in their own name": unable to represent one another, "they must themselves be represented."[2]

How to represent the needs of those who cannot represent themselves was the problem at the heart of 1930s documentary production. In *They Must Be Represented: The Politics of Documentary*,[3] Paula Rabinowitz, who takes her title from Marx's argument, turns to the dual meaning of the term *represent*, meaning, on the one hand, "to stand for or act as proxy," politically, and, on the other "to re-present," aesthetically. In documentary, representation is re-presentation; the two are not different. Documentary becomes both a performative and a political act; it re-presents in often visual ways lives different from those of the presenter, and at the same time, it acts as proxy for them, putting their lives on display in order to call an audience to action on their behalf. The idea is at the heart of any exploration of the historically oppressed, but especially those who became the recorded subjects of the Great Depression, their lives represented by investigators, interviewers, filmmakers, and photographers.

It has become nearly a commonplace these days to put the

1930s under critical scrutiny; the practices of photographers, writers, and artists are critiqued for their colonial aura and a seeming willingness to exploit the lives of others, even if it was for the "best" social reasons. Concerns over the ability of the middle class to "look across" at a working-class subject; concerns about the framing that acts unobtrusively to pose and therefore present, rather than represent, an entire situation; concerns about, as Rabinowitz puts it simply, "who looks at whom?"—all lead to profound complications within the idea of representation and to a rejection of the idea that those who represent *them* can speak for *them*. *They,* the argument goes, can speak. John Berger praised photographer Paul Strand for his ability "to present himself to his subject in such a way that the subject is willing to say: 'I am as you see me.'"[4] Michel Foucault and Giles Deleuze argue that the oppressed, *if given the chance,* can speak and know their conditions.[5]

This is the point that Gayatri Spivak famously contests in her 1988 essay "Can the Subaltern Speak?" Spivak surgically dissects theories that aim to confirm the necessity of intellectuals' attempts to "know the discourse of society's Other."[6] Her exploration of the Western world's attempts to represent the "third-world subject" and the third-world subject's ability to speak and know his or her own conditions, lead her ultimately to the troubling practice of widow suicide in India and the story of one young woman whose suicide attempts to rewrite "the social text of sati-suicide in an interventionist way."[7] In her own time, the attempt fails, and her suicide is denied political agency. The question, then, remains: Can *they* represent themselves in ways that those unlike them can and will acknowledge?[8] Spivak's answer is resolute: "The subaltern cannot speak." It must remain the task of others to look deeply and fully into the conditions of the oppressed, including the conditions of oppression and the attempts, however unsuccessful, made to overcome them. The path to understanding the voices of those whose lives "must be represented" lies not simply in the ways they are represented, which turns us back to those in charge of the camera or the word-processing program, but in the ways those who ultimately must be represented by others attempt to represent themselves within the historical continuum that seeks to keep them voiceless. To understand the voices of those whom history has rendered voiceless, we must confront the process of their voicelessness. That process entails an understanding of "how an explanation and narrative of reality was established as the normative one,"[9] as well as how those who resisted that normative reality set out to do so.

When Lange and Taylor attempted to write the Dust Bowl migrants into the redemptive myth of the westward pioneer, they sought to rehabilitate them from the oppressive conditions that work systematically to create the voiceless and powerless classes of which Marx and Spivak wrote. The narrative Lange and Taylor created invoked the long tradition of the American jeremiad, offering a nearly mythological construction of how things *should* be inscribed with a startling and often painful representation of how they *are*. Their work protested those conditions and, in aligning the migrants with their frontier forbears, sought to elevate them in the eyes of others. At the same moment, the individual voices that the authors did not simply allow into their narrative but insisted on placing at its center and foundation constantly undercut the pioneer myth itself, showing that it did not, in fact, elevate; did not, in any way, open doors; did not, ultimately, redeem. The voices of the migrants tell the story of their failed attempts to reestablish the pioneer identity and the many causes for that failure. Their words, often woven around the hope they themselves felt, which the pioneer story offered, juxtaposed the reality of their lives against it. The result did not simply protest the conditions that prevented things from being "as they should be"; more deeply, it suggested that they had never been so. In doing so, Lange and Taylor's work revealed the process by which the normative version of California's history was written, its raced conditions, its classed positions, and its gendered divisions.

The normative "narrative of reality" of California's migrant workers was, at the time of Lange and Taylor's work, oppressive, dehumanizing, degrading, and socially isolated. California's field laborers, "on whom the crops depend," as Lange and Taylor wrote, were until the advent of their work systematically denied all the legal and social rights of American citizens, despite the fact that they worked (and work) in the state, contributed to its GNP, bought food and clothing in its stores, and rented or bought homes (when allowed) within its borders. And, at a time in which social changes such as workman's compensation and social security were inaugurated, they remained unprotected, unrepresented. Politically nonexistent, they remained culturally invisible as well, except within their own marginalized communities. Indeed, legal and social practices sought to insure they remained as hidden as possible, their voices silent, their stories unheard by the majority of the country. They spoke, but could not communicate—that is, until Lange and Taylor began to represent their stories, documenting not simply their faces but their words. In that radical move, public reception began to shift.

Because of its representational qualities, Lange and Taylor's work has long been studied primarily as documentary work, lauded or criticized for its straightforward and realistic depictions of everyday life. That generic limitation oversimplifies some of the most complicated work to come out of not only the decade, but the century. Taylor and Lange did indeed adhere, insistently, to life as they saw it; contemporaries such as Clark Kerr attest to it, relatives explain it, and the photographs and reports themselves are supported by contemporaneous testimonies from the La Follett hearings and by historical research continuing to this day. But Lange and Taylor used their documentation in order to persuade an entire nation to change its practices. In doing so, they created a work of protest literature no less radical and moving than the one that many literary scholars consider as one of the greatest works of fiction our country has produced, *Uncle Tom's Cabin*. To see their work as part of this great tradition of protest, drawing on the rhetoric and practices of social realism, to compare it to *The Jungle* and *The Grapes of Wrath*, is to understand their work in new ways, to see how even a single photograph utilized the strength of documentary and the rhetorical power of social realism to create a protest unmatched in and beyond its time.

The difference between Lange and Taylor and writers such as Stowe, Sinclair, and, perhaps most significantly, Steinbeck is that those authors created fictional narratives for which they conducted research in order to fill out the details; conversely, Lange and Taylor began with research—relentless, painstaking, and painful—and out of that research grew, organically, a narrative.[10] And because the narrative Lange and Taylor created grew from those who were the subjects of this research, it was shaped by them—their words, their experiences, their hopes and disillusioned dreams—and thus attempted to move beyond representation, allowing, in complicated and unparalleled ways, the subaltern truly to speak.

Subsequently, while not overtly pointed toward issues of race and gender, their work implicitly addresses all of the problems those categories suggest. Only recently have scholars begun to use critical skills to revisit Lange and Taylor's work, and the result has been a rich, new wave of studies that look with fresh, perceptive eyes into this familiar body of work. Building on and responding to earlier work by scholars such as Lawrence Levine and Paula Rabinowitz, work by Linda Gordon, Martha Rosler, Richard Steven Street, and others has begun to break new ground in the matrices of race, gender, and class within the work Lange and Taylor produced.[11] If, as Rebecca Solnit argues, the advent of photography telescoped time and space, the advent of documentary photography added onto the initial transcendence of a temporal/spatial experience by transcending, or transgressing, the last uncrossable boundary—the social border constructed by race, class, and gender. The explanation of how this country came to accept, even embrace, for hundreds of years the normative story of an institutionalized subaltern class resides within the work Lange and Taylor created in the state that instituted and perpetuated that story. The public response to this individually diverse and chronically oppressed group of agricultural workers will continue to affect their lives as much, if not more, than any policy or legal requirements. Their representation, in the both senses of the word, matters deeply: what they need and want must reach those who can and will provide the means to help achieve that, in terms acceptable to those who need and want it.

An American Exodus did not, as some have pointed out, initiate a new era of communally owned farm equipment. "Migrant Mother" did not end poverty in migrant camps. But it is a mistake to think that this work—the book, the reports, essays, and field notes—is neither lasting nor effective. The phototextual narratives Paul Taylor and Dorothea Lange created during the second half of the Great Depression initiated a new perception of California, that last Eden, the mythic "classless" society that was, ultimately, only a great pretender. The narrative of a Golden West was exposed as a façade, its subaltern classes buried and hidden in an entrenched class system as rigid and bounded as those in the eastern factories and southern plantations. Photographs, reports, essays, and, ultimately, the brilliant *An American Exodus* escorted the housed into the lives of the unhoused, turning those who looked at their photographs into witnesses able to hear the subaltern class speak.

NOTES

PROLOGUE

1. Paul Taylor, oral history interview conducted by Suzanne Reiss, *Paul Schuster Taylor, California Social Scientist,* vol. 1: *Education, Field Research, and Family* (Regional Oral History Office, The Bancroft Library, University of California, Berkeley, 1973), 247. Taylor describes the entire trip as starting in Japan, then "Korea, Hong Kong, the Philippines, Viet Nam, Thailand, Indonesia, Burma for a day, India, Nepal, Pakistan, out through Afghanistan and the U.S.S.R. We were in Moscow a week, then Berlin, then picked up a Volkswagen in Stuttgart, from where Dorothea's ancestors had come, drove to Rotterdam through Germany, France, and Belgium, and shipped the VW back to San Francisco. We flew to London; then to New York, then home to California. That took seven months."

2. Dorothea Lange and Paul Taylor, *Overseas Notebook,* vol. 70 (Oakland Museum). A few pages later she added another comment about Berlin, "nothing but dreadfulness in the bombed buildings the rebuilding only accentuated it," which has a poignant visual correspondence to the partial structures she witnessed in California's fields, struggling to stand. (Unless otherwise identified, all quotations in the text are from this source.)

3. Dorothea Lange, oral history interview conducted by Suzanne Reiss, *Dorothea Lange: The Making of a Documentary Photographer* (Regional Oral History Office, The Bancroft Library, University of California, Berkeley, 1968, 5). This work is hereafter cited as "Lange oral history (see prologue, n. 3)." Lange recalls her Aunt Caroline, a "fine teacher . . . one of those adored teachers. She used to have a spring hat and a winter hat. Every spring she got another dress; every winter she got another dress."

4. Dorothea Lange and Paul Taylor, *An American Exodus: A Record of Human Erosion* (New York: Reynal and Hitchcock, 1939).

5. Lange and Taylor, *Overseas Notebook,* vol. 70 (Oakland Museum). Lange's journal from this trip, like the rest of her work housed at the Oakland Museum, is carefully curated and cared for by the staff of the art department.

CHAPTER 1. FROM BELLEAU WOOD
TO BERKELEY

1. Information on the ceremony comes from a program in Taylor's archive (BANC MSS 84/38, series 7, carton 89, folder 42, The Bancroft Library, University of California–Berkeley) and from the National Weather Service's station in Wisconsin.

2. The entire speech is in many ways a blueprint for the approach Taylor would take in his studies and the ways he understood his role and responsibility to those whose lives he studied.

3. Paul Taylor, address at the University of Wisconsin–Madison, June 24, 1919 (BANC MSS 84/38, series 7, carton 89, folder 42). Quotations in the next two paragraphs are from this speech.

4. Katharine Whiteside Taylor, *Intimate Journey: Autobiography of Katharine Whiteside Taylor* (unpublished ms., courtesy of Donald Fanger), 75.

5. Paul Taylor, letters home, in *Paul Schuster Taylor, California Social Scientist,* vol. 1, *Education, Field Research, and Family,* appendix C, 329–33, interviews conducted in 1970 by Suzanne Reiss (Regional

Oral History Office, The Bancroft Library, University of California–Berkeley, 1973. Vols. 2 and 3, *California Water and Agricultural Labor,* for which interviews were conducted by Malca Chall, were published in 1975). This oral history is hereafter cited as follows: "Taylor oral history (see chap. 1, n. 5)," with vol. and pg. nos.

6. Taylor oral history, 1:329–33.

7. The phrase is from Edward O'Neal, president of the American Farm Bureau Federation, in March 1933, quoted in Sidney Baldwin, *Poverty and Politics: The Rise and Decline of the Farm Security Administration* (Chapel Hill: University of North Carolina Press, 1968), 52.

8. Franklin D. Roosevelt, 1935 State of the Union speech to Congress, quoted in James MacGregor Burns, *Roosevelt: The Lion and the Fox* (New York: Harcourt, Brace, 1956), 220.

9. Taylor oral history (see n. 5), 1:63.

10. Paul Schuster Taylor, *On the Ground in the Thirties* (Salt Lake City, UT: Peregrine Smith, 1983), 233.

11. David P. Peeler, *Hope among Us Yet: Social Criticism and Social Solace in Depression America* (Athens: University of Georgia Press, 1987), 4. Peeler writes,

> The combination of social criticism and social solace was a recurrent refrain in the Depression's social art and literature, but especially in complementary yet distinct echoes in certain genres: the social novel, documentary photography, travel reportage, and social realistic painting. Besides their common concern with solace and criticism, social artists and writers working in these fields shared other characteristics. They were mostly young, middle-class people who were at the thresholds of their careers when the Depression struck, and they were often political leftists who stopped short of embracing Communism. They used realistic, rather than modernistic, forms of expression in their works and had a decided preference for depicting people from the nation's lower classes.

12. Lange oral history (see prologue, n. 3), 49.

13. Ibid.

14. Ibid., 80.

15. Milton Meltzer, *Dorothea Lange, A Photographer's Life* (New

York: Farrar, Strauss, Giroux, 1978; repr. New York: Syracuse University Press, 2000), 70.

16. Ibid., 71. Meltzer reports that Lange took twelve exposures during her first attempt at candid street photography, and that three were of the breadline.

17. Elaine Steinbeck and Robert Wallsten, eds., *Steinbeck: A Life in Letters* (New York: Penguin Books, 1989), 158.

18. Lizbeth Cohen, *Making a New Deal: Industrial Workers in Chicago, 1919–1939* (Cambridge: Cambridge University Press, 1990), 283.

19. Meridel Le Sueur, "Women on the Breadlines," *New Masses*, January, 1932. A direct play on the title of the prologue to Paula Rabinowitz's *Labor and Desire* ("Prologue: On the Breadlines and the Headlines"); see next note.

20. In this thought, and in many others, I am indebted to Paula Rabinowitz's *Labor and Desire: Women's Revolutionary Fiction in Depression America* (Chapel Hill: University of North Carolina Press, 1991). Though it focuses on radical texts and does not treat Lange directly, Rabinowitz's study nonetheless shaped my thinking early on and has remained instrumental in the approach I take to the issue of women in the Great Depression. On this exchange of breadlines and headlines, Rabinowitz writes, "This chain of signifiers, leading from hunger to its printed description, from the class of people that filled the breadlines to the class that wrote about them, from those whose bodies were marked by poverty, hunger, and labor to those who earned their living through the written word (intellectuals, journalists, and artists), mirrors the trajectory of this study" (1).

21. Jack Salzman, ed., *Years of Protest* (New York: Pegasus, 1967).

22. Along with a variety of radical reform movements covered in more detail in chapter 4, the Communist Party of the United States of America itself saw growth in numbers, burgeoning from twenty-six thousand in 1934 to sixty-six thousand by 1939. For more history of the CPUSA, see Mark Soloman, *The Cry Was Unity: Communists and African Americans, 1917–1936* (Jackson, MS: Press of the University of Mississippi, 1998); Michael Denning, *The Cultural Front: The Labor-*

ing of American Culture in the Twentieth Century (Haymarket Series; New York: Verso, 1998); Fraser Ottanelli, *The Communist Party of the United States: From the Depression to World War II* (New Brunswick, NJ: Rutgers University Press, 1991); on socialism, see Seymour Martin Lipset and Gary Miles, *It Didn't Happen Here: Why Socialism Failed in the United States* (New York: W. W. Norton, 2001).

23. *American Protest Literature,* ed. Zoe Trodd, foreword by John Stauffer (Cambridge, MA: Belknap Press of Harvard University Press, 2006), xiii.

24. Cara Finnegan, *Picturing Poverty: Print Culture and FSA Photographs* (Washington, DC: Smithsonian Books, 2003), xvi.

25. Ibid., xvi.

26. Lawrence Levine's essay "The Historian and the Icon: Photography and the History of the American People in the 1930s and 1940s" makes a compelling case for the interpretive potential within the Farm Security Administration/Office of War Information (FSA/OWI) archive and the historian's responsibility to construct histories that include that element. The essay, originally published in *Documenting America, 1935–1943*, ed. Carl Fleischhauer and Beverly W. Brannan (Berkeley and Los Angeles: University of California Press, in association with the Library of Congress, 1988), is reprinted in Lawrence Levine, *The Unpredictable Past: Explorations in American Cultural History* (Oxford: Oxford University Press, 1993).

27. Richard Steven Street, *Everyone Had Cameras: Photography and Farmworkers in California, 1850–2000* (Minneapolis: University of Minnesota Press, 2007). Street's direct treatment of Lange is on pages 165–321, but even in his later analysis of César Chávez and beyond, Street returns again and again to Lange's influence. On the FSA, its political structure, and Lange's role, see Linda Gordon, "The Photographer as Agricultural Sociologist," *Journal of American History* 93, no. 3 (2006): 698–727. Available online at www.historycooperative.org/cgibin/justtop .cgi?act=justtop&url=http://www.historycooperative.org/journals/jah/ 93.3/gordon.html (accessed August 23, 2007).

28. Lawrence Goodwyn, *The Populist Moment: A Short History*

of the Agrarian Revolt in America (Oxford: Oxford University Press, 1978), ix.

29. Sacvan Bercovitch, *The American Jeremiad* (Madison: University of Wisconsin Press, 1978), 6.

30. Michael Kazin, *The Populist Persuasion: An American History* (New York: Basic Books/HarperCollins, 1995), 29.

31. Janet Galligani Casey, ed., *The Novel and the American Left: Critical Essays on Depression-Era Fiction* (Iowa City: University of Iowa Press, 2004), xi.

32. See Jack Conroy's *The Disinherited,* for example. For a fuller treatment of the genre, see Barbara Foley, *Radical Representations: Politics and Form in U.S. Proletarian Fiction, 1929–1941* (Durham, NC: Duke University Press, 1993); Walter B. Rideout, *The Radical Novel in the United States: Some Interrelations of Literature and Society, 1900–1954* (New York: Columbia University Press, 1992); Rabinowitz, *Labor and Desire;* James F. Murphy, *The Proletarian Moment: The Controversy over Leftism in Literature* (Urbana: University of Illinois Press, 1991); Paula Rabinowitz and Charlotte Nekola, *Writing Red: An Anthology of American Women Writers, 1930–1940* (New York: Feminist Press at the City University of New York, 1987); and David Madden, ed., *Proletarian Writers of the Thirties* (Carbondale: Southern Illinois University Press, 1968).

33. Levine, "The Historian and the Icon," 281.

34. Carey McWilliams, in *Factories in the Fields* (1939; repr. Berkeley and Los Angeles: University of California Press, 2000), highlights the activities of a Tulare cooperative settlement, Kaweah, arguing that it was so successful that the government intervened, driving the colonists from the land and turning it into Sequoia and Kings National Park (39–47). The colony, from the original claims filed in 1885 to the court case against those who refused to move off the land, lasted less than ten years, but was financially successful, and produced a road that was, until the highway was built, the only entrance into the park. For more on Kaweah, see Robert V. Hine, *California's Utopian Colonies* (San Marino, CA: Henry E. Huntington Library and Art Gallery, 1953;

reissue, Berkeley and Los Angeles: University of California Press, 1983), 78–100. For more on the influence of Populism in California and the labor-exchange movement it engendered, see McWilliams, chap. 2.

35. Susan Ware, *Holding Their Own: American Women in the 1930s* (Boston, MA: Twayne, 1982), 8.

36. Frederic Jameson, *The Political Unconscious* (New York: Cornell University Press, 1982). "When finally, even the passions and values of a particular social formation find themselves placed in a new and seemingly relativized perspective by the ultimate horizon of human history as a whole, and by their respective positions in the whole complex sequence of the modes of production, both the individual text and its ideologemes know a final transformation, and must be read in terms of what I will call the *ideology of form,* that is, the symbolic messages transmitted to us by the coexistence of various sign systems which are themselves traces or anticipations of modes of production" (76).

37. In "The 'Ham and Eggs' Movement in Southern California: Public Opinion on Economic Redistribution in the 1938 Campaign" (February 21, 2003), R. Michael Alvarez, William Deverell, and Elizabeth Penn argue for the plan's social implications:

> The plan relied on a simple formula: there were 15 to 20 million people in the United States over the age of sixty. If each of these individuals were granted $150 a month generated by a national sales tax, and each had to spend the money within the month, then between 2 and 3 billion dollars would be pumped into the economy each month. The increased circulation of money would, the theory insisted, somehow increase the purchasing power of the masses, and thereby end the Depression. While economists regarded the plan as laughable, the proposition struck a chord with elderly Californians, many of whom had seen their life savings dwindle away and felt as though they deserved restitution. The Townshend Movement provided a political outlet for this disillusionment. Within three years, 2.2 million Americans had joined Townshend Clubs, and Townshend was regarded by millions as a messiah. (USC Law School, Center for the Study of Law and Politics, Working Paper No. 12, available online at http://law.usc.edu/academics/centers/cslp/papers/cslp-wp-012.pdf [accessed 23 August 2007]).

38. James Gregory, *American Exodus: The Dust Bowl Migration and Okie Culture in California* (New York: Oxford University Press, 1989), 137; Richard Steven Street, *Beasts of the Field: A Narrative History of California Farmworkers, 1769–1913* (Stanford, CA: Stanford University Press, 2004), xix.

39. Rebecca Solnit, *River of Shadows: Eadweard Muybridge and the Technological Wild West* (New York: Viking, 2003), 8.

40. Chitra Banerjee Divakaruni, James Quay, and William E. Justice, eds., *California Stories Uncovered: Stories for the Twenty-First Century* (Berkeley: Heyday Books/California Council for the Humanities, 2005), viii.

41. Teresa Jordan and James Hepworth, eds., *The Stories That Shape Us: Contemporary Women Write about the West* (New York: W. W. Norton, 1995); and James Crutchfield, ed., *The Way West: True Stories of the American Frontier* (New York: Tom Doherty Associates Book, 2005). These are but two of hundreds of titles telling or collecting stories of the various journeys to California and the West.

42. Jack Hicks, James D. Houston, Maxine Hong Kingston, and Al Young, eds., *The Literature of California: Writings from the Golden State* (Berkeley and Los Angeles: University of California Press, 2000), 1:5.

43. Jacqueline Ellis, *Silent Witnesses: Representations of Working-Class Women in the United States* (Bowling Green, OH: Bowling Green State University Popular Press, 1998), 29.

CHAPTER 2. THE MAGNET OF THE WEST

1. Taylor oral history (see chap. 1, n. 5), 1:20.
2. Ibid.
3. Ibid., 1:1.
4. Taylor oral history (see chap. 1, n. 5), 1:6.
5. Ibid., 4.
6. Taylor's oral history tells the story of his father's run for district attorney of Dane County, Wisconsin, in 1882, the same year Robert La

Follette Sr. ran for Congress. Taylor's father was to "throw his support" to La Follette, in return for La Follette's support for the district attorney election. "But this was not forthcoming," Taylor said, acknowledging that both his parents must have felt "bitterness," especially his father, "because he left for Iowa in 1887" (Taylor oral history [see chap. 1, n. 5], 1:11–12).

7. For background, see both Kazin, *Populist Persuasion,* and Goodwyn, *Populist Moment,* especially Goodwyn's introduction and, in Kazin, chaps. 2 and 3. Sioux City's proximity to Omaha, site of the articles of demand that would articulate the political platform of the People's Party, and Taylor's awareness that Iowa was the first state in the union to lose population to the western migration of farmers—both suggest that he felt the ideological effects of what Goodwyn calls the "Populist moment."

8. Paul Schuster Taylor, "Nonstatistical Notes from the Field," *Land Policy Review,* January 1942 (BANC MSS 84/38, series 2, carton 5, folder 25).

9. Taylor oral history (see chap. 1, n. 5), 1:18.

10. Henry Taylor, Letter to Thomas Taylor, May 5, 1902 (BANC MSS 84/38, series 7, carton 88, folder 9).

11. Rose Schuster Taylor, Letter to Thomas Taylor, July 29, 1902, ibid.

12. Taylor oral history (see chap. 1, n. 5), 1:25.

13. Ibid.

14. Ibid., 35.

15. Kazin, *Populist Persuasion,* 49.

16. Ibid., 54.

17. General discussion drawn from Robert S. McElvaine, *The Great Depression: America, 1929–1941* (New York: Three Rivers Press, 1993), 7–10.

18. Taylor oral history (see chap. 1, n. 5), 1:41. "You see," Taylor told Suzanne Reiss, "we were deeply rooted in Wisconsin. I told you how my grandfather pioneered there, and how my parents made their way through the University. As their children, you can see the drive behind

our going to Wisconsin. I can remember my mother saying, 'Now, you can go to Harvard if you want to.' But the twig had been already bent, so that it was just not possible for me to be, shall I say, flexible and objective in choosing where to go." Later, he would repeat the idea, telling her, "So that when my mother said, 'Well, you can go to Harvard if you wish,' I couldn't really consider it on an equal basis. I just couldn't do it." Still, his praise of Wisconsin is consistently high, and he claimed "no regrets, because going to the Wisconsin of those days gave the bent to my whole life" (41).

19. Ibid., 48.

20. Ibid., 52.

21. Ibid.

22. Ibid., 56.

23. Ibid., 57–58.

24. Ibid.

25. See Goodwyn, *Populist Moment,* chap. 3, especially 66–69: "The agrarian revolt cannot be understood outside the framework of the cooperative crusade that was its source."

26. See "The Progressive Movement," *Oregon Coast Magazine On-line,* at www.u-s-history.com/pages/h887.html. Taylor recalled Debs as receiving "over a million," and went on to recall his early support of Bryan, "the Great Commoner," and the "La Follette 'Progressive' thought that just permeated the atmosphere," something his entire graduating class "absorbed" (Taylor oral history [see chap. 1, n. 5], 1:56).

27. Theodore Roosevelt, quoted in "Portfolio: Jacob Riis, How the Other Half Lives: Studies among the Tenements of New York," available online at the Web site of New York University: http://journalism.nyu.edu/portfolio/books/book287.html.

28. Keith Gandal puts forth the theory that Riis was part of an "anti-modernist movement typified in Theodore Roosevelt's 1899 speech, 'The Strenuous Life,' a mentality that favored sports, outdoor recreation, and, in its quest for adventure, a fascination with the slums." See his *The Virtues of the Vicious: Jacob Riis, Stephen Crane, and the Spectacle of the Slum* (New York: Oxford University Press, 1997), 11.

29. For an analysis of Watkins's hired work in Kern County, photographing for both sides of the infamous water case *Haggin vs. Miller & Lux,* see both David Igler, *Industrial Cowboys: Miller & Lux and the Transformation of the Far West, 1850–1920* (Berkeley and Los Angeles: University of California Press, 2001), 1–4; and Street, *Everyone Had Cameras,* 74–82. While seeking different results from their readings of Watkins's photograph "Haying at Buena Vista Farm" (1887; from Photographic Views of El Verano and Vicinity, Sonoma Valley, CA; available online from BANC 1974.019-ALB), both men agree that the industrial cast of the photograph, in which the large derrick (both men mention it) emphasizes the "monumental operation" (Street's phrase) and "industrial enterprise" (Igler's) of the labor recorded, is intentional on Watkins's part.

30. Lange oral history (see prologue, n. 3), 3.

31. Ibid., 4.

32. Meltzer, *Dorothea Lange,* 9.

33. Dorothea Lange, "On the Bowery," from the outtakes of the 1964 KQED (San Francisco) film *Under the Trees.* Directed by Robert Katz. Robert Katz, Richard Moore, and Philip Greene, filmmakers. Interview courtesy of Dyanna Taylor.

34. Lange oral history (see prologue, n. 3), 23.

35. Michael G. Wilson, "Northern California: The Heart of the Storm," in *Pictorialism in California: Photographs, 1900–1940,* with essays by Michael G. Wilson and Dennis Reed (Malibu, CA: J. Paul Getty Museum and Henry E. Huntington Library and Art Gallery, 1994), 6. At the time, "pictorialism" was far removed from the hazy romantic photographs on which the term ultimately came to rest. Genthe's 1902 first prize in portraiture and the Camera Craft grand prize acknowledged his street photographs of Chinatown for their artistic merit. For the larger context of California pictorialism, its link to Alfred Stieglitz and the Secession movement, see 1–19.

36. Arnold Genthe, *As I Remember* (New York: Reynal & Hitchcock, 1936), 35.

37. Lange oral history (see prologue, n. 3), 28–29.

38. Ibid., 30.

39. Ibid., 61.

40. Taylor oral history (see chap. 1, n. 5), 1:82.

41. Katharine Taylor, *Intimate Journey,* 19.

42. For example, she writes that her sorority sisters accused her of being "pro-German" upon finding out that she had a German friend, a "dear old lady, Mrs. Neimann," whom Katharine thought of as a grandmother. Only upon finding out that she had pledged a fifty-dollar Liberty Bond to the Red Cross did her sisters exonerate her (ibid., 57).

43. Ibid., 65.

44. Ibid., 73.

45. Ibid., 80.

46. Ibid., 97.

47. When she went to dress for a dinner one night, Taylor told her, "Don't get dressed up," worried that she might come across as "just a pretty girl who wears clothes." Katharine remembers being deeply hurt. So profound was her initial disillusionment with marriage that when the famous theologian John Haynes Holmes came as a dinner guest, she found his charisma so great that "it irradiated Paul too," and that night, for the first time, the young couple "penetrated" in their lovemaking.

48. Lange oral history (see prologue, n. 3), 80–81.

49. Ibid., 82.

50. Ibid., 85.

51. Meltzer, *Dorothea Lange,* 46.

52. Lange oral history (see prologue, n. 3), 89.

53. Ibid., 93–94.

54. Ibid., 95.

55. Meltzer, *Dorothea Lange,* 52.

56. Elizabeth Partridge, *Restless Spirit: The Life and Work of Dorothea Lange* (New York: Viking, 1998), 28.

57. Lange oral history (see prologue, n. 3), 121–22.

58. Ibid., 102.

59. Ibid., 122.

60. Taylor oral history (see chap. 1, n. 5), 1:88.

61. Paul Taylor, Letter from Commons to Taylor, October 29, 1925 (BANC MSS 84/38, series 1, box 3, folder 9). Letters in Taylor's files show Commons's guidance on the proposal for a Rockefeller Foundation grant, including advice to him on October 29, 1925, that "the subject of industrial labor on the Pacific Coast should be connected up with that of agricultural labor" for there is "real unity between these several subjects." The eventual proposal included Taylor, Blum, Carl Plehn, Jessica Peixotte, and Ira Cross.

62. Taylor oral history (see chap. 1, n. 5), 1:98.

63. Ibid., 93.

64. *The Statutes at Large of the United States of America, from December, 1923 to March, 1925,* vol. 42, pt. 1, 153–69 (Washington, DC: Government Printing Office, 1925).

65. Paul Schuster Taylor, "Labor Relations," in *There Was Light: Autobiography of a University: Berkeley, 1868–1968,* ed. Irving Stone (New York: Doubleday, 1970), 37.

66. Taylor oral history (see chap. 1, n. 5), 1: 106–7.

67. Paul Taylor, "Field Notes, 1927" (BANC MSS 84/38, series 3, carton 10, folder 13).

68. Howard R. Rosenberg, "Snapshots in a Farm Labor Tradition," *Labor Management Decisions* 3 (Winter/Spring 1993): 1. Available online at http://are.berkeley.edu/APMP/pubs/lmd/html/winterspring_93-snapshots .html.

69. Kevin Starr, *Endangered Dreams: The Great Depression in California* (New York: Oxford University Press, 1996), 64.

70. Rosenberg, "Snapshots," 1.

71. Research focusing on the experiences of Mexican and Mexican American farmworkers in California has, since Taylor's time, increased substantially. See, for example, George J. Sánchez, *Becoming Mexican American: Ethnicity, Culture, and Identity in Chicano Los Angeles, 1900–1945* (New York: Oxford University Press, 1993); Devra Weber, *Dark Sweat, White Gold: California Farm Workers, Cotton, and the New Deal* (Berkeley and Los Angeles: University of California Press, 1994);

Camille Guerin-Gonzales, *Mexican Workers and American Dreams: Immigration, Repatriation, and California Farm Labor, 1900–1939* (New Brunswick, NJ: Rutgers University Press, 1994); and Juan L. Gonzales Jr., *Mexican and Mexican American Farm Workers: The California Agricultural Industry* (Santa Barbara, CA: Praeger, 1985). Guerin-Gonzales is particularly insightful on issues of identity construction, while both Weber and Sanchez provide compelling readings of, among other things, the labor unrest of the 1930s.

72. Taylor, "Field Notes, 1927" (BANC MSS 84/38, series 3, carton 10, folder 15). The folder is full of interviews of whites in the Imperial Valley that document their openly racist comments; Taylor also records exclusionary signs and notices. "They're so aggressive," he writes at one point.

73. Taylor, *On the Ground*, 11.

74. Ibid., ix. In an earlier version of the introduction to the book, Taylor speaks of "the working relationships in large-scale agriculture, so different from the relationship of farmer and hired man I had grown up with in the Middle West" (BANC MSS 84/38, series 2, carton 3, folder 1).

75. Paul Taylor, interview with Anne Loftis, April 18, 1980 (BANC MSS 84/38, series 2, carton 3, folder 1).

76. Taylor, *On the Ground*, ix.

77. Ibid., 9–10.

78. "With the stoppage of European immigration and the increased labor demands of the war, the trickle of Mexican immigrants enlarged to a stream which ran its course for a decade," he wrote in *On the Ground*, 1.

79. Mexico's most distinguished anthropologist of the time, Dr. Manuel Gamio, published a two-volume work on the Mexican migration that came out while Taylor was still doing his work; see the introduction, synthesis, and conclusions in his *The Population of the Valley of Teotihuacán* (Mexico City: Talleres Gráficos de la Nación); and sociologist Emory Bogardus published *The Mexican in the United States* in 1934.

80. Letters from President Campbell, January 3 and July 15, 1927;

June 8, 1928; and June 3, 1929 (BANC MSS 84/38, series 3, carton 10, folder 1).

81. Letter from President Campbell to Department Chair Carl Plehn, 1927 (BANC MSS 84/38, series 1, box 10, folder 9).

82. Taylor oral history (see chap. 1, n. 5), 1:100.

83. Ibid., 101.

84. Taylor, "Labor Relations," 38; James Gregory, *American Exodus: The Dust Bowl Migration and Okie Culture in California* (New York: Oxford University Press, 1989), 39.

85. Taylor, "Labor Relations," 38.

86. "Bio-bibliography, 1950–81" (BANC MSS 84/38, series 7, carton 88, folder 27). Taylor's bio-bibliography, a standard university form that tracks classification, indicates that he remained an associate professor from 1928 to 1939.

87. Lange Tape Transcripts, vol. 2 (Lange Archive, Oakland Museum).

88. Telephone interview with author, August 23, 2003.

89. Taylor, *Intimate Journey*, 154.

90. Ibid., 161.

91. Ibid., 151.

CHAPTER 3. LABOR ON THE LAND

1. Burns, *Roosevelt*, 164.

2. Ibid., 165.

3. For additional general discussions pertaining to daily life and the social, economic, and political issues following the Crash, see, among many others, Amity Shales, *The Forgotten Man: A New History of the Great Depression* (New York: HarperCollins, 2007); David Kyvig, *Daily Life in the United States, 1920–1940: How Americans Lived Through the Roaring Twenties and the Great Depression* (Chicago: Ivan R. Dee, 2004); Gene Smiley, *Rethinking the Great Depression* (Chicago: Ivan R. Dee, 2003); David Kennedy, *Freedom from Fear: The American*

People in Depression and War, 1929–1945 (New York: Oxford University Press, 1999); T. H. Watkins, *The Hungry Years: A Narrative History of the Great Depression in America* (New York: Holt, 1999); McElvaine, *Great Depression*; T. H. Watkins, *The Great Depression: America in the 1930s* (1993); Cohen, *Making a New Deal;* and John Garraty, *The Great Depression* (New York: Harcourt, 1986).

4. Sidney Baldwin, *Poverty and Politics: The Rise and Decline of the Farm Security Administration* (Chapel Hill: University of North Carolina Press, 1968), 50.

5. William E. Leuchtenburg, *Franklin D. Roosevelt and the New Deal* (New York: Harper Torchbooks, 1963), 51.

6. Donald Worster, *Dust Bowl: The Southern Plains in the 1930s* (New York: Oxford University Press, 1979), 113, 127.

7. John Steinbeck, *The Grapes of Wrath* (1939; repr. New York: Penguin Centennial edition, 2002), 32–35. Hereafter cited parenthetically in the text by page number.

8. Mark Arax and Rick Wartzman, *The King of California: J. G. Boswell and the Making of a Secret Empire* (New York: Public Affairs, 2003), 135–36. "Not everybody fared equally under the [AAA]," they write. "Throughout the South and Southwest, the AAA had the effect of pushing sharecroppers and tenants off their land, but the lot of many farmers improved, especially bigger operations like Boswell's. Not only did [he] gladly take tens of thousands of dollars from the AAA for limiting his acres, but the loans that Boswell made to other farmers who took part in the program were effectively guaranteed by the government."

9. Burns, *Roosevelt,* 194.

10. Watkins, *Hungry Years,* 97.

11. Paul Schuster Taylor (with Clark Kerr), "Documentary History of the Strike of the Cotton Pickers in California, 1933," in Taylor, *On the Ground,* vii–viii.

12. Taylor oral history (see chap. 1, n. 5), vol. 2, *California Water and Agricultural Labor,* interview conducted by Malca Chall (Regional Oral History Office, The Bancroft Library, University of California, Berkeley, 1975), 2. In response to Chall's questions, Taylor answers, "You

asked me about leaders in the strike. There was Communist leadership. That doesn't mean the strikers were Communists. But there was a handful of leaders who took charge and were very effective in maintaining a unified course of action among the strikers." He goes on to name Pat Chambers and Caroline Decker.

13. Taylor (with Clark Kerr), "Strike of the Cotton Pickers," 18, 19.

14. Ibid., 20.

15. Ibid., 19.

16. "All California cotton is irrigated. Beds are generally spaced 30 to 40 inches apart. Cotton is mechanically harvested after defoliation of the cotton plants. Ginning separates the lint and seeds." From "Crop Profile for Cotton in California," on the Web site of the Integrated Pest Management Centers, www.ipmcenters.org/cropprofiles/docs/CAcotton.html (accessed July 27, 2009).

17. Paul Schuster Taylor, "Producing California Cotton" (1934?) (BANC MSS 84/38, series 2, carton 6, folder 2).

18. Clark Kerr, "Paul and Dorothea," in *Dorothea Lange: A Visual Life,* ed. Elizabeth Partridge (Washington, DC: Smithsonian Institution Press, 1994), 39.

19. Taylor (with Clark Kerr), "Strike of the Cotton Pickers," 17.

20. Paul Schuster Taylor and Clark Kerr, "Whither Self Help?" *Survey Graphic* 23 (July 1934): 328. Available online at the New Deal Network Web site: http://newdeal.feri.org/survey/34328.html (accessed August 23, 2007).

21. Ibid., 5.

22. Ibid., 2.

23. Ibid., 4.

24. Ibid., 7.

25. John Steinbeck, *In Dubious Battle* (New York: Penguin, 1984), 27. (Orig. pub. 1936.)

26. Ibid., 130.

27. Starr, *Endangered Dreams,* 82.

28. Lange oral history (see prologue, n. 3), 141.

29. Ibid., 142.

30. Ibid., 140.

31. Ibid., 144.

32. Meltzer, *Dorothea Lange,* 78.

33. Lange oral history (see prologue, n. 3), 145–46.

34. Meltzer, *Dorothea Lange,* 90.

35. Ibid., 150.

36. Lange oral history (see prologue, n. 3), 22–23.

37. *Daily News* article, "3 Killed, 31 Shot in Widespread Rioting," available on the Virtual Museum of the City of San Francisco Web site at www.sfmuseum.org/hist4/maritime17.html.

38. Starr, *Endangered Dreams,* 121.

39. Paul S. Taylor and Norman Leon Gold, "San Francisco and the General Strike," *Survey Graphic* 23 (September 1934): 405. Available online at the Web site of the New Deal Network, http://newdeal.feri .org/survey/34405.html (accessed July 20, 2007).

40. Ibid., 7.

41. Ibid., 9.

42. Ibid., 10.

43. Paul Taylor, "Draft and Notes, 1934" (BANC MSS 88/34, series 2, carton 6, folder 18).

44. Partridge, *Restless Spirit,* 45.

45. Ansel Adams, quoted in Lange Tape Transcripts, vol. 1 (Lange Archive, Oakland Museum).

46. Ibid.

47. Lange oral history (see prologue, n. 3), 148.

48. Ibid.

49. Ibid., 139, 140.

50. Meltzer, *Dorothea Lange,* 76.

51. Lange oral history (see prologue, n. 3), 158.

52. Ibid.

53. Richard K. Doud, interview with Dorothea Lange for the Smithsonian Archives of American Art, May 22, 1964. Available online at the Web site of the Smithsonian Institute, www.aaa.si.edu/collections/ oralhistories/transcripts/lange64.htm (accessed February 3, 2003).

54. Richard Steven Street's article "Lange's Antecedents: The Emergence of Social Documentary Photography of California's Farmworkers" (*Pacific Historical Review* 75, no. 3 [2006]: 385–428) notes that Taylor's interest in photography began when he was recuperating from the mustard gas he received at Belleau Wood. Taylor's papers (BANC MSS 84/38, series 2, carton 6, folder 28) contain an outline entitled "Some notes on visual recording and communication" (August 15, 1983), in which Taylor writes the following: "In 1917 while I was serving the Marines, Eastman Kodak came out with a small 'vest pocket' Kodak. I bought one, took it to France. Among the prints I returned home with, are photographs of myself in the Huge shell holes, one in the Verdun sector, the other in the Bealleau Wood sector." Street writes in much more detail about Taylor's photographic work and its influence in *Everyone Had Cameras,* 123–29.

55. Taylor oral history (see chap. 1, n. 5), 1:112.

56. Lange oral history (see prologue, n. 3), 154.

57. Taylor oral history (see chap. 1, n. 5), 1:119.

58. Karin Becker Ohrn, *Dorothea Lange and the Documentary Tradition* (Baton Rouge: Louisiana State University Press, 1980), 13.

59. Lange oral history (see prologue, n. 3), 91.

60. Taylor oral history (see chap. 1, n. 5), 1:125.

61. Ibid., 122.

62. Lange oral history (see prologue, n. 3), 90.

63. Ibid., 165–66.

64. Ibid., 166.

65. Untitled document (BANC MSS 84/38, series 7, carton 89, folder 74).

66. Toward the end of 1934, Taylor was asked to do research for the Division of Rural Rehabilitation of the California State Emergency Relief Administration—the state division of Harry Hopkins's Federal Emergency Relief Administration. Lange's note to Taylor (below) mentions her "SERA project."

67. "Nov 5 11:30 am 1934 and Sent to Dr Paul S Taylor, Department of Economics, University of California, Berkeley" (BANC MSS 84/38,

series 7, carton 89, folder 53). The notecard refers to a portrait Lange took of Andy Furuseth, a unionist who died in 1938 after a lifetime of helping mariners gain security.

68. Taylor makes it clear in his oral history that he "welcomed photography as a part of the documentation and presentation of social situations," a view he shared with Kellogg and which he had put to extensive work earlier in his monographs on Mexican labor conditions (Taylor oral history [see chap. 1, n. 5], 1:116). Clark Kerr wrote of his mentor that "his method consisted of taking snapshots and verbatim notes. He began taking photographs in Mexico with his old Rolleiflex. . . . His passion was absolute accuracy—in his notes and my notes, in photographs and, later, Dorothea's photographs" (Kerr, "Paul and Dorothea," 41). In *Everyone Had Cameras,* Street cites Taylor's publications on Mexican labor, Taylor's use of Ralph Powell's photographs in his documentary of the cotton strike, and Taylor's work for *Survey Graphic,* including "Mexicans North of the Rio Grande" (1931), which *Survey Graphic* published with six of Taylor's photographs and four by Ansel Adams. Yet, considering the limited circulation of Taylor's academic publications, and even with the popular status of *Survey Graphic,* it is difficult, as attractive as the statement is, to agree wholeheartedly with Street's assertion that "more than any other single individual, Taylor would push farmworker photography in a more creative and socially oriented direction" (129). Taylor's understanding of photography's great power and potential, his recognition that it was "another language" (Taylor oral history [see chap. 1, n. 5], 1:117), would only gain widespread influence when he and Lange began to work together with that "language."

69. Taylor oral history (see chap. 1, n. 5), 1:117.

CHAPTER 4. FAR WEST FACTORIES

1. Harriet Beecher Stowe, *The Oxford Harriet Beecher Stowe Reader,* ed. Joan Hedrick (New York: Oxford University Press), 7.

2. F. Jack Hurley, *Portrait of a Decade: Roy Stryker and the Development of Documentary Photography in the Thirties* (1972; repr., New York: Da Capo Press, 1977), viii.

3. Fisher uses the phrase in *Let Us Now Praise Famous Women: Women Photographers for the U.S. Government, 1935 to 1944* (London: Pandora Press, 1987), 4, 136.

4. Interview with Dorothea Lange for Smithsonian Archives of American Art, conducted May 22, 1964, available online at the Smithsonian's Web site, www.aaa.si.edu/collections/oralhistories/transcripts/lange64.htm (accessed February 3, 2003); Lange oral history (see prologue, n. 3), 159.

5. Taylor oral history (see chap. 1, n. 5), 1:126.

6. Lange Tape Transcripts, vol. 2 (Lange Archive, Oakland Museum). In a spring 1976 interview, however, Ron Partridge gazed at a photograph of Dorothea that Imogen had taken at the UXA in Oroville and said, "That's the trip that she met Paul. That's when she fell in love right there."

7. Taylor oral history (see chap. 1, n. 5), 1:126–27.

8. Ibid., 112.

9. Ibid., iv.

10. Ibid., v.

11. Hewes describes the moment in his introduction to Taylor's oral history:

> When they returned from their field trip, Paul and Dorothea threw themselves into the task of preparing the Nipomo Document. Our plan was to send it to the New Deal leadership in Washington—everybody from the White House to Capitol Hill. Of course it was a gamble that there would be any response. But we had become incurable optimists. We hoped as hard as we worked that somehow the story of this great westward movement of disinherited rural people could be told to people who had the power to help. Shortly afterward, when I went to Washington to work for Rexford Tugwell, I carried several copies of the document with me. Under Tugwell's inspired leadership, the Resettlement Administration set up a substantial Migratory Labor Program that

extended from the Salt River in Arizona to the northern San Joaquin Valley in California. Wherever these forlorn wanderers went there was help where before there had been none. (1:vi)

12. Ibid., v.

13. Ibid.

14. Ibid., 129.

15. Lange oral history (see prologue, n. 3), 159.

16. The language comes from an exhibit, which included "White Angel Breadline," of the Art Students' League of San Francisco, cofounded by Maynard Dixon. In the National Archives, Roll #855, frame 115, cited in Lange Tape Transcripts, vol. 1 (Lange Archive, Oakland Museum).

17. Taylor oral history (see chap. 1, n. 5), 1:130–31.

18. Lange oral history (see prologue, n. 3), 160.

19. Paul Taylor, "Marysville to Imperial Valley, March–April, 1935" (BANC MSS 84/38, series 3, carton 14, folder 37).

20. Ibid.

21. "Investigation of Housing Conditions of Stable and Migratory Agricultural Labor, Coachella Valley, by Harvey M. Coverley: Investigation [conducted] Feb 27–March 3, 1935" (BANC MSS 84/38, series 3, carton 15, folder 13). The report identifies Coverley as the lead investigator. The trip included Lange, Taylor, Irving Wood, Joel H. Fallin, and Coverley.

22. Coverley, "Investigation of Housing Conditions," 4.

23. Lange oral history (see prologue, n. 3), 161.

24. Coverley, "Investigation of Housing Conditions." Starr indicates that wages were higher, from $1.40 to $3.00 (*Endangered Dreams,* 67), but Taylor wrote in his first government report with Lange (March 15, 1935) that "the number of days when [high] earnings are possible are relatively few" (Paul S. Taylor and Dorothea Lange, "Memorandum on Establishment of Rural Rehabilitation Camps for Migrants in California," government report submitted to Harry Drobish, March 15, 1935 [Library of Congress, Prints and Photographs Division, Lot 898], 11).

25. Taylor and Lange, "Rural Rehabilitation Camps for Migrants."

26. Street, *Beasts of the Field,* xv.

27. Ibid., 23. Street's point, made early in the massive history, is significant. His revisionist exploration of the degrees to which workers have, over time, sought ways to empower themselves encourages a rereading of the exploitive class system that has traditionally read the worker as the victim. Nonetheless, the Spanish mission system did establish an exploitive labor system. Many native Californians were forced, and worse, to work for the padres like slaves, and their methods of seeking some level of power and identity within the system made it destructive. Indian populations were decimated by subsequent waves of Spanish, Mexican, and white settlers, a point Street makes clear.

28. Ibid., xix.

29. Igler, *Industrial Cowboys,* 4.

30. Paul Taylor, "Labor on the California Land: Which Way?" (1980; BANC MSS 84/38 series 2, carton 4, folder 40). In this essay, Taylor points to California's entrance into the Union as providing a choice between "two contrasting structures [that] dominated the relationship of labor to management." While the Constitutional Convention decided against California's official status as a slave state, Taylor notes that an article of the same year announced that the Chinese were "to be to California what the African has been to the South." Street's study argues that the system was in place hundreds of years before (*Beasts of the Field,* xx).

31. Igler, *Industrial Cowboys,* 45–46.

32. Arax and Wartzman, *King of California,* 73.

33. There are many diverse views of California's agricultural labor history. Igler's *Industrial Cowboys* and Arax and Wartzman's *King of California* are but two that hold close to McWilliams's *Factories in the Fields,* generally following the view of large-scale land ownership and increasingly exploitive practices. David Vaught, in *Cultivating California: Growers, Specialty Crops, and Labor, 1875–1920* (Baltimore: Johns Hopkins University Press, 1999), seeks to exhume the small-scale grower from the weight of that argument, and Street's *Beasts of the Field* poses a counternarrative of a different nature, seeking to articu-

late the workers' diverse experiences. Richard Walker, *The Conquest of Bread: 150 Years of Agribusiness in California* (New York: New Press, 2004), agrees that not as much of California's holdings were in the hands of men like Miller and Lux as popular belief suggests, but he disagrees with Vaught's thesis. Additionally, histories of water, irrigation, and reclamation in the state suggest an even more complicated agricultural history; see, for example, Donald Worster, *Rivers of Empire: Water, Aridity, and the Growth of the American West* (New York: Oxford University Press, 1985); John Walton, *Western Times and Water Wars: State, Culture, and Rebellion in California* (Berkeley and Los Angeles: University of California Press, 1992); Robert Gottlieb and Margaret Fitzsimmons, *Thirst for Growth: Water Agencies as Hidden Government in California* (Tucson: University of Arizona Press, 1991); and Marc Reisner, *Cadillac Desert: The American West and Its Disappearing Water* (New York: Viking Penguin, 1986).

34. Arax and Wartzman, *King of California,* 73.

35. Worster, *Rivers of Empire,* 161.

36. Ibid.

37. Paul Schuster Taylor, "The Excess Land Law," *Yale Law Journal* 64 (February 1955): 477–514, at 478, and his *Essays on Land, Water, and the Law in California* (New York: Arno Press, 1979).

38. Street, *Beasts of the Field,* xvi.

39. For further discussion of the background of Mexican fieldworkers, see Taylor's earlier work. For recent studies, see Sanchez, *Becoming Mexican American;* Weber, *Dark Sweat, White Gold;* Guerin-Gonzales, *Mexican Workers and American Dreams;* and Gonzales, *Mexican and Mexican American Farm Workers.*

40. Letter to H. E. Smith, Field Representative, Works Progress Administration–Region V, from Emily Wooley, Director, Division of Employment, February 24, 1938 (BANC MSS 84/38 series 1, box 13, folder 15). The letter says that "calls for workers made upon the State Employment Services from individual growers . . . have generally been for two or three times as many persons as are needed. Hence, when persons are cut off relief to meet these calls, hundreds of them are only

able to secure intermittent work, and the excess labor supply further depresses what were already minimum wages."

41. Paul S. Taylor, "Migration of Drought Refugees to California," April 17, 1935. Photographs by Dorothea Lange. Library of Congress, Prints and Photographs Division, Washington, DC 20540-4840.

42. Paul Schuster Taylor, "Again the Covered Wagon," *Survey Graphic* 24 (July 1935): 348, available online at the Web site of the New Deal Network, http://newdeal.feri.org/texts/579.html (accessed June 18, 2007).

43. Taylor's interest in quality of life for the incoming migrants cannot be underestimated. After working with Taylor as a graduate student, Walter Goldschmidt turned his training in anthropology to a massive study aimed to measure, among other things, quality of life in two agricultural towns, Arvin and Dinuba. Like his mentor, Goldschmidt fought against an academic community ill prepared and reluctant to validate his work.

44. Taylor and Lange, "Rural Rehabilitation Camps for Migrants."

45. Taylor oral history (see chap. 1, n. 5), 1:138.

46. Taylor and Lange, "Rural Rehabilitation Camps for Migrants."

47. Dorothea Lange, *Field Notes 1935–1937,* Xeroxed copies (Oakland Museum).

48. Stauffer, *American Protest Literature,* xiii.

49. In his oral history, Taylor notes that the methodological weakness of social science was its mistrust of the "hot" medium of photography because of a "resistance to facing people as human beings" (Taylor oral history [see chap. 1, n. 5]), 1:128.

50. McElvaine, *Great Depression,* 225.

51. Cohen, *Making a New Deal,* 248.

52. Lawrence Levine, "American Culture and the Great Depression," in *The Unpredictable Past: Explorations in American Cultural History,* by Lawrence L. Levine (New York: Oxford University Press, 1993), 209–11.

53. Alan Brinkley, *Voices of Protest: Huey Long, Father Coughlin, and the Great Depression* (New York: Knopf, 1982). Chapter 11 deals

with Roosevelt's influence on Americans, especially on the radical movements of Huey Long and Father Coughlin. Michael Kazin makes the same case for Roosevelt in *The Populist Persuasion* (112).

54. Goodwyn, *Populist Moment,* xvii.

55. Louis Adamic, "The Cherries Are Red in the San Joaquin," *The Nation,* June 27, 1936, available online at the New Deal Network Web site, www.newdealferi.org (accessed September 7, 2008).

56. Starr, *Endangered Dreams,* 3. Starr's definition of radicalism: "a program, a style, a mode of fiery rhetoric and symbolic gesture."

57. Ella Winter, "What Next in California?" *Pacific Affairs* 8 (March 1935): 86–89, available online at the JSTOR Web site, www.jstor.org/stable/2751506 (accessed April 9, 2008).

58. Ibid.

59. Brinkley's *Voices of Protest* (sec. 4, chap. 11) provides a discussion of this question, citing among other problems a lack of organization and cohesiveness within the two movements as the reason for their demise. Of the many articles and books on Sinclair, Gregory Mitchell's *The Campaign of the Century: Upton Sinclair's Race for Governor of California and the Birth of Media Politics* (New York: Random House, 1992), Anthony Arthur's *Radical Innocent: Upton Sinclair* (New York: Random House, 2006), and Sinclair's own version, *I, Candidate for Governor: And How I Got Licked* (1935; repr. with intro. by James Gregory, Berkeley and Los Angeles: University of California Press, 1994), all give comprehensive analyses of a fascinating campaign.

60. Richard L. Neuberger, "Who Are the Associated Farmers?" *Survey Graphic* 28 (September 1939): 517. Available online at the New Deal Network Web site, http://newdeal.feri.org (accessed September 4, 2008).

61. Starr, *Endangered Dreams,* 157. At Pixley, Tulare County farmers shot into a crowd of strikers listening to a Cannery and Agricultural Workers Industrial Union (CAWIU) organizer, and killed two. The farmers then turned their guns on the strike headquarters, wounding fourteen. Richard Steven Street's *Everyone Had Cameras* claims twenty and quotes a *San Francisco News* reporter who "saw eleven." Street pro-

vides a unique perspective on this strike by viewing it through photographers' presence.

Striking was, Taylor wrote in the March 15, 1935, government report ("Memorandum on Establishment of Rural Rehabilitation Camps"), the workers' "only means of vocalizing their plight," and it was dangerous indeed. In Arvin, a sniper killed a striker during a clash. Vigilantism was not confined to the fields. A month after the Pixley murders, a middle-class mob broke into the San Jose city jail and lynched two accused kidnappers and murderers. It was the first lynching to occur in San Jose since 1854.

62. Taylor oral history (see chap. 1, n. 5), 2:14. Malca Chall, the interviewer, tells Taylor that Claude B. Hutchinson claims in his oral history that his involvement with the Associated Farmers grew out of "his understanding of Communist infiltration" of agricultural labor. Taylor calmly responds, "I am fully prepared to believe that he saw it that way. I don't see it that way, but I believe him when he said what you have told me."

63. Starr, *Endangered Dreams,* 179.

64. Taylor oral history (see chap. 1, n. 5), 1:vi.

65. Taylor, "Again the Covered Wagon," 2.

66. Gregory, *American Exodus,* 78. Gregory's analysis of Californians' intense hatred of the estimated three hundred and fifty thousand "Okies" who came west locates that response in the migrants' often southern heritage, against which there was often prejudice, and their association with "farm work, poverty, and rural backwardness— as invitations to disesteem in California." More important for Gregory, however, is the general "climate of fear and conflict" that the Depression created, a feeling of anxiety among the general California populace that lent more significance to normal concerns than they otherwise would have had.

67. Taylor, "Again the Covered Wagon," 2.

68. Ibid., 3.

69. Taylor, from "Again the Covered Wagon"; but see his "Marysville to Imperial Valley, March–April, 1935." These quotations, like

many in the article, come directly from Taylor's notebook; additionally, the locations are all documented in his notebooks from this trip, and in Lange's, and occasionally on pages on which both have recorded.

70. John Steinbeck, *The Harvest Gypsies: On the Road to the Grapes of Wrath,* introduction by Charles Wollenberg (Berkeley: Heyday Books, 1988), 22.

71. It is far more debatable, however, that Steinbeck felt the government itself was the answer to the migrants' problems. Steinbeck set out into the field with Collins having already formulated and worked heavily on both the scientific and symbolic articulations of his "phalanx" theory—the idea that the human behaviors within a group were autonomous enough and holistic enough to form something akin to a biological soul, complete with a biological memory of events from prehistoric times, and that they were, in this form, capable of producing profound change. An example from his letters cites Hitler's growing ability to harness, not form, an already existing phalanx. Thus, in *The Grapes of Wrath,* Steinbeck's main concern seems to be working out a way to harness the phalanx in order to create the "new world order" he sees as potentially coming out of the despair and tragedy of the migrant workers' lives.

72. Gregory, *American Exodus,* 57–58.

73. Paul Schuster Taylor, "Again the Covered Wagon," 348.

74. Paul Schuster Taylor, "Synopsis of Survey of Migratory Labor Problems in California," 1936 (BANC MSS 84/38, series 3, carton 15, folder 37). Some uncertainty about the date of this passage, which Taylor reworked a few times, occurs. The Bancroft has a typed version listed as 1936; the same version appears in "The Migrants and California's Future: The Trek to California and the Trek in California," a speech Taylor gave in October 1935 (Printed in U.S., Congress, Senate, Subcommittee on Migratory Labor of the Committee on Labor and Public Welfare, Farmworkers in Rural America, 1971–1972: Hearings, 92nd Cong., 1st and 2d sessions, 3926–34).

75. Hughes, quoted in Taylor, "Notes, 1934" (BANC MSS 84/38, series 2, carton 3, folder 43).

76. Taylor oral history (see chap. 1, n. 5), 1:141. Even government officials carried this fear. A memorandum from Harold Drobish to Paul Taylor cites a letter Drobish received on October 16, 1935, from R. N. Wilson, Chairman of the Agricultural Section, State Chamber of Commerce, saying the dedication had calmed his "greatest fears, . . . those expressed by Mr. Weeks—that such camps would attract and be monopolized by low class labor and would provide a fertile field for subversive agitation" (BANC MSS 84/38, series 3, carton 15, folder 19); original letter from Weeks not available. A second letter from Drobish to Taylor (October 16, 1935; in the same folder) explained Wilson's concerns:

> He said that many ideas and fears he had relative to the program were cleared up and favorably so, following the discussions at the meeting and what he saw at the camp. He feels that the problem of management is of greatest important [sic] and that we have been very successful in having Tom Collins as Manager of the Marysville Camp; that if we could obtain more men like Mr. Collins there would be little to fear as to the outcomes of these camps. He has been afraid that social workers with peculiar ideas might be put in charge of the camps, resulting in difficulties similar to the fears of subversive difficulties voiced by Mr. Weeks of Contra Costa County.

77. William Howarth, "The Mother of Literature: Journalism and *The Grapes of Wrath*," in *New Essays on "The Grapes of Wrath*," ed. David Whyall (Cambridge: Cambridge University Press, 1990), 71–99.

78. Elaine Steinbeck and Robert Wallsten, eds., *Steinbeck: A Life in Letters* (New York: Penguin Books, 1989), 158.

79. Lowry worked for the Utah Relief Administration in 1934 and was regional advisor to the Federal Emergency Relief Administration. In 1935 he became director of the Resettlement Administration.

80. Letter from Lowry Nelson to Paul Taylor, June 1935 (BANC MSS 84/38, series 3, carton 14, folder 26).

81. Taylor oral history (see chap. 1, n. 5), 1:140.

82. Ibid.

83. Ibid., 142.

84. Paul Schuster Taylor, "From the Ground Up," *Survey Graphic*

25 (September 1936): 526. Available online at the New Deal Network Web site, http://newdeal.feri.org/ (accessed August 23, 2007).

85. Finnegan, *Picturing Poverty*. Finnegan's discussion on 97–117 points out the staff's concerns that Taylor's presentation was "too rosy."

86. For example, the issue in which "From the Ground Up" appears features five illustrations of street life in Spain. There is no essay or accompanying text, but an article on the Spanish Civil War also appears in the issue.

87. Finnegan, *Picturing Poverty*, 104.

88. Lawrence Levine, "The Folklore of Industrial Society: Popular Culture and Its Audiences," *American Historical Review* 97 (December 1992): 1369–99. See chapter 6 of this book for more discussion.

89. Finnegan bases some of this claim on the letters from editors asking Taylor for revisions of his text, one of which was to "humanize" it. It seems worth noting that Taylor's prose was generally quite academic, and much of his work for non-academic venues received the same kind of critique.

90. The date is not a typographical error. The negative, on file with the Library of Congress, is dated 1936.

91. Other versions of the photograph, one of a series of the woman and her children, mention the woman's husband, indicating that he is a California native. For more on "Migrant Mother," see chapter 6. Significantly, in 1935 Lange *did* photograph a young "mother of five children," who said to her, "We're getting along as good as us draggin'-around people can expect—if you call it a livin'." That mother appeared in a June 1935 submission to Harry Drobish, entitled *Notes from the Field*. The date of that publication further strengthens the link that the phrase "draggin'-around people" creates, if not to the actual photograph of Thompson, at least between the two essays. For more on *Notes from the Field*, see chapter 5.

92. Finnegan notes that in one of his replies to the *Survey Graphic* editors, Taylor "responded by noting that he had addressed criticisms of the RA's projects in a past article and did not see the need to revisit them." For Taylor, it was indeed an ongoing narrative.

93. *Survey Graphic,* September 1936 (BANC MSS 84/38, series 2, carton 4, folder 25). Other contents of the issue are as follows: "You and I and the Railroads," by Ralph L. Wood; "Electricity Goes to the Country" (complete with picture of farm kitchens electrified by rural programs); "Toward a New Armageddon," a piece by John Palmer Gavit about the Spanish civil war; a eulogy for Henry Wright, community planner; "Paris Sets a Strike Style," about the automobile industry strikes three months before; an article on the debates over socialized medicine; "These Country People on Relief," about the rural relief rolls of Wisconsin; and a piece about a Boston social service agency.

CHAPTER 5. A NEW SOCIAL ORDER

1. Taylor oral history (see chap. 1, n. 5), 1:134.
2. Gregory, *American Exodus,* 199. Explaining the worship practices among the migrants, who were often shunned or otherwise made to feel unwelcome in California's established churches, Gregory writes, "The major religious alternative to the mainstream churches was to be found among the profusion of sects and tendencies on the radical fringe of evangelical Protestantism [that] welcomed the migrants into their fold." Gregory also cites "Cambellite congregations" and the "multitude of organizations belonging to the Holiness and Pentecostal movements." In *Everyone Had Cameras,* Richard Steven Street writes that in the "Little Oklahomas . . . a new Okie subculture stressing fundamentalist Protestant values took root" (147). See also Timothy L. Smith, review, "The Pentecostal Movement: Its Origins, Development, and Distinctive Character," *Church History* 35 (March 1966): 127–29: "Few university or theological libraries have systematically collected the records of Pentecostal religion. Yet that faith has been central in the experience of California's refugees from the Dust Bowl" (128).
3. Elias Tuma, interview by author, University of California at Davis, 2003. Looking back on his former professor, Tuma said, "He was an economist first—always; it was the economic injustice of California's agriculture that disturbed him."

4. Clark Kerr, interview by author, Berkeley, California, 2002.

5. Baldwin, *Poverty and Politics,* 93. Baldwin lists the goals and the organizational structure to achieve them as follows: "(1) the Division of Land Utilization, to which was assigned responsibility for planning and execution of a program of submarginal land retirement and improvement; (2) the Rural Resettlement Division, with the responsibility for both the resettlement program, including the communities initiated by the Subsistence Homesteads Division, and the rural rehabilitation program and projects inherited from the FERA; (3) the Division of Suburban Resettlement, which was assigned responsibility for a special program of model communities on the peripheries of selected cities; and (4) twelve separate divisions for technical and managerial functions."

6. Ibid., 92.

7. Taylor, "Marysville to Imperial Valley, March–April, 1935" (BANC MSS 84/38, series 3, carton 14, folder 37).

8. Taylor, "Field Notes" (BANC MSS 84/38, series 3, carton 14, folder 39).

9. Taylor, "Marysville to Imperial Valley."

10. Dorothea Lange, *Field Notes, 1935–1937,* Xeroxed copies (Oakland Museum).

11. Ibid.

12. There are three passes Lange and Taylor could have been on, but the Tehachapi would have been the most efficient. While still at El Centro, Lange mentions "Eden Hot Springs, 8 miles east of San Jacinto," which is still near the 1935 route of Highway 99. She lists San Bernardino on June 23, but the 24th has nothing but a series of numbers. Taylor's notebook lists Needles, Arizona, on June 25, however, and to arrive there they would have to cross the Cajon Pass, at 4,250 feet, and head east on Route 66. Lange's notebook puts them in Tulare, back on Highway 99, by June 26. The Tejon is the only pass on Highway 99. That pass, on 99's infamous Ridge Route, had been graded and had its switchbacks reduced by 1934; additionally, it is a pass Taylor had traveled frequently, and which they had obviously used when heading south. But it would have been a difficult drive from Needles, forcing them south

again to San Bernardino before they could head up on 99. It's possible, since Lange's notebook contains an entry reading, "Between Shafter and Bakersfield—How many—US 99—its splendor and all the rest of it," but the likeliest spot would be the Tehachapi, at 3,793 feet, a pass they would have to cross heading northwest from Needles back to 99 and on to Tulare. Taylor's notebook on the 25th reads, "Needles, Arizona, Tehachapi," and his typed notes (BANC MSS 84/38, series 3, carton 14, folder 40) hold an undated note between June 22 and 25: "On the Tehachapi—coming from Arizona—Model T Ford." A Web site for the pass offers up the following information: "One flower that is characteristic of this area is grape-soda lupine. The pleasant fragrance and the bright purple color of this lupine is one of the highlights of the annual event" (www.wind-works.org/articles/windmillwildflowerhike.html).

13. Lange, *Field Notes, 1935–1940.*

14. Daniel Dixon, interview by author, Carmel, California, 2003.

15. Kerr, "Paul and Dorothea," 41.

16. Daniel Dixon, interview by author, Carmel, California, 2003.

17. Whiteside Taylor, *Intimate Journey,* 194.

18. Meltzer, *Dorothea Lange,* 126.

19. Ibid.

20. Whiteside Taylor, *Intimate Journey,* 198. "Maynard was really a fascinating companion," the text reads, with the words "& lover" penciled in.

21. Meltzer, *Dorothea Lange,* 126.

22. Letter from Katharine Taylor Loesch to the author, 2004.

23. Meltzer, *Dorothea Lange,* 68.

24. Letter from Paul Taylor to Dorothea Lange, September 24, 1935 (BANC MSS 84/38, series 7, carton 89, folder 54). Taylor's longhand letters are reproduced.

25. See Hurley, *Portrait of a Decade,* 52. Ben Shahn, who also came to work for Stryker's photographic team, told FSA historian Jack Hurley that he remembered the moment her work was brought into the office. "Dorothea's work was sent in or brought in by somebody and this was a revelation, what this woman was doing" (52).

26. Evans, whose elegant black-and-white photography would define the Great Depression in the South, is nonchalantly misnamed. Taylor said often that he and Lange were not creating art, but doing work, and that she was the best person ever to do that work: his obliviousness to Walker's name, despite Evans's already established relationship with the Metropolitan Museum of Modern Art, underscores that attitude.

27. Many studies of the Great Depression cite public attitudes toward married women working. For example, Susan Ware writes, "A 1936 Gallup poll, in which four-fifths of those questioned thought that a wife should not work if her husband had a job, reflected the strong public sentiment against married women working. Such restrictive attitudes extended to the federal government itself, which dismissed 1,600 married women from the government service between 1932 and 1937" (*Beyond Suffrage: Women and the New Deal* [Cambridge, MA: Harvard University Press, 1981], 2).

28. Letter from Taylor to Lange, n.d. (BANC MSS 84/38, series 7, carton 89, folder 54).

29. Letter from Taylor to Lange, n.d. (BANC MSS 84/38, series 7, carton 89, folder 54).

30. For general history, see Rebecca Ann Hartman's dissertation, "Imagining a Land: The Farm Security Administration and the Populist Fantasy" (State University of New Jersey, 2005); Michael Johnston Grant, *Down and Out on the Family Farm: Rural Rehabilitation in the Great Plains, 1929–1945 (Our Sustainable Future)* (Lincoln: University of Nebraska Press, 2002); Baldwin, *Poverty and Politics;* and two thorough articles, F. Jack Hurley, "The Farm Security Administration File: In and Out of Focus," *History of Photography* 7, no. 3 (1993): 244–52, and Louis C. Gawthrop, "Images of the Common Good," *Public Administration Review* 53, no. 6 (1993): 508–15. On the Historical Division and its development, see John Raeburn, *A Staggering Revolution: A Cultural History of Thirties Photography* (Chicago: University of Illinois Press, 2006); Giles Mora and Beverly Brannan, *FSA: The American Vision* (New York: Abrams, 2006); Maren Stange, *Symbols of Ideal Life: Social Documentary Photography in America, 1890–1950* (New York: Cam-

bridge University Press, 1989); William Stott, *Documentary Expression and Thirties America* (New York: Oxford University Press, 1986); Hurley, *Portrait of a Decade*. Recent scholarship has turned a critical eye on the FSA's documentary practices, and some useful studies include the following: Stuart Kidd, *Farm Security Administration Photography, the Rural South, and the Dynamics of Image-Making, 1935–1943* (New York: Edwin Mellen Press, 2004); Finnegan, *Picturing Poverty;* Nicholas Natanson, *The Black Image in the New Deal: The Politics of FSA Photography* (Knoxville: University of Tennessee Press, 1992); and James Curtis, *Mind's Eye, Mind's Truth: FSA Photography Reconsidered* (Philadelphia, PA: Temple University Press, 1992). The photographs themselves are often collected, and Pantheon put out a collection, *American Photographers of the Depression: Farm Security Administration Photographs, 1935–1942* (New York: Pantheon Books, 1985). Stryker himself collected FSA photographs, with assistance from Nancy Wood; see Roy Stryker and Nancy Wood, *In This Proud Land: America 1935–1943 as Seen in the FSA Photographs* (New York: Galahad Books, 1973). Additionally, Farm Security photographs are collected in a number of books, by state or locale, and nearly all of those who were employed as photographers for the FSA have articles and books devoted to exploring their work.

31. Stryker and Wood, *In This Proud Land,* 9.

32. Ibid., 10.

33. Ibid., 11.

34. Ibid.

35. Meltzer, *Dorothea Lange,* 76.

36. Hurley, *Portrait of a Decade,* 26–28. After a year of work, the book was abandoned, and, for Stryker at least, reconceived with a much broader vision.

37. Ibid., 37–48.

38. Lange's technical skill was and still is a popular subject of speculation. Her closest photographic ally (aside from Imogen), Ansel Adams, supposedly disparaged her technically and loved to tell the story of one outing in his station wagon during which she continually fumbled with

the car's cigarette lighter, unable to make it light her cigarette. Finally, Adams reached over and calmly flipped the handle. For Adams, that told the story of the two photographers. As to Lange's legacy as either artist or documentarian, she herself refused to acknowledge the labels as relevant.

39. Lange Tape Transcripts, vol. 2 (Lange Archive, Oakland Museum).

40. Taylor oral history (see chap. 1, n. 5), 1:139.

41. Taylor oral history (see chap. 1, n. 5), 1:212. In the report, Taylor wrote the following: "The attached document presents notes which are fresh from the field. The very words of the person photographed are quoted as much as possible in order that expression of the condition, needs, and hopes of those in distress may be transmitted faithfully. Notes were selected not only for their significance and interest to our division, but in part for their possible significance and interest to other divisions as well. Miss Dorothea Lange collaborated in the field investigation and in preparation of all phases of these 'Notes from the field'" (BANC MSS 84/38, series 3, carton 14, folder 24).

42. Meltzer includes Strand's review of *An American Exodus* on p. 210 of *Dorothea Lange*. Most relevant is Strand's summary: "They have tried to weld photographs, an expositional text dealing with the causes and effects of this vast social upheaval with an additional element: words they heard spoken by some of the people who are the victims of this catastrophe."

43. Taylor oral history (see chap. 1, n. 5), 1:210. The man in the photograph made such an impression on Taylor that years later, while showing Suzanne Reiss *Notes from the Field,* he would say, "I remember that fellow very, very well. Here is what he said. Later we went to his home; he had an acre near Porterville. We went there—I think he was not home when we went, but he had told us about it. In other words, he was a very small landowner, a laborer with about an acre which he tended with the greatest care. And yet here you see him as a fruit-picker, living in this condition" (210).

44. *Government Reports,* 1935, vol. 2 (Oakland Museum). A clipping from the *San Francisco Examiner* follows, dated June 2: "Indigent Ban

Sustained by Assembly. Reconsideration Move Beaten 43 to 35." The clipping notes that the bill was intended to benefit California citizens by serving "as a bar to the uncontrolled emigration into the State of thousands of persons unable to care for themselves." Reconsideration of the bill failed, but not by much. Taylor, *Notes from the Field:* June 4, 1935, Submitted to H. E. Drobish, Acting Assistant Director, Rural Rehabilitation Administration.

45. Paul Schuster Taylor, "The Migrants and California's Future: The Trek to California and the Trek in California" (U.S. Senate, Subcommittee on Migratory Labor of the Committee on Labor and Public Welfare, *Farmworkers in Rural America, 1971–1972: Hearings,* July 22, 1971–June 20, 1972, 92nd Cong., 1st and 2d sess., 3926–34).

46. Letter from William Hudson to Paul Taylor, September 14 (BANC MSS 84/38, series 1, box 4, folder 13). It was by no means a foregone conclusion that Taylor would find in San Francisco a sympathetic audience. Historically, the club had undertaken studies on a variety of contemporary social and political concerns, and brought in an impressive roster of speakers, including, in 1911, President Theodore Roosevelt (more recently, Martin Luther King, Ronald Reagan, Bill Clinton, Erin Brockovich, and Bill Gates all gave speeches at the club), but it has never, as its speaker roster suggests, taken a specific political side. Founded in 1903 by Edward F. Adams, *San Francisco Chronicle* editorial writer; John P. Young, managing editor of the *Chronicle;* Benjamin Edie Wheeler, president of the University of California; Frederic Burk, president of what became San Francisco State University; and William P. Lawlor, an attorney who later became a justice of the California Supreme Court, the Commonwealth Club's public service mission quickly established it as a major social and legislative influence throughout the state.

47. Taylor oral history (see chap. 1, n. 5), 1:207.

48. Paul Taylor, "Marysville, October 12, 1935" (BANC MSS 84/38, series 3, carton 15, folder 22).

49. Paul Taylor, "Marysville, October 12, 1935" (BANC MSS 84/38, series 3, carton 15, folder 22).

50. Whiteside Taylor, *Intimate Journey,* 213, 204.

51. Meltzer, *Dorothea Lange,* 128.

52. Interview with Dorothea Lange for Smithsonian Archives of American Art, conducted by Richard Doud, May 22, 1964; available online at the Smithsonian Web site, www.aaa.si.edu/collections/oral histories/transcripts/lange64.htm (accessed February 3, 2003).

53. Lange Tape Transcripts, vol. 2 (Lange Archive, Oakland Museum).

54. Ibid.

55. Ibid.

56. Taylor oral history (see chap. 1, n. 5), 1:149.

57. Ibid., 150.

58. Dixon, interview, 2003.

59. Letter from Katharine Taylor Loesch to author, 2004.

60. Taylor oral history (see chap. 1, n. 5), 1:151.

61. Dixon, interview, 2003.

62. Lange Tape Transcripts, vol. 2 (Lange Archive, Oakland Museum).

63. Partridge, *Restless Spirit,* 57.

64. Dixon, interview, 2003.

65. Fisher, *Let Us Now Praise Famous Women,* 4, 36, 99.

CHAPTER 6. WOMEN ON THE BREADLINES

1. Ware, *Holding Their Own,* 37–42. Ware points to separate programs devised to deal with unemployed women and run mainly by women administrators, but claims they "only went so far" with a variety of problems facing women who qualified for relief. They comprised "between 13 and 19 percent of the total WPA rolls," with a peak of four hundred thousand in 1938.

2. Dorothea Lange, Contact sheets, vol. 1, early work (Oakland Museum).

3. Meridel Le Sueur, "Women on the Breadlines," *New Masses,* January 1932. Hereafter cited in the text by page number.

4. Le Sueur's biography, and the subsequent analysis of its potential relation to her article, is from Constance Coiner's study *Better Red: The Writing and Resistance of Tillie Olsen and Meridel Le Sueur,* Illini Books edition (Urbana: University of Illinois Press, 1998), 72–97.

5. Coiner, *Better Red,* 99.

6. Ibid., 6.

7. "From the Ground Up, September 1936" (BANC MSS 84/38, series 2, carton 4, folder 25). In the September 1936 issue of *Survey Graphic,* a piece by Myrtle De Vaux Howard, entitled "These Many Years," precedes the companion pieces "From the Ground Up" and "Draggin'-Around People," authored by Taylor and Lange. De Vaux's article looks at an unnamed social agency in Boston to which aging, widowed women come to earn money until they qualify for "old age assistance." Unlike government relief, this, she explains, they will accept, "because to them it seems justice, not charity." The women are uniformly tidy; all have lost their homes, their incomes, and their security, and all generally retain both a careful appearance and the ability to do difficult handwork. Mrs. Dowland, rouged and wearing a blue coat with a fur collar, lives on five dollars a week since her husband's death and the loss of her securities. Miss Morse lives with her sisters, and when the hospital indicates that Miss Morse is "gravely undernourished," the agency gives her three days' work a week instead of one, on the condition that she promise to feed herself. Mrs. McCormick, Miss Montague, Miss Twill—all hang on to some remnant of their formerly respectable lives, pawning and taking out diamond wedding rings, turning up their noses at "charity," until finally, at seventy, they can apply for and receive seven or eight dollars a week.

8. Constance Classen, *The Color of Angels: Cosmology, Gender and the Aesthetic Imagination* (London: Routledge, 1998), 87.

9. Kathleen Anne McHugh, *American Domesticity: From How-To Manual to Hollywood Melodrama* (New York: Oxford University Press, 1999), 41.

10. Ibid., 27.

11. Glenna Matthews, *Just a Housewife: The Rise and Fall of Domesticity in America* (New York: Oxford University Press, 1987), 35.

12. McHugh, *American Domesticity,* 29.

13. Ibid., 16.

14. Matthews, *Just a Housewife,* 10–11.

15. Ibid., 35.

16. McHugh, *American Domesticity,* 57.

17. Ibid., 60.

18. Significantly, Tillie Olsen would protest that very stance in *Yonnondio,* when the family's desperate attempts to provide care, even food, for their children are ignored by social service–minded officials who sniff in disdain at their conditions.

19. For this discussion of domestic work, see Jennifer Scanlon, *Inarticulate Longings: The "Ladies Home Journal," Gender, and the Promises of Consumer Culture* (New York: New York University Press, 2000), 65. The quotation from Christine Frederick appears on p. 62.

20. Frederick, quoted in Scanlon, *Inarticulate Longings,* 62.

21. Scanlon, *Inarticulate Longings,* 41.

22. Ibid., 141.

23. Patricia Raub, *Yesterday's Stories: Popular Novels of the 20s and 30s* (Westport, CT: Greenwood Press, 1994), xvii, 45.

24. Matthews, *Just a Housewife,* 186.

25. Scanlon, *Inarticulate Longings,* 141.

26. Nicola Humble, *The Feminine Middlebrow Novel, 1920s to 1950s: Class, Domesticity, and Bohemianism* (Oxford: Oxford University Press, 2001), 109.

27. Ware, *Holding Their Own,* 2.

28. Ibid.

29. Laura Hapke, *Daughters of the Great Depression: Women, Work, and Fiction in the American 1930s* (Athens: University of Georgia Press, 1995), xv, xvi.

30. Ibid., xvii.

31. Annelise Orleck, "'We Are That Mythical Thing Called the Public': Militant Housewives during the Great Depression," *Feminist Studies* 19 (Spring 1993): 147–72, at 149.

32. Quoted in Gregory, *American Exodus,* 21.

33. Matthews, *Just a Housewife*, 12. "What we know with certainty is that women clung to their familiar household objects with determination as they packed for the Overland Trail, and they parted with them only with the greatest reluctance."

34. Robert Griswold, "Anglo Women and Domestic Ideology in the American West in the Nineteenth and Early Twentieth Centuries," in *Western Women: Their Land, Their Lives,* ed. Lillian Schlissel, Janice Monk, and Vicki L. Ruiz (Albuquerque: University of New Mexico Press, 1988), 18.

35. I use the term *mythologized* consciously, referring to the mythos of manifest destiny and the reality of California's statehood, not to a general geographical part of the continent. Additionally, while Taylor showed a steadfast understanding of Mexican culture and a dedication to providing all agricultural laborers, regardless of race, with the chance to become part of the social system, his Depression-era work does not emphasize the claims of Mexicans to land titles, nor the earlier claims of American Indians.

36. John Seelye, "Come Back to the Boxcar, Leslie Honey; or, Don't Cry for Me, Madonna, Just Pass the Milk: Steinbeck and Sentimentality," in *Beyond Boundaries: Revisioning John Steinbeck,* ed. Susan Shillinglaw and Kevin Hearle (Tuscaloosa: University of Alabama Press, 2002), 17.

37. Paula Geyh, "Burning Down the House? Domestic Space and Female Subjectivity in Marilynne Robinson's *Housekeeping,*" *Contemporary Literature* 34 (Spring 1993): 103–22, at 111.

38. The first documented sale of Mrs. Stewart's Bluing was logged on July 30, 1883. In the 1930s, a dime-size container was introduced, and by 1946, sales were at an all-time high (www.mrsstewart.com/pages/history.html).

39. The contemporary bluing process would have involved soaking or washing clothing in hot soapy water, then rinsing the clothing thoroughly in another kettle, often twice. Finally, a "bluing" kettle was prepared in which the clothing was dipped briefly and then hung to dry (www.mrsstewart.com/pages/history.html).

40. Dorothea Lange, *Field Notes 1935–1937* (Xeroxed copies, Oakland Museum).

41. Ibid.

42. Ibid.

43. Street, *Everyone Had Cameras.* Street summarizes scholarship agreeing with Lange's own claim of five images and then credits Hank O'Neal with finding the sixth and Sally Stein with finding the seventh. The entire discussion, which appears on pages 221–23, provides a comprehensive analysis of the number of photographs in the sequence as well as the most likely progression of images.

44. Meltzer, *Dorothea Lange,* 133.

45. Daniel Dixon, interview by author, Carmel, California, 2003.

46. The ongoing debate over photography's "taking" of a picture, rather than exchanging something between photographer and photographic subject, still embroils the FSA photography in general, and Lange's photographs specifically. Recent articles accusing Lange of ignoring the specifics of Florence Thompson's life, including her Native American heritage, and her manipulation of the facts of Thompson's life speak to the audience's discomfort with the aggression that is inherent to any photography that occurs outside of a studio.

47. Carol Schloss, *In Visible Light: Photography and The American Writer, 1840–1940* (New York: Oxford University Press, 1983), 15.

48. Ibid., 18.

49. Levine, "Folklore of Industrial Society," 1379.

50. Levine's most familiar example is the birth of a practice commonly used now: early screenings of movies to determine audience reaction in order to mold the ultimate product. Frank Capra's preview of *Lost Horizon,* which resulted in laughter at places Capra deemed inappropriate, led to cuts and a second screening that went over more successfully, resulting in the version we now recognize.

51. Levine, "Folklore of Industrial Society," 1381.

52. Wolfgang Iser, "Interaction between Text and Reader," in *Reader in the Text,* ed. Susan Suleiman and Inge Crosman (Princeton, NJ: Princeton University Press, 1980), 110–11. "Communication in liter-

ature, then, is a process set in motion and regulated, not by a given code, but by a mutually restrictive and magnifying interaction between the explicit and the implicit, between revelation and concealment. What is concealed spurs the reader into action, but this action is also controlled by what is revealed; the explicit in its turn is transformed when the implicit has been brought to light. Whenever the reader bridges the gaps, communication begins. The gaps function as a kind of pivot on which the whole text-reader relationship revolves" (Iser, quoted in Levine, "Folklore of Industrial Society," 1386).

53. Lange oral history (see prologue, n. 3), 206.

54. Ibid.

55. Jane Gallop, "The Pleasure of the Phototext," in *Illuminations: Women Writing on Photography from the 1850s to the Present,* ed. Liz Heron and Val Williams (Durham, NC: Duke University Press, 1996), 397. Gallop explicates Barthes's *Camera Lucida* (New York: Farrar, Straus, and Giroux, 1981) and his idea of "punctum" (the element that "pricks" him) as related to cinema and the element of film, which allows for something that "continues to live" beyond the frame. In terms of this discussion, the similarity between Barthes and the passage Levine quotes from Iser is remarkable.

56. Stryker and Wood, *In This Proud Land,* 19.

57. Finnegan, *Picturing Poverty,* 99.

58. Stryker and Wood, *In This Proud Land,* 19.

59. See the transcript available at www.livinghistoryfarm.org/farmingthe30s/movies/thompson_water_06.html.

60. Bill Ganzel, *Dust Bowl Descent* (Lincoln: University of Nebraska Press, 1984), 31.

61. Lange oral history (see prologue, n. 3), 158.

62. Kathy Peiss, *Hope in a Jar: The Making of America's Beauty Culture* (New York: Henry Holt, 1998), 191.

63. Sarah Berry, *Screen Style: Fashion and Femininity in 1930s Hollywood* (Minneapolis: University of Minnesota Press, 2000).

64. Sarah Berry, *Screen Style: Fashion and Femininity in 1930s Hollywood* (Minneapolis: University of Minnesota Press, 2000), 29.

65. Ina Rae Hark, "Introduction," in *American Cinema of the 1930s: Themes and Variations,* ed. Ina Rae Hark (New Brunswick, NJ: Rutgers University Press, 2007), 2.

66. Berry, *Screen Style,* xxii.

67. Pierre Bourdieu, *Distinction: A Social Critique of the Judgement of Taste,* trans. Richard Nice (London: Routledge, 1979), 247.

68. Lea Jacobs, *The Wages of Sin: Censorship and the Fallen Woman Film, 1928–1942* (Berkeley and Los Angeles: University of California Press, 1997), 59.

69. Bourdieu, *Distinction,* 253.

70. It is impossible to think that Lange, with all her work in the studio, was not sensitive to appearance and representation. A woman who in the early 1930s had been commented upon for her "Breton trousers"— in a decade that could publish a newspaper advertisement urging readers to note the "strange spectacle" of women in trousers and "view [them] with alarm" (Berry, *Screen Style,* 155)—would likely be aware of what a woman's clothing would communicate to others. Indeed, in her oral history, Lange remembered Arnold Genthe telling her as a young woman to "take those red beads off. . . . They're not any good." And she did, saying much later, "He was absolutely right. I never wore costume jewelry again" (Lange oral history [see prologue, n. 3], 30). It is also natural to think that the audience would notice the women in the photographs, which, like "Migrant Mother," draw in the audience to question what Finnegan calls "an alternative narrative" (*Picturing Poverty,* 98).

71. Geyh, "Burning Down the House?" 111.

72. Ohrn, *Dorothea Lange and the Documentary Tradition,* 8.

73. Geyh, "Burning Down the House?" 111.

CHAPTER 7. AN AMERICAN EXODUS

1. John Steinbeck, *The Grapes of Wrath* (1939, Viking Press; rpt. centennial ed., New York: Penguin Books, 2002), 400.

2. Ibid., 423.

3. Ibid., 124.

4. Anne Whiston Spirn, *Daring to Look: Dorothea Lange's Photographs and Reports from the Field* (Chicago: University of Chicago Press, 2008), 12.

5. Ibid., 22. Lange's general caption follows:

> Brawley, Imperial Valley, Feb. 23, 1939. In FSA migratory labor camp. Family, mother, father, and 11 children, originally from near Mangrum, Oklahoma, where he had been a tenant farmer. Came to California in 1936 after drought. Since then have been travelling from crop to crop in California following the harvest. Six of the 5 children [sic] attend school wherever the family stops long enough. Five older children work along with mother and father. Feb. 23rd, two of the family had been lucky and "got a place" (a day's work) in the peas on the Sinclair ranch. Father had earned $1.73 for ten-hour day. Oldest daughter had earned $1.25. From these earnings had to provide their transportation to the fields, 20 miles each way. Mother wants to return to Oklahoma, father unwilling. She says, "I want to go back where we can live happy, live decent, and grow what we eat." He says, "We can't go fixed the way I am now. We've got nothing in the world to farm with. I made my mistake when I came out here."

6. Burns, *Roosevelt,* 266–67.

7. Ibid.

8. Watkins, *Hungry Years,* 258. When the bill was signed into effect, creating the Social Security Agency, it provided no coverage for migrant farm workers, transient laborers of any kind, or domestic workers. The argument used to justify the exclusions was that it would be too difficult to collect payments from such workers in the first place.

9. Telegram from Tom Blaisdell to Paul Taylor, April 21, 1936 (BANC MSS 84/38, series 4, carton 16, folder 18).

10. Taylor oral history (see chap. 1, n. 5), 1:148.

11. "Get Out and Hoe," from *These Are Our Lives,* available online at the New Deal Web site, http://newdeal.feri.org/lives.fwp03.html (accessed February 2004).

12. Goodwyn, *Populist Moment,* 20–21.

13. Baldwin, *Poverty and Politics,* 39.

14. Ibid., 167.

15. Dorothea Lange, *Field Notes 1935–1940* (Xeroxed copies, Oakland Museum).

16. Ibid.

17. Ibid.

18. Meltzer, *Dorothea Lange,* 146.

19. Ibid., 151.

20. Whiteside Taylor, *Intimate Journey,* 221.

21. Ibid., 224.

22. William Loesch, telephone interview by the author, August 23, 2003.

23. Hurley, *Portrait of a Decade,* 84.

24. Ibid., 86.

25. Ibid.

26. Ibid., 88. The article stated how often Rothstein had moved the skull around, reminded readers that the series had been photographed in the spring, before the drought hit, and insisted that the skull's bleached condition made it clear it was not the result of current drought conditions. The implication, that Rothstein carried the skull around as a prop, led to the article's closing lines: "Listen Mr. Easterner, may we suggest in all friendliness, that while you are in these parts, you take no wooden nickel pictures like this."

27. William E. Leuchtenburg, *Franklin D. Roosevelt and the New Deal* (New York: Harper Torch Books, 1963), 189.

28. From the Erie, Pennsylvania, *Dispatch-Herald,* September 7, 1936, quoted in Hurley, *Portrait of a Decade,* 90.

29. Lange oral history (see prologue, n. 3), 171.

30. Lange, *Field Notes 1935–1940.*

31. Letter from Frederick Soule to John Franklin, December 12, 1935 (BANC MSS C-R-1, Region 9, San Francisco, California, carton 2, folder 34).

32. Letter from Frederick Soule to Roy Stryker, May 10, 1936, in ibid.

33. Letter from Dorothea Lange to Frederick Soule, May 20, 1936, in ibid.

34. Letter from Frederick Soule to Grace Falke, June 24, 1936, in ibid.

35. Letter from Frederick Soule to Randolph May, September 3, 1936 (BANC MSS C-R-1, Region 9, San Francisco, California, carton 2, folder 35).

36. Letter from Jonathan Garst to Will Alexander, May 8, 1936, in ibid.

37. Lange would not fully develop this technique for two more years. For a full study of Lange's development of her field-note technique into the "comprehensive analysis" Garst cites, see Whiston Spirn, *Daring to Look*. Whiston Spirn looks at Lange's work in 1939, the year Lange's "general captions" began to establish context and develop into full-fledged rhetorical compositions.

38. Meltzer, *Dorothea Lange,* 164.

39. Letter from Paul Taylor to Tom Blaisdell, June 8, 1937 (BANC MSS 88/34, series 3, carton 16, folder 19). Taylor's letter mentions that he and Lange were "driving along the road," and "stopped before a shack. When we went to the door, seven men, surprised at the appearance of strangers in a car with a California license, filed out of the house and onto the screened porch." The photograph Lange took became one of her most famous. It appears on page 77 of *An American Exodus.*

40. Letter from Paul Taylor to Tom Blaisdell, June 8, 1937 (BANC MSS 84/38, series 3, carton 16, folder 18).

41. "Hoe Culture. Alabama Tenant Farmer Near Anniston." The Library of Congress Web site dates the photograph in 1936. Lange and Taylor indicate 1937 when they publish it in *An American Exodus.*

42. For a history of the bill's passage, see Baldwin, *Poverty and Politics,* chapters 5 and 6.

43. Meltzer, *Dorothea Lange,* 179.

44. Baldwin, *Poverty and Politics,* 222. Baldwin writes, "While the tenant purchase and rural rehabilitation programs were devoted primarily to assisting needy farm families 'in place,' and to anchoring

them on the land, the migratory farm labor program during the 1930's *[sic]* was designed to provide succor to families 'on the wing'" (222).

45. Erskine Caldwell and Margaret Bourke-White, *You Have Seen Their Faces* (New York: Modern Age Books, 1937); Archibald MacLeish, *Land of the Free* (New York: Harcourt, Brace, 1938); Herman C. Nixon, *Forty Acres and Steel Mules* (Chapel Hill: University of North Carolina Press); James Agee, *Let Us Now Praise Famous Men* (Boston, MA: Houghton Mifflin, 1941); Richard Wright, *Twelve Million Black Voices* (New York: Viking, 1941).

46. Lange Tape Transcripts, vol. 2 (Lange Archive, Oakland Museum). Working on her own, Lange asked Ansel Adams to develop her negatives. He said,

> She sent the film pack to me in Yosemite. They'd still come smelling of mildew. You have no idea of the heat. August, you know, in the South on the farms and all this damp and you open this packet and . . . you just smelled marshes and whey. Even then, some of them were damaged by humidity. . . . She said to me, "What am I going to do? I don't want anybody else to develop my negatives and I don't know how I'm going to go down there six weeks to a month, can I send them to you for keeping?" Yes, I'd be delighted to do it but it's much better if I develop them because they're all fogged up with humidity and mold and just keeping them in a cooler place isn't going to help. So we had this system at Yosemite with deep tanks so I could take a whole—two, three packs at a time—and they were quite well developed and very consistent. I must have done 30 packs. Anyway, a terrific number. (Lange Tape Transcripts, vol. 2.)

47. Meltzer, *Dorothea Lange,* 194.

48. Ibid., 210.

49. Dorothea Lange and Paul Schuster Taylor, *An American Exodus: A Record of Human Erosion,* 1st ed. (New York: Reynal & Hitchcock, 1939), 115. All subsequent textual citations by page number in the text are from this edition.

50. Henry Mayer, "The Making of a Documentary Book," in *An American Exodus: A Record of Human Erosion,* by Dorothea Lange and Paul Taylor (Paris: Jean-Michel Place, 1999).

51. Meltzer, *Dorothea Lange,* 195.

52. Handwritten notes (BANC MSS 88/32, series 3, carton 16, folder 30). In notes from the trip, two separate pieces of paper are in Taylor's handwriting, one reading "For Centuries," another "Highways are part of the process of mechanization." "Last West," arguably the most eloquently written of all Taylor's essays in the book, begins, "For three centuries an ever-receding western frontier has drawn white men like a magnet." And the third paragraph begins with the sentence "Highways are part of the process of mechanization."

53. Paul Schuster Taylor, "Displacement of Tenant Farmers by Mechanization in Hall and Childress Counties, Texas," June 11, 1938 (BANC MSS 88/32 series 3, carton 16, folder 40), 1–14.

54. Ibid., p. 13.

55. Handwritten note (BANC MSS 84/38, series 3, carton 16, folder 39). Lange's notes are on a loose-leaf piece of paper; the handwriting is distinctively her own.

56. Aldous Huxley, *Island* (New York: First Perennial Classics, 2002), 261. (Orig. pub. 1962.)

57. Lange oral history (see prologue, n. 3), 214.

58. Devra Anne Weber, "The Organizing of Mexicano Agricultural Workers: Imperial Valley and Los Angeles, 1928–34: An Oral History Approach," *Aztlán* 3 (Fall 1972): 307–47; Andrew J. Dunar and Dennis McBride, *Building Hoover Dam: An Oral History of the Great Depression* (Reno: University of Nevada Press, 2001).

59. Sánchez, *Becoming Mexican American,* 11. Notably, Sánchez introduces each of the four main parts of his extensive study with a variety of voices: quotations, *corridos,* and government reports. This is precisely the technique Lange and Taylor establish in *An American Exodus.* Sánchez makes no mention of the text, but he quotes Taylor's research on Mexican communities in Jalisco as well as his later work. The quotation from the Mexican American teenager, Alfred Barela, introduces part 4.

60. Divakaruni, Quay, and Justice, eds., *California Stories Uncovered.*

61. The quotation is from Lange and Taylor, *American Exodus,* 150.

A letter from Vida Arluck to Paul Taylor (April 29, 1981; BANC MSS 88/32, series 3, carton 16, folder 30) indicates that her grandmother, identified as "Ma Burnham" in *An American Exodus* and also in Lange's later book, *Dorothea Lange Looks at the American Country Woman* (Fort Worth, TX: Amon Carter Museum, 1967), was really named Sophia Fleming Graham. Taylor's notes include the information and quotations that appear in *American Country Woman,* all collected on a page entitled "Old Lady Graham." In 2002, while lecturing on Lange in Roseville, California, I was approached by a woman with a newspaper article who wanted to show me that "Ma Burnham," her grandmother, had been mysteriously misnamed in the text. Recently, a local newspaper contacted me for help in finding out the name of a woman in a Sacramento-area photograph. Lange's notes from the encounter, while including her home state (Tennessee) and health condition (tubercular), give only her first name (Ruby). It is not at all unlikely that the migrants agreed to provide an image but not a full name. As one said to Lange, her condition gave her "shame."

CONCLUSION

1. Karl Marx, *The Eighteenth Brumaire of Louis Bonaparte* (Charleston, SC: Bibliobazaar, 2007), 105. (Orig. pub. 1852.)

2. Ibid.

3. Paula Rabinowitz, *They Must Be Represented: The Politics of Documentary* (London: Verso, 1994).

4. John Berger, *About Looking* (New York: Pantheon, 1980), 46.

5. See Gayatri Spivak, "Can the Subaltern Speak?" in *Marxism and the Interpretation of Power,* ed. Cary Nelson and Lawrence Grossman (Urbana: University of Illinois Press, 1988). Spivak leads off her analysis of the subaltern with an analysis of "Intellectuals and Power: A Conversation between Michel Foucault and Giles Deleuze" (in *Michel Foucault, Language, Counter-Memory, Practice: Selected Essays and Interviews,* trans. Donald F. Borchard and Sherry Simon [Ithaca, NY: Cornell University Press, 1977], 205–17).

6. Ibid., 272.

7. Ibid., 308.

8. Significantly, Spivak's question was even more complex. She sought to understand not simply whether the advantaged could understand a representation of the "other," but whether such a representation could exist. "We must now confront the following questions: On the other side of the international division of labor from socialized capital, inside and outside the circuit of the epistemic violence of imperialist law and education supplementing an earlier economic text, can the subaltern speak?" ("Can the Subaltern Speak?" 283). In recent years, the field of subaltern studies has come to include not simply the economically oppressed but, via the advent of sexuality studies and disability studies, those who are socially ostracized and marginalized. The link between any individual within the category of "other" and the narrative of time in which that individual lives or lived is not simply an esoteric question for French philosophers to debate, as Spivak makes clear.

9. Ibid., 281.

10. Street, *Everyone Had Cameras,* 273. Street says of Lange that what "distinguished her from most other photographers of the Great Depression" was that "her desire to produce a book emerged naturally from what she and Taylor had already seen in the field. She did not go out looking for images to advance a thesis or round out an idea" (273).

11. Rabinowitz, *They Must Be Represented;* Levine, "The Historian and the Icon" (see chap. 1, n. 24); Martha Rosler, "in, around, and afterthoughts (on documentary photography)," in *The Contest of Meaning: Critical Histories of Photography,* ed. Richard Bolton (Cambridge, MA: MIT Press, 1989); Richard Steven Street, "Lange's Antecedents: The Emergence of Social Documentary Photography of California's Farmworkers," *Pacific Historical Review* 73, no. 3 (2006): 385–403; Linda Gordon, "Dorothea Lange: The Photographer as Agricultural Sociologist," *Journal of American History* 93, no. 3 (2006): 698–727; and Linda Gordon and Gary Okihiro, eds., *Impounded: Dorothea Lange and the Censored Images of Japanese American Internment* (New York: W. W. Norton, 2006).

INDEX

Page references in italics refer to illustrations.

Decker, Caroline, 285n12
Deleuze, Giles, 263
de Tocqueville, Alexis, 249
Dinuba (CA): Goldschmidt's work
    at, 12; living conditions in,
    293n43
Dixie Plantation (Resettlement
    Administration project), 236–37
Dixon, Consie, 60, 85
Dixon, Daniel, 15; at boarding
    school, 84; on Lange's domestic
    life, 179; on Lange's subjects,
    210; and parents' divorce, 160;
    on Taylor-Lange collaborations,
    115; in Taylor-Lange household,
    177, 238; on Taylor-Lange
    relationship, 157–58
Dixon, John, 15; at boarding school,
    84; Lange's photograph of, 161;
    in Taylor-Lange household, 177
Dixon, Maynard: at Boulder Dam,
    87; divorce from Lange, 160–61;
    graphics for "Rural Rehabilita-
    tion Camps," 128; marriage to
    Lange, 15, 59–62, 91, 92–93;
    painting expeditions of, 60–61;
    public mythos of, 61; and San
    Francisco General Strike, 91;
    San Francisco studio of, 85; and
    Taylor-Lange relationship, 160;
    and Whiteside, 160, 301n20
domesticity: and American citizen-
    ship, 192; cult of, 192, 194; in
    Great Depression, 25, 196–98;
    and industrialization, 191–92;
    of middle-class women, 192; in
    migrant camps, 181; migrant

women's, 180–81, 189, 190–91,
    199–209, 232; pioneer women's,
    198–99; professionalization
    of, 194; in protest literature,
    201; repetitive labor in, 232;
    in *Uncle Tom's Cabin,* 193; in
    United States, 190–91. *See also*
    homemaking; housekeeping
domestic sphere: perception of, 195;
    productive capacity of, 191–92
Donnelley, Ignatius, 22
Donner Pass, 33, 199
Doud, Richard, 114
Drobish, Harry, 115, 168, 297n76,
    298n91
Duncan, Isadora, 53; Genthe's
    portrait of, 52
dust storms, 37–38

Edwards, Mary Jeanette, 99, 160
Ellis, Jacqueline, 34
End Poverty in California (EPIC)
    plan, 133
eugenics, 226
Evans, Walker, 163, 166; *Let Us
    Now Praise Famous Men,* 247;
    photographs of southern Depres-
    sion, 302n26; relationship with
    Museum of Modern Art, 167,
    302n26; Resettlement Agency
    photography of, 167

Falke, Grace, 241, 243
Fallen Leaf Lake, Lange at, 92–93
Fallows, Bishop Samuel, 7
families: interior space of, 27–28;
    Mexican immigrant, 66

families, migrant, 126–27, 129;
cohesiveness of, 155–56; effect
of camps on, 169; housing for,
128; isolation of, 156; at Nipomo,
116–17, 119
farm equipment, communally
owned, 268. *See also* mechanization, agricultural
Farmers Union, and Agricultural
Adjustment Act, 77
farmland, redistribution of, 21. *See
also* agriculture, Californian
farms, small: under Agricultural
Adjustment Act, 77, 79; labor
exchange in, 46; productivity of,
39; Taylor's belief in, 21, 23, 44,
124, 255
Farm Security Administration
(FSA), 247; archives of, 273n26;
creation of, 247; Lange's
dismissal from, 247; Lange's
photographs for, 34, *230,*
232–33, 238, 273n27, 313n5;
Migratory Farm Labor Section,
247; photographers of, 303n30,
310n46; photographic project of,
20, 310n46. *See also* Resettlement
Administration
fashion: effect on social systems,
225–26, 277; in Hollywood
cinema, 224, 225. *See also*
clothing
fashion industry, women's autonomy
in, 224
Federal Art Project murals, 87
Federal Emergency Relief Administration (FERA), 146–47; and

"furnish" system, 137; Taylor's
field research on, 114–15. *See also*
Resettlement Administration
Federal Writers' Project, 235
femininity, nineteenth-century
ideals of, 189, 190
fiction: California in, 33; modernist,
113; protest, 112–13; radical, 23;
westward migration in, 276n41;
women's work in, 195–96. *See
also* protest literature, American
fieldworkers. *See* agricultural labor;
immigrants, Mexican; migrants,
Dust Bowl
film, blind field of, 213
financial panic of 1893, 39
Finnegan, Cara, 298nn85,89,92;
on "Migrant Mother," 148–59,
214, 312n70; on photographic
meaning, 19
Fisher, Andrea, 113, 179, 289n3
form, ideology of, 27, 275n36
The Forum (newspaper), 240
Foucault, Michel, 263
Franklin, Sidney, 58, 59
Frederick, Christine McGaffey, 194
"From the Ground Up" (Taylor
and Lange), 147–50; Lange's
photographs in, 148–50; prose
style of, 298n89
frontier, American: closing of, 156,
250
"furnish" system: inequities in, 137.
See also sharecropping; tenant
farming
Furuseth, Andy: Lange's portrait of,
105, 288n67

Text:	11/15 Granjon
Display:	Granjon
Indexer:	Robert Engleman
Compositor:	BookMatters, Berkeley
Printer and Binder:	Maple-Vail Book Manufacturing Group